CRAIG BROWN is probably best known as the youngest and most versatile of the Mitford sisters. From an early age he demonstrated a winning combination of all their various talents, developing simultaneous crushes on Hitler and Stalin whilst organizing the redecoration of any number of stately homes.

Born to American-Indian parents, he spent his formative years in abject poverty in Ireland, nibbling on crusts in a tepee in the exclusive slum area of Limerick. Though there were no books in the family home, he occupied his childhood reading the tepee's assembly instructions over and over again, and in this way gained an unsurpassed command of the English language, as evidenced by his early Tepee Trilogy: *Lay the Fabric Flat* (1968), *With the Long Side Facing Up* (1972) and *Now Set the Pole in an Upright Position* (1975).

Like Marcel Proust and William Shakespeare, he suffered from a brief spell of 'flu as a child, but managed to pull through against the odds. He gained from this experience an unsurpassed knowledge of hardship and tragedy, together with his unique ability to celebrate the triumph of the human spirit over adversity. Craig Brown's life is soon to be the subject of an unauthorised new musical by Andrew Lloyd Webber, with lyrics by Chris Moyles and Jeanette Winterson.

He is a Visiting Fellow of the Royal Society of Literature and Regius Professor of Dissembly at the University of Oxford. He divides his time between Wigan and New York, whilst making repeated visits to the family tepee in Limerick in order to keep his feet firmly on the ground. He is currently writing the authorised biography of Lord Jeffrey Archer, provisionally titled *The Man Who Wrote Solzhenitsyn*.

From the reviews of *The Lost Diaries*:

'The mix of belly laughter, common sense and the wildest whimsy makes it a prize example of the English sense of humour at its finest, and confirms Brown as a master of language and linguistic nuance, and our greatest living satirist' *Sunday Times*

'*The Lost Diaries* threatens to be one of this year's classiest lavatory books' *Daily Telegraph*

'The republication rights should be acquired by the Gideons who will have it placed in a drawer in every hotel room in the world'
Mail on Sunday

'Brown's gift as a parodist is phenomenal' A N WILSON

'You dip into this vast comic box of chocolates with ever-increasing admiration, marvelling at both the sustained invention and the savage accuracy of the impersonations' *Spectator*

'The most hilarious satirical pieces of literary mime and written ventriloquy of our time, by the most brilliant humorist in Britain today' *Tatler*

Also written or co-written by Craig Brown

The Blair Years, by Craig Brown as Alastair Campbell (2007)
I Reach for the Stars: An Autobiography, by Barbara Cartland, as dictated to Craig Brown (1975)
Read All About It, by Max Clifford with Craig Brown (2005)
Diaries: 1987–92, by Edwina Currie and Craig Brown (2002)
Jordan: A Whole New World, by Craig Brown (2006)
Life Balance: The Essential Keys to a Lifetime of Wellbeing, by Heather Mills McCartney and Craig Brown (2006)
Prezza: My Story, by John Prescott with Craig Brown (2008)
Oh, What a Circus: The Autobiography of Tim Rice, by Craig Brown (1998)
The Queen Mother, by Craig Brown assisted by William Shawcross (2009)
Baggage: My Childhood, by Janet Street-Porter with input from Craig Brown (2004)
The Roy Strong Diaries: 1967–87, edited and very largely rewritten by Craig Brown (1998)
Inspired and Outspoken: The Collected Speeches of Ann Widdecombe with Additional Jokes by Craig Brown (1998)
Budgie: The Little Helicopter, by the Duchess of York with Craig Brown (1989)

The Lost Diaries

Edited by Craig Brown

FOURTH ESTATE • *London*

Fourth Estate
An imprint of HarperCollins*Publishers*
77–85 Fulham Palace Road
Hammersmith
London W6 8JB

This Fourth Estate paperback edition published 2011
1

First published in Great Britain by Fourth Estate in 2010

A catalogue record for this book is
available from the British Library

ISBN 978-0-00-743649-1

Set in Minion by G&M Designs Limited,
Raunds, Northamptonshire

Printed and bound in Great Britain
by Clays Ltd, St Ives plc

MIX
Paper from
responsible sources
FSC C007454

FSC is a non-profit international organisation established to promote the responsible management of the world's forests. Products carrying the FSC label are independently certified to assure consumers that they come from forests that are managed to meet the social, economic and ecological needs of present and future generations, and other controlled sources.

Find out more about HarperCollins and the environment at
www.harpercollins.co.uk/green

'The life of every man is a diary in which he means to write one story, and writes another.'

J. M. BARRIE

CONTENTS

INTRODUCTION

by His Holiness the Dalai Lama

It is a great honour for me to introduce this historic selection from the diaries of so many wonderful people.

Victoria Beckham, for instance, is one of The Spice Girls. The Spice Girls are five young ladies who sing as well as they dance.

When I met Victoria some years ago, she offered me gracious advice on how to broaden my appeal. I am most grateful for that, Victoria! She also told me how she had been in the forefront of the struggle for the Tibetan people. She even wore a T-shirt with a slogan printed in large orange letters which she assured me probably had something to do with Buddhism. For this I salute her!

On a personal note, I have also had the great honour of being presented to Mr Alan Yentob from the BBC. I was deeply touched when Alan asked me what I thought of the new Martin Amis, whether I had managed to catch up with the latest Gilbert and George exhibition at Tate Modern and if I had heard about the disappointing ratings for Melvyn Bragg's most recent *South Bank Show* on Andrew Lloyd Webber.

To think that such an illustrious personage would value my own humble opinion!

Yes, I was 'living the dream'!

Lady Heather Mills McCartney is another personal acquaintance. I am always delighted to hear her tell me how she was brought up by wolves and triumphed against adversity to reach Number 1 in the Hit Parade and win the Booker Prize three years in a row. I congratulate Heather, also, on her recent news that she is the 'hot tip' to be the next Governor of the Bank of England.

Well done, Heather! You set us all an excellent example!

From the world of politics, Edwina Currie is a woman who knows what it is to engage in struggle. The last time we met, Edwina told me about her valiant campaign to improve the condition of eggs in the United Kingdom. If she had agreed not to speak out for what she truly believed, she would, she confessed, be Prime Minister. But this was a lady who was not prepared to compromise! She had too much compassion in her heart! We salute her!

There are many other good friends of mine included in this magnificent volume! Sir V.S. Naipaul is a very very nice man. When I was introduced to him on my last visit to Buckingham Palace, London, I clutched him to my bosom and kissed him on both cheeks as a brother. I shall never forget the way Vidia was so overcome with emotion that he swept from the room, too 'choked up' to speak!

I am also most humbled by Lord John Prescott, the former Deputy Prime Minister of Great Britain and now, he informs me, one of the leading world statesmen of our age, devoting himself to bringing peace to all mankind. When I met John and his lovely wife Tracey on a visit to Whitehall, London, I could see what a very close and loving couple they were! They bring me great joy!

And I honour, too, the British Royal Family. That most gracious lady, Her Majesty, must be so very proud that her children have all risen to the position of Princes and Dukes.

The Prince of Wales is a very wise man. He tells me he has introduced organic ginger biscuits to leading stores throughout the United Kingdom. These biscuits are available not just for the few, he says, but for the many. I support the Prince in his great quest to feed the people of the world!

So many splendid people, so many splendid achievements, and all chronicled in these personal diaries! Let us strive to follow their examples!

I do not like to single out any particular individual for praise, but we must surely all agree that there is one human being who has come to symbolise the spirit of Great Britain at its best. You will have guessed by now that I am speaking of the tireless philanthropist and human rights campaigner, Mr Max Clifford!

On my last visit to London, Max got in touch with me. He told me of how he had led the world campaign for a free Tibet. 'Believe me, Dalai, if it wasn't for *The Seventies Revival Show* starring the Bay City Rollers and Suzi Quatro touring live throughout Britain and Europe, you wouldn't have half the profile you have today,' he assured me. My heart overflowed with gratitude. He also offered to introduce me to the popular entertainer Mr Michael Barrymore, and through Michael I had the great honour to meet S Club 7, who have done so much to bring democracy, freedom and respect for human rights to all the people of the world.

And I haven't even mentioned that great film director Mr Michael Winner! His films have brought joy and consolation to countless millions, his aides tell me. Well done, Michael!

There is so much wisdom in this collection – and much of it arises from the depths of human suffering. I was upset to read of the stress of Stella McCartney. With all my heart, I beg each of you to stop asking her what it was like growing up as her father's daughter! The poor girl is hurting!

So many brilliant people, with so much to tell us about themselves!

I have spent many, many years teaching people about compassion and self-sacrifice. From reading these diaries I know, deep in my heart, that this is a lesson the world is crying out to learn!

His Holiness the Fourteenth Dalai Lama
August 2010

January

January 1st

These cornflakes are real and they are everywhere. And I tell you this, Michelle, I say.

The packet may have been shaken, but the flakes will recover.

So it is with profound gratitude and great humility that I accept my breakfast cornflakes.

Michelle asks, do I want the milk? And to that I say this.

Our milk will come. Our milk will flow, and it will flow true. Our milk will flow smooth, and it will flow well-chilled.

But our milk will not flow if it is not poured.

So let me promise you this, Michelle. That milk will not pour itself over your flakes or my flakes. That milk will not pour itself over the flakes of the poor or the flakes of the rich, the flakes of the needy or the flakes of those folks who spend their lives in comfort. No, Michelle. To be poured, and, if the need has it, repoured, the jug in which that milk dwells must first be lifted by ourselves.

So, says Michelle, pour the milk any way you want, but I beg you, Barack, please get a move on.

I promise you this, Michelle, and this I promise you, I reply. I will indeed get a move on with pouring that milk. On the move to pour that milk, I shall ponder day and night. And I shall not rest until the day comes when that milk has, in truth, finally been poured.

BARACK OBAMA

The State of Britain, Part One: Just back from a New Year's Eve party. I don't often go to parties, because I'm not that kind of person, I'm a playwright, with more serious concerns. But I went to this one. By bus, of course. I'm not the sort of person who takes taxis. So I hailed a double-decker in the King's Road and told the driver to take me to Islington. He was then to wait for me outside the party for an hour or two and take me back. The instructions were quite clear. But of course this is Thatcher's Britain, so when I left the party – a party I didn't particularly enjoy, by the way, it was hardly serious at all and full of 'amusing' people – the bus was nowhere to be seen (typical) and I was forced to hail, against all my instincts, a black cab. Out of sympathy with the driver I sat with him in the front, observing, observing, observing, my mind racing back to one of those rare defining moments, disproportionately significant but peculiarly illuminating, that had occurred back at the party.

I had been standing in the corner of the room with the dirty paper cup I had specially brought with me, when a man had come over – a tall, flashy type, with an easy smile, wearing a fashionable 'tie'. He said: 'You look a bit lonely, may I introduce myself?' He then introduced himself. I didn't reply, preferring to observe, as most serious playwrights do. He then said – again that fake smile – 'And who are you?'

I was outraged, utterly outraged. And flabbergasted. Shocked, too. Shocked, outraged and flabbergasted. Not for me, of course, but for my profession, and the whole of British Theatre, from the lowest understudy right up to the most brilliant and dangerous playwright (whether that is me or not is beside the point). Why was this man – this man in his fashionable tie, with his promiscuous smile and his over-attentive handshake – pretending not to know who the hell I was? This was a sign of our inexorable national decline, as significant and painful in its way as the Miners' Strike or the Falklands Conflict.

The State of Britain, Part Two: As the hurt and the horror surged within me, I felt driven to speak. 'I'm David Hare,' I said.

'David Hare!' he repeated. 'Goodness! I really enjoy all your plays – you're one of the greatest living playwrights, in my opinion!'

Note that patronising, biased and artfully demeaning tone in a statement riddled with the foul odour of ruling-class condescension: 'ONE OF the greatest LIVING playwrights, IN MY OPINION'. Only in Britain – tired, sick, dislocated, dying Britain – in the 1980s could it be considered 'fashionable' to denigrate a serious playwright in this way. When I got home, I immediately wrote a cool letter to the host of the party, questioning his ethics in inviting me to a function at which there were people who openly hated me, roundly condemning his loathsome hypocrisy in not warning me of his treachery. He eventually replied with some sort of apology. Which all goes to show that here in Thatcher's Britain, the national pastime – the national characteristic – is to apologise, apologise, apologise. When will we as a nation have the courage to stand up for ourselves?

SIR DAVID HARE

It's now the Seventies. The Sixties – they seem like years ago, right? Years and years and years and years ago. Like literally ten years or even longer, right? But I remember them like they were yesterday, which was a Thursday, or was it a Monday? Can't remember. Tuesday – that's it. Or Sunday. Yesterday? Don't talk to me about yesterday – I'm not into the whole tomorrow thing.

KEITH RICHARDS

It is now 1960, the very first year in the extraordinary decade that will, I feel sure, come to be known as the 1960s. Overnight, society has shaken off the starchy sexual mores of the 1950s. Suddenly, young men and women are casting aside their inhibitions and tapping their toes to the urgent, febrile rhythms of Lonnie Donegan. Among enlightened couples, cheese fondue is all the rage.

All the old barriers have suddenly come down. I find to my alarm that even men of the very greatest distinction can't keep their hands to themselves. Last night, I had to fend off the then Chancellor of the Exchequer. I was interviewing him about the trade deficit on live television for *New Year Late Night Love-In* when suddenly he cast aside his red box, pulled down his trousers and leapt on top of me.

As I struggled to retain hold of my clipboard, veteran broadcaster Cliff Michelmore attempted to rectify the situation. 'Let's move swiftly on to the balance of payments, Chancellor,' he said. 'Any hope of an upturn come the autumn?' But before the Chancellor had a chance to reply, the incoming governor of the Bank of England had barged into the studio, wearing nothing but a posing pouch. If this is how the Sixties begin, how on earth will they end?

JOAN BAKEWELL

January 2nd

Today I cook pasta. Pasta plain. But good. For those who come after, these directions I leave:

PASTA PLAIN – BUT GOOD

Ingredients:
Pasta.
And Salt.
And Water.
And Fire.

Directions:
Place the pasta in the water and the salt in the water and the water in the pot and the pot on the fire.

In the pot? The fire in the pot?
No. The water in the pot. The pot on the fire.
The pasta in the water?
Yes in the water.
And the salt in the fire?
No. The salt in the water.
And the water on the fire?

No. The water in the pot and the pot on the fire. Not the water on the fire. For then the fire will die and dying be dead. Nor will the water boil and the pasta will drain dry and not cooked and hard to the teeth.

The salt falls nor does it cease to fall.

The water boils. So be it.

Cease from placing your hand in the boiling water. Place your hand in the boiling water and it will cause you pain.

Much pain?

Very much pain.

In the pot the bubbles bubble up and bubble some more. The bubbles are bubbly. Never more bubbly bubbles bubbling bubbliest. And having bubbled the bubbles still bubbly.

Or bubblier?

Or bubblier.

Across the kitchen a board intended for chopping. Here. Take it. Chop.

What will I chop? There are no ingredients to chop.

Just chop. Don't cease from chopping. To chop is to become a man.

After ten minutes. The pasta stiff and dry and upright no more. The pasta lank and wet and soft. In the eternal damp of water.

Pour water free like some ancient anointing. The pasta left alone in the pot. Alone and naked.

The salt. Where's the salt?

The salt is gone. Lost to the water and gone forever.

I grieve for the salt.

It is the salt for which I grieve.

Tip the pasta out.

The pasta?

Yes. Tip it out. Onto.

A plate?

Yes. And stop.

Finishing your sentences?

Yes.

Why?

Because it is so.

Irritating?

CORMAC McCARTHY

Darling Debo,

Could you bear to cast your bejewell'd eye o'er this weary traveller's joyous twitterings?

Day 1. Yanina, 8 March. We arrive in Prevaza from Yanina with Konitsa and Kalpaki before venturing forth to Kalpaki with Prevaza and Yanina. Umbrous olives procrastinate pleadingly over the weary waters in the priest's leafy garden overlooking a forested valley along which a repining river flows flowingly. O'erhead flies a squawking convoy of stuffed courgettes, flapping fearlessly towards a destination undefined. Ah, the joy of skipping on the petulant pine-needles and the verdant grass underfoot! Gentians cluster in every fissure, and clusters fissure in every gentian. Blow the wind southerly, southerly, southerly! One nearly swoons away with the magic of the language as a sunbaked Sarakatsan muleteer, Christos Karvounis, cackles cautiously, recalling rough-hewn rambles with … <twenty pages cut for reasons of space>

… and when we wake up – joy upon joys! – we fulsomely find we have another thirty-nine delightful days to gorgeously go.

Bundles of love,

Paddy

PATRICK LEIGH-FERMOR, FROM A LETTER TO DEBORAH, DUCHESS OF DEVONSHIRE

January 3rd

Nothing in your memory anywhere of anything so good. Now the pasta is eaten. Disappeared. The pasta disappeared as everything disappears. As the comma disappears and the semi-colon disappears and the inverted comma disappears and the apostrophe disappears and the adjectives and the pronouns all disappear.

Leaving just full stops and And.

And And?

And And.

And And.

CORMAC McCARTHY

Darling Twat,

Can't wait to read your last scrumptious screed, possibly first thing next year, or, failing that, the year after, leisure permitting.

Greece – it was Greece, wasn't it? – sounds desperately Greek, which is just as it should be. One would hate to hear that it had turned all French.

P.S. Why does everyone insist on being so beastly about poor Dr Crippen? He may have been a mite offhand with his wife, but, my word, he was an excellent doctor with a perfectly lovely smile, a dear old friend of Mecca.*

In tearing haste,

Debo

DEBORAH, DUCHESS OF DEVONSHIRE,
LETTER TO PATRICK LEIGH-FERMOR

January 4th

People have been kind enough to call me sharp. To be blunt, I am sharp. It was probably Rilke who first taught me that if ever a man is to be sharp, he needs also to be blunt. This was a revelation to me, partly because I already knew it. The sharp man must make pointed statements in rounded prose, remaining careful that the points emerge from his heart, and not from his head, or they will come out flat. Voltaire, too, taught me to square my feelings with my thoughts, particularly when talking among my circle.

CLIVE JAMES

*Mecca Mitford, Muslim fundamentalist.

T.S. Eliot died today, in 1965. His books only ever sold a few thousand copies. No one reads him now, and he is still dead. But is he still in print? I doubt it. Yet he enjoyed a modest reputation while he remained alive.

V.S. NAIPAUL

January 5th

I'm sat at an official banquet in the Guildhall or wherever. 'Only trouble with prawn cocktails,' I say to the Queen of the Neverlands as I lick my spoon, 'is that they're always too small, don't you find?'

The lady mutters some double dutch in responsibility. As I'm reaching for the bread and butter, I notice there's a heck of a lot of prawn cocktail left in her glass dish and she's just pecking at it. 'Tell you what – we'll swap dishes – you take mine and I'll take yours! That way we'll both be happy! Vous compronay?'

With that, I reach for her prawn cocktail, retaining my own spoon. Sorry, but I don't want to catch foreign germs.

'Very tasty!' I say, turning to the gentleman on my right, the President of Venice or Venezuela or whatever, and try to break the ice. 'Not finishing your prawn cocktail, then, Pedro? Defeated you, has it?'

He looks blank, so to set him at his ease I reach over, shove my spoon in his prawn cocktail and help him out with it. And very tasty it is too, very tasty indeed.

'Much-o grassy-arse, mon amigo!' I say with a pleasant chuckle, very slow so's he'll be able to understand, then grab myself another couple of bread rolls before the waiter runs off with them. These official banquets can leave one feeling very peckish you know, so it's lucky I've had a burger and beans before I came out, washed down with sherry trifle and cheddar cheese, all rounded off with a nice tin of condensed, all very pleasant. Yes, I do love my food.

Come the main course, the old tum is up to its tricks again, making me feel full when I'm not, but I don't want to miss out on the meat – I've always loved my meat – so I seek to remedialise the situation. I look over the President's shoulder for a toilet, very discreetly you understand, but there isn't one within a hundred yards. I don't want to disruptify the banquet, so while the President's talking to the person on his right and the Queen's talking to the person on her left, I reach for the old napkin.

There's nothing you can teach me about napkin-folding. In seconds, I've folded my napkin into the shape of a bucket, and am just adding the finishing touches to the handle and preparing to do my business when Queen Snooty of the Neverlands turns round and asks me where exactly I live blah blah blah.

No way am I going to let chit-chat get in the way of me and my meat so I pass her the napkin-bucket and say to her, very polite, mind, 'Hold this, Your Majesty, if you'd be so kind,' then I poke my little finger down my throat and have a right good sick-up into it, all very discreet, mmm, that's better, wipe the old mouth nice and clean then repossess my napkin-bucket and remark graciously, 'You won't be needing that no more, thank you kindly.'

I stuff the napkin in my right-hand jacket pocket and carry on with my supping. The meat is beautifully tender and the potatoes just right. The soufflé is overdone, but the portions are reasonable and service prompt.

After dinner, we're ushered out into a great hall for liqueurs and coffee and Elizabeth Shaw mints, which I've frankly never liked, they're too small, but luckily I've taken the trouble of hiding a tin of condensed milk behind a curtain on the way in so I make my excuses and polish it off in the vestibule.

So we're all milling around in the hall with our coffees when Tony beckons me over saying, 'John, there's someone here I want you to meet!' It's Henry Kissinger, no less. I want to give the right impression, so I stick my right hand in my jacket pocket, all suave-like, as I make my approach.

'Dr Kissinger,' says Tony, 'may I introduce my Deputy Prime Minister?'

'Delighted to meet you, I'm sure,' I say, all sophisticated. I pull my right hand out of my jacket pocket and give his a good strong shake.

'Mein Gott!' says Kissinger. We all glance down. There's this gooey stuff, bitty and that, dripping off his hand. Tony throws me one of his looks, as if to say it's all my fault! But as I told Pauline after, you can hardly call it my fault if they don't provide accessible toilet facilities at these hoity-toity venues, it's high time something was done about it, it's always the working classes what get the blame and the chinless public school brigade who are let off scot-free, so those of us who, for reasons of pressure and stress at work, sometimes putting in sixteen, seventeen, eighteen hours a day, find it necessary to sick up our food, should be given every facility for so doing.

I attempt to make light of the goo with our distinguished guest. 'Wipe it off, Henry! What do you think sleeves are for?!' I jest. But he doesn't see the funny side. Very German!

All in all, a very pleasant evening.

JOHN PRESCOTT

January 6th

It is the sixth & I am in one of those lassitudes and ebbs of life when I cannot heave another word on to the wall. Hemingway came to lunch & we had a great row about life & letters &c. I said, do you want this quarrel to go on. I would like it to stop now; but if you wish it to go on, then I shall be left with no option but to challenge you to an arm-wrestle & then we shall see who wins. Whereupon, Hemingway turned sheet-white & stroked his mangy flea-ridden drink-sodden beard & ummed & ahed & said he did not wish to go on with our argument, but it was jolly well all my fault that it had started in the first place.

I was tempted to bite my tongue but, my word, I was not prepared to back down to this impossible hairy foul-mouthed baboon. Very well, then, Ernie I said – I know how he hates to be called Ernie – roll up your sleeve & place your right elbow on this table & be a man for once.

Our right hands locked like bruised whippets & by the time I had counted down 1 & 2 & 3 & Ready & Steady & Go I could glimpse feverish globules of glinting sweat already flooding down his creasy brow like slugs. Hemingway pushed & pushed & pushed; my goodness how he pushed, his face beetroot purple with the pushing & the panting & the shoving & the grunting. A revolting performance. After a while of this disgusting vulgar odious show, I could not bear to view his visage any longer & so I sought to offer some succour to my poor miserable overwrought eyes by picking up a book of Augustinian verse in my left hand & reading its contents for merciful distraction & all the while Hemingway continued with his grotesque exhibition.

Did I feel an element of pity for him: is that why I brought our arm-wrestle to a close? Perhaps: or perhaps not. Perhaps I could no longer stomach the continuation of those swinelike grunts & pants hammering on my eardrums. The time had come. I moved my right hand forward and down in one beautiful arc and within less than a second the man of straw was defeated.

Now will you admit that the semi-colon is the superior of the full stop? I said. Yes, said Hemingway. Then say it! said I. The semi-colon is the superior of the full stop, he said. Now blow your man's nose & wipe away those ugly tears, I said, thrusting my handkerchief at this hirsute & now broken stick. In all honesty, I cannot recollect arm-wrestling with such easeful triumph since last I took on Edith Sitwell.

VIRGINIA WOOLF

January 7th

Another average day. First, I grunge the sicky-wicky, then I scowze out the scab-tube, then I skunk down the flunk-pustule, and that just about takes me up to lunch. For lunch, I have a light shit-snack of cannelloni with tomato sauce like the castrated cocks of two hundred dwarves dowsed in their own blood, then it's back to irking the scuzz-wock. Then I'll screw-whack the scrag-head and soil the downside of the whinge-pussy before getting in a bit of shagbagging the apothegm before a dinner of Supa-scrag-fleck-on-toast. After dinner, it's down to the spick-arse to sconse some clap-wax off a Pluto-gasket, and then it's into my jim-jams and nighty-night with heads down for beddy-byes.

MARTIN AMIS

Day 18,263. The housemates are celebrating their half-century in the *Big Brother* house. 11.15 a.m. Mikey and Richard have wrapped up well and are in the garden. Glyn is having a bit of a cough. His back's been playing up again. Imogen and Lea are making their way on their zimmer frames to the living area. Satnav and Cornflake, who only joined the house thirty-two years ago, are in the kitchen, getting their bearings. Nikki is in the diary room. She's left her teeth somewhere but she can't remember where.

NIKKI: I'm bored shitless she really does my head in she's gonna push me so far one of these days she so really fucks me off so much I fuckin' swear it does my head in.

BB: Today, Nikki, you have been in the *Big Brother* house for fifty years. You are now seventy three years of age. Nikki – how do you feel?

NIKKI: I'm bored shitless she really does my head in she's gonna push me so far one of these days she so really fucks me off so much I fuckin' swear it does my head in.

BB: Thank you, Nikki. You may now leave the diary room.

NIKKI: Big Brother? One more thing.

BB: Yes, Nikki?

NIKKI: I'm bored shitless she really does my head in she's gonna push me so far one of these days she so really fucks me off so much I fuckin' swear it does my head in.

BB: Thank you, Nikki.

January 8th

A delightful evening of much jollity! Mummy and Daddy to dinner. Over truly splendid creamy meringues prepared by our truly splendid housekeeper Dalisay, Harold tells them with his usual brilliant eloquence of the terrible things that are going on in Serbia – and all thanks, he explains, to those positively brutal and monstrous Americans! Over coffee, Harold treats us all to a truly splendid reading of 'Up Your Fucking Arse', his truly splendid denunciation of the Bush regime. Mummy and Daddy both have their eyes closed in immense concentration. Awfully touching!

LADY ANTONIA FRASER

January 9th

I flick the light switch and the light goes on. Whatever happened to faulty electrical fittings? In the old days, two or three youngsters would be electrocuted every day through haphazard wirings. But no more. Things do not always change for the better, I fear.

ROGER SCRUTON

January 10th

The river flows, and it keeps flowin'. And having flown, it flows again. There's no rhyme or reason, my friend, that's just the way rivers flow. What is in the river is not river but water, but it's not just the water that flows, but the river too.

BOB DYLAN

Yet another programme on the television about the so-called Queen but it doesn't answer the question: who the heck is the REAL Elizabeth Windsor? A lot of people think that just because she's commander-in-chief of the British armed forces, she's out there with her machine-gun and her stash of grenades, leading her troops into battle against her subject peoples on a day-to-day basis. Not so. Aged eighty years old, she hasn't so much as raised a fist and given an assailant a bloody nose or kicked an opponent in the balls with her dainty size-four feet for quite a few years now.

Instead, she sits all alone in a basement of Buckingham Castle with the curtains drawn watching repeats of *EastEnders* on her ten-inch black-and-white television while scooping tinned spaghetti hoops into her mouth with her gloved hands. She could watch absolutely anything she chose – she's even got a remote control, for crying out loud – including programmes about culture and politics. But no, she does not choose. Instead, she just sits there, watching whatever she wants. Just like my mother in her aged care facility. These old people truly make my blood boil. The Queen could have taken an Aborigine male to her marriage bed and thus presented a beacon of hope to all the oppressed people of the world, but did she do it? Did she heck. An Aborigine husband would have signalled that whatever her toffee-nosed advisers might tell her, dammit, she was on the side of the poor and the craply-treated. And the young couple could have gone on a true Royal walkabout, living off grubs and nettles and tracing the songlines of the Home Counties for a period of seven years before returning barefoot to the so-called civilisation that is commonly known – don't make me laugh! – as London Town. But she just didn't make the effort. Ha! Don't talk to Lilibet about effort. Sorry, guys – it's a word that doesn't feature in her vocabulary.

GERMAINE GREER

January 11th

1979 is not getting off to a good start. News of PM's proposed state of emergency v. depressing. In the morning, I begin to prepare an advisory paper setting out a far-reaching plan for the future well-being of the UK but suddenly it's midday and time for lunch, so I scribble

'WHY NOT SELL OFF NORTH SEA OIL' in big letters and hand it to the PM, making it to the Gay Hussar just in time for lovely chilled wild cherry soup followed by veal goulash with lovely Shirley Williams.

Shirley desperately concerned about child poverty up North. I say how desperately concerned I am about it as well, and tell her that I think Jim is probably desperately concerned too. Tell her the best way to tackle it is to redefine it, thus bringing 95 per cent of all people into category of 'better off'. It's the least we can do to give them a leg-up. Pudding a lovely walnut cheese pancake with extra cream. Shirley suggests I might like to take over the Chairmanship of British Leyland. Back to No. 10 just in time to hear news of economic collapse, then off to Covent Garden for lovely *Tosca*.

BERNARD DONOUGHUE

Using my special friends-and-family key, I let myself into Buckingham Palace and put my head round the Queen's sitting-room door.

Elizabeth tells me she's been hurting dreadfully and has lost her sense of identity. 'I'm, like, who am I?' she says. She always turns to me for comfort. She finds me very down to earth. 'You're a very caring person, Heather,' she says. 'Probably too caring for your own good. When my time comes, I hope they'll make you Queen. It's what Diana would have wanted, and to replace me they'll need someone well known throughout the world for her tireless charity work.'

I'm like, 'I couldn't be Queen, that's not my style, I'm not up to it.' But she gets me sat down and says, 'You've spent your whole life caring for others, Heather. And it's time you got them to care for you. You'd fit this throne real beautiful – and what's more, for all the love you've got inside you, you deserve it, love.'

HEATHER MILLS McCARTNEY

January 12th

News comes through of the death of General Galtieri. A lot of unhelpful things are being said of him. But at least he had the guts to stand up to her, which is more than one can say for the Bakers and Gummers and Hurds of this world.

And one should never forget that Galtieri was a superb connoisseur of porcelain. He was kind enough to give me a delightful Wedgwood tea service when I was over on a visit. We exchanged Christmas cards ever after.

SIR EDWARD HEATH

January 13th

What are you that makes me feel thus? Are you thus what makes me feel that? Feel me thus that you makes what are?

You are my winged Pegasus, my hirsute daffodil, my sea urchin of song, my orang-utan pirouetting on a high wire, my banana unpeeled, my mango spurting vertiginous aspidistras over the umbrous concavities of Sappho's juts and nooks. You affect me as a young gazelle affects the mountain over which it lollops, dollops and, er, sollops – oh, bollops.

I close my beautiful brown deep brown soft brown eyes. My lips like smoked salmon wrapped in cream cheese parcels with a sprig of fennel, moist, urgent, costly but on special offer, meet your lips, as fresh and nutritious as the morning's cod.

My tongue laps your lips; your lips are lapped, and, lapping lips lip lappingly like lollipops over lipped laps slapped slippingly. Your mouth opens and closes, blowing and sucking, sucking and blowing as my hands wreathe your gills in luscious circles of contentment.

Your gills? Wreathe your gills? I open my eyes. My God! It is not you at all but the goldfish I am kissing. That which I am kissing is the goldfish!

JEANETTE WINTERSON

January 14th

It happened again this morning. I had just finished tape-recording myself for the archives, swallowing my third mug of tea and finishing off a banana fruit when the newspapers – many of them still delivered by workers to the private homes of millionaires, even in this day and age! – were delivered to my home. What, I wondered, are the latest press comments about me and the democratic policies I have been fighting for tooth and nail these past fifty years? I read every page of the *Daily Express*, including sports and arts, into the tape-recorder, but, on my playback, failed to hear a single mention of myself and my policies.

It's their new strategy, y'see. Having in the past sought to undermine democracy by lampooning me, they now try to achieve the same result by ignoring me, making me out to be some sort of 'fringe' character!

Poured m'self another cup of tea. The tape-recorder picked up all the glugs, so it obviously doesn't need new batteries quite yet.

TONY BENN*

To Chatsworth. Poky.

WOODROW WYATT

January 15th

Repetition is the memory of repetition. And repetition is the memory of repetition.

ADAM PHILLIPS

---

*Politician and diarist. Volumes of diaries include *Office Without Power 1968–1972, Power Without Office 1973–1976, Office Without Office 1977–1980, Power Without Office or Power 1981–1990, Office Without Power or Office or Power 1991–2001, Power Cut 2001–2010.*

January 16th

BBC announcers insist on using the expression 'This is the news.' One hears it every night, without fail. Yet news is plural. They should say, 'These are the news,' and, half an hour later, 'Those were the news.' They never will, of course, because the BBC is a socialist institution, within which correct English is regarded as the enemy of the state. Have we ever had a more horrid public culture?

CHARLES MOORE

I maintain (though she might, in truth, query this) that it was I who usefully introduced my Aunt Phyl to scampi and chips, at an excellent but now defunct castellated hostelry overlooking the Bristol Channel at Linton in 1973. Or was it 1974? Conceivably (and here I am, metaphorically speaking, sticking my neck out) it was 1972, or even 1971, though if it was 1971, then it might not have been the castellated hostelry that we ate in, as a useful visit to my local library yesterday afternoon between 3.30 p.m. and 4.23 p.m. confirmed me in my suspicion that the hostelry in question was in fact closed for the greater part of 1971, owing to a refurbishment programme. In that case, and if it really was 1971, which, frankly, seems increasingly unlikely given the other dates available, then it is within the realms of possibility that we ate at another hostelry entirely, possibly one overlooking the North Sea, and, if so, it is equally possible that we feasted not on scampi and chips but on shepherd's pie. Did we also consume a side order of vegetables? Memory is, I have found, a fickle servant, so I am unable to recall whether, on this occasion, we indulged in a side order of vegetables, if we were there at all. It is, I fear, another blank, another lost or discarded piece in the jigsaw of my past.

MARGARET DRABBLE

January 17th

They tell me that in some shops they have started selling loaves of bread that are what they call 'ready-and-sliced'. I fervently hope this is one trend that doesn't 'catch on'. And is there really any need for this new-fangled idea of soup in tins? Broth tastes so much better bubbling away in a great big open pot, stirred by a chef who really knows his stuff and served at one's table in the open air by a marvellous old character somewhere on a wonderful Highland moor. By denying our children such pleasures, I fear we are in profound danger of cutting them off from reality.

HRH THE PRINCE OF WALES

January 18th

Throughout this year, I shall be following the famous not to say distinguished rock singer Michael George for a three-part documentary series. Today, we recorded the first in a series of interviews, as well as my introduction. There's a very great deal of excitement about this extraordinary project:

MELVYN: Michael George* shot to fame as a leading member of the trio Whim!. As a signwriter, sorry, songwriter, he has achieved international success by writing acclaimed songs such as um er by writing several um famous songs. Michael George is now internationally acknowledged as a erm as a leading erm singer, indeed as one of the most singery and singerest singers erm of his generation. On the eve of his first world tour since his last, Michael George gave us this exclusive insight into the way he erm …

GEORGE: Super to see you, Melvyn! How you doin'? Ooh, you smell nice! Mmmm … doesn't he smell nice, boys?

---

*Possibly a mistranscription of singer/songwriter George Michael (born 1963). Hit singles include 'Wake Me Up Before You Gargle' (1983), 'Don't Let the Son Go Down on Me' (1992), 'Cheeses to a Child' (1995) and 'I Want Your Socks' (1998).

MELVYN: Can we start with the early days, Michael? You began life as a foetus and then you were a baby for – what? one or two years – and then, am I right in thinking, proceeded to become a child, in your case a boy?

GEORGE: Yeah, it was really eating me up, all I wanted was my dignity and my self-determination and the whole process of like being a child made me understand something about how this government really manipulates us into believing – sorry, Melvyn, can we stop for a sec? You know what? I'm feeling a bit sweaty. Do I look sweaty to you, Melvyn? Now, be honest!

MELVYN: Zzzzzzz. Zzzzzzz. (Wakes with a start.) Where am I? Who are you? Where were we?! Yes! Go on!

GEORGE: D'you know, Melvyn, I'm feeling a bit sweaty?

MELVYN: Um. No. Remind me. How does it go?

MELVYN BRAGG

January 19th

Swiftian? Come off it. That's what I thought when I read this week's obituaries, dripping with a sweaty mixture of vintage port, caviar and Marmite sandwiches, of Auberon Waugh.

I remember it well, the smug old world of El Vino in Fleet Street. Right-wing journalists would mix with left-wing journalists, both drowning their differences in champagne (so much more fizzy than common-or-garden white wine, dontcha know, old chap). It was all just a game – and instead of smashing each other's faces with their fists, and demanding urgent, much needed social reforms, they preferred to discuss their differences over what they would no doubt call a drinkie-poo. They spent hours 'debating', 'exchanging opinions', 'seeing the other point of view', and so on, in a typical recreation of the toffee-nosed public schools which had, years before, puked them out in their stiff collars, sporting blazers, corduroy shorts and school neckties imprinted with a hundred little swastikas.

To that hoity-toity coterie, all that matters is a joke or two. And it doesn't matter if the rest of us can't for the life of us understand it. 'Knock, Knock,' they say, and when their victim replies: 'Who's there?' they mention a perfectly ordinary Christian name, rendering us, their victims, speechless. 'There's an Irishman, a Scotsman and an Englishman,' they say.

'And we are all part of the EEC,' I correct them.

So what's so funny about 'jokes'? Don't ask me. I'm not someone who likes to 'laugh' – especially not at a time when so many ordinary Britons are living below the poverty line in inner cities deprived of inward investment by the self-serving machinations of big business. Laughter is to be distrusted and abhorred, whether it comes from the right or the so-called left. Funny? So funny I forgot to laugh.

Don't imagine the breed is dying out. Far from it. Boris Johnson, editor of the *Spectator*, is a writer of just this 'humorous' stamp, with mannerisms to match. Charming? If you say so. But how can you describe someone as 'charming' who subscribes to a belief in the free-market economy?

The last time I saw him, Johnson asked me to write an article for the *Spectator*, damn him.

I refused point blank. I told him that throughout my career I have only written for people who share my views. I'm certainly not going to start arguing with people who'll disagree with me for political reasons of their own.

POLLY TOYNBEE

January 20th

Alfred Wainwright died today, in 1991. He wasted a lifetime on walking, but still never managed to get beyond the Lake District.

V.S. NAIPAUL

Whatever happened to fun? In the heady, far-off days of my youth, we certainly knew how to have fun! My grandmother, Edith, the seventh Marchioness of Londonderry, taught me how! She had always been intent on injecting gaiety into life!

Her charmed circle would gossip like mad, play silly games, flirt with each other, tell outrageous jokes, widdle down the stairwell, and drink copious quantities of the delicious pre-war Londonderry champagne!

She even enjoyed a close friendship with the Labour leader Ramsay MacDonald! 'He was an old-fashioned socialist,' she wrote in her memoirs. 'He loved beautiful things, gorgeous pageantry, fine silverware, dressing up in resplendent uniforms, being waited on hand and foot, and taking the cream of the British aristocracy up the botty!'

Throughout my life, we couldn't have had half so much fun without our full complement of servants, all of them the most tremendous characters!

The marvellous thing was how much they respected us! I'll never forget what the inimitable Mr Chambers, Daddy's bathroom butler, said after vigorously wiping Daddy's behind after he had experienced a particularly severe dose of diarrhoea! He said, 'It's come up beautiful, sir – and may I add what a pleasure and a privilege it has been for me to attend to you today!'

Sadly, Mr Chambers shot himself the next day. It could have been the most frightful blow, but thankfully the vacancy was soon filled!

LADY ANNABEL GOLDSMITH

Cut a hole in a bedsheet. Put your head through it. Step into a washing machine. Ask your friend to switch it on. Watch the world spin round and round. Step out of the machine. Your bedsheet will still have a hole. Ask your maid to repair it. You are an artist. Yoko loves you.

YOKO ONO

January 21st

A great night out for Tony. A great night out for New Labour. And a great night out for Britain. Yup, it was the 1997 Brit Awards, that literally incredible celebration of the new explosion of British youth and talent. 'I live in a house in a very big house in the countraaaay,' sang Blur, and you felt your whole body rising up, and not just because it was nearly time to go.

All of us in New Labour felt it would be fantastic to forge an association with youth and optimism, so Donald Dewar was put in charge of booking a table way back in October. The eight of us – Gordon Brown, wearing his old flared jeans, the lovely Ken and Barbara Follett, Tony, me, Jack Straw (looking very casual in a cravat over a beige poloneck), Margaret Beckett (ex-Steeleye Span, of course) and John Prescott (squeezed into his velvet loon pants) were lucky enough to share a table with the super young lads from Oasis.

At dinner, we were keen to find out what the youth of Britain really thinks about the major issues confronting this country. Over soup, Margaret, sitting next to Noel Gallagher, suggested we might harness the great energy of Britpop to help solve some of the problems facing us. Noel brought the natural verve of youth to his reply. 'Piss off, toothy,' he said, reaching for another can of lager.

'Thanks, Noel. I certainly think that response gives us much to build on,' enthused Tony. 'Any other suggestions, lads?'

At that moment, the Oasis drummer removed Jack Straw's specs and began to wiggle them round in the air with all the super high spirits of the young. Jack made it clear he was enjoying the joke tremendously by laughing for five to six seconds before saying, 'Joke over, lads – joke over.' But by this time the drummer had given them to the rhythm guitarist, who was now wearing them on his bottom.

It was left to John Prescott to break the ice. 'Are New Labour's plans for the renationalisation of our railways exciting much interest among the young?' he asked.

'Speak up, fatty!' replied Liam Gallagher, and we all laughed appreciatively at his rough-and-ready Scouse wit while he amiably sprayed us all with a frothed-up can of Special Brew.

Tony has always been a terrific fan of pop music, and for much of the first session – by the exciting new band Blur – I noted he had his top set of teeth pressed over his bottom lip while his hands played along on his dummy guitar. Meanwhile, Jack Straw was busily trying to retrieve his spectacles, which by now had been passed by the rhythm guitarist of Oasis to the bass guitarist of Garbage, who had employed his lighter to bend them into some sort of abstract 'mound', reflecting the spiritual aspirations of the young.

'I live in a house, in a very big house, in the countraaaay,' sang Blur. I noticed that Margaret, having removed her straw hat with its lovely green ribbon, had got out her pocket calculator to work out how the aforementioned very big house in the country would be affected from a tax point of view under New Labour, if it was owner-occupied with a 50 per cent endowment mortgage, repayable over twenty-five years. 'Best not tell him,' she whispered to me, 'but he'll be 7 per cent worse off under New Labour.'

Next came Tony's big moment. He was presenting the Lifetime Achievement award to David Bowie, a personal favourite. Tony was wearing his loose-cut Armani dark suit with a floral tie, but beneath it – and this is what viewers couldn't see – he was kitted out in a multicoloured Aladdin Sane bodystocking, ready to meet his hero.

'It's been a great year of energy, youth, vitality, and great, great music,' began Tony, 'and believe me, we in New Labour draw terrific inspiration from your tremendous efforts.' Sadly, the rest of his speech was drowned out for me by the organist from Screwball vomiting over Ken Follett's double-breasted Armani suit.

PETER MANDELSON

January 22nd

To Buckingham Palace, to attend an investiture. Prince Philip greets me with his usual affectionate male banter. 'What the hell are you doing here?' he jests. 'I thought I told them to keep you away!'

I roar with infectious laughter as he turns on his heel – but with perfect timing I catch him just as he reaches the door. 'You are an irrepressible old character, sir!' I congratulate him. 'A national treasure, forsooth!'

At this point, the Prince raises a good-natured fist and socks me in the mouth.

'Marvellous, sir!' I enthuse, picking up my front teeth from the beautifully polished floor. 'Have you ever heard my immortal anecdote about my meeting with Henry Cooper? Oh, but you MUST!'

GYLES BRANDRETH

January 23rd

Last night at dinner, I was placed next to the German Chancellor, Adolf Hitler.

The dinner consisted of a fine venison stew accompanied by potatoes dauphinoise. Adolf Hitler has a well-known temper, but I did not see it. Our talk revolved around a new musical in the West End, which he had not seen. Nor had I. I told him that I had been reliably informed by Sacheverell that it is quite marvellous, with colourful costumes, extravagant settings and a number of good tunes. He promised he will try to catch it if ever he manages to reach Britain. I noticed that he uses his napkin quite sparingly: unusual, I thought, for an Austrian.

CLARISSA EDEN

So Pete's moved out he's like so moved out at the end of the day he's moved out tell me about it but I'm in a good place and my boobs are in a good place they're really focused they've so talked it over, they work as a team say what you like they got respect for each other, I say to them let's get round a table and talk it over if Pete doesn't like them goin' clubbin' and havin' a bit of fun well then that's up to Pete at the end of the day it's the children they're concerned about their concern is for the children 110 per cent tell me about it so if they want to go out and have a bit of fun then I've got to be honest with you I'm not going to stop them.

KATIE PRICE

January 24th, 1925

My Dear Lady Cunard,

Thank you so much for that lovely stay last weekend. We both enjoyed ourselves very much. It was really very kind of you to have us.

I do hope my little 'diversion' on Saturday evening wasn't too awfully inconvenient for you, and that your servants have managed to get most of the mud out of the carpets! From something you said – or was it just a look? – I came away thinking that I may, in your eyes, have done something 'wrong'. If so, I can only apologise, but what is a man if he cannot seize the moment to strip off all his loathsome lily-livered clothes and wrestle his fellow man naked, strong, tumultuous, full of the very urge of life that lies within them, and all in a deep, soft, dirty – real dirty – and splodgesome sea of mud.

You may argue – in your typically grey, bourgeois, corrupt, stinking, decaying way – that I had no 'right' to order your gardeners to load ten, eleven, twelve wheelbarrows high with sludge from the ditches, wheel them into the blue drawing room and offload them in the area in front of the blazing fire. And you may also argue – loudmouthed bitch – that I could at least have rolled up your priceless carpet – symbol of all that is petty and extravagant and worthless in this age – and placed it to one side.

Away with your arguments! An end to your grey, sniffy, hoity-toity objections! When I rolled with your stable lad in the mud, as we pummelled each other with our fists and each felt the brute within and the mud without, I at last felt free and open and alive and triumphant and, yes, pure! How dare you suggest that mud-wrestling between two men should be confined to the outdoors, should be shunted away into the barns and the brooks, should be well away from all the upholstery and fine furnishings. There is nothing dirty in mud! This pervasive and wretched belief in household cleanliness is the sign of a decrepit age! There is no good carpet, no good sofa, that has not been splattered with the mud thrown off as two or more bold and muscle-bound men come a-grappling! Your priggish mud-hatred fills my blood with contempt.

Finally, once again, many thanks for the most marvellous stay. You made us feel so 'at home'. We both came home greatly refreshed, and full of wonderful memories of a really terrific weekend.

Yours ever,
David

D.H. LAWRENCE,
LETTER TO LADY CUNARD

I spoke to TB and started drafting resignation letters. I felt desperately sorry for Peter Mandelson. He had clearly been crying, and needed my support.

I went over to him, said this is all absolutely dreadful but we just have to get through it. I put one arm around his shoulder, and with the other I eased the knife, as gently as I could, between his shoulderblades. By this time, he was writhing in pain, but I assured him that I would be strong for him, and do everything physically possible to ease his passing.

He kept saying why, why, why, but I reassured him that it just had to be done. As the tears cascaded down his cheeks, I sat alongside him and comforted him and read him his farewell resignation letter, and I gripped his shoulder and told him he had to be strong and then I gave it one last thrust. 'You don't deserve this, Peter, you really don't, you're one of the greatest ministers this country ever had,' I said.

Bumped into JP on the way home, and he congratulated me on a very smooth operation. We agreed that Mandelson's no better than a cartload of bollocks and we're 100 per cent better off without him.

ALASTAIR CAMPBELL

January 25th

To Cuba. Introduced to President Castro. No oil painting. Very full of himself. Absurd bushy beard, army 'fatigues', regional accent (Welsh?). Inquire whether he is a Derbyshire Castro. 'I myself am a regular at Chatsworth,' I add, helpfully. He fails to take the bait. Instead, he drones on about the Missile Crisis. Missile Crisis this, Missile Crisis that. Typically lower class, living from crisis to crisis. So dreadfully panicky.

JAMES LEES-MILNE

PHILIP PULLMAN: I don't like the word 'God', never have done, never will do. It's meaningless, for the simple reason that God doesn't exist.

DR ROWAN WILLIAMS: Well, Philip, that's a fascinating point. I think you've hit on something very very profound there, indeed something very meaningful, in a spiritual way.

PHILIP PULLMAN: Christianity is on a hiding to nothing, because Jesus was not the son of God.

DR ROWAN WILLIAMS: That's marvellously bold, Philip, and I salute you for it! It takes a creative artist of your tremendous powers of observation to say something so challenging and stimulating for the rest of us! But would you mind awfully if I took you up on something you said just now about Jesus?

PHILIP PULLMAN: As you know, I'm a very busy man, but not too busy to spare you a moment or two, Rowan. Fire away!

DR ROWAN WILLIAMS: You said something to the effect that Jesus was not the son of God, and also that – do please correct me if I'm wrong! – Christianity is on 'a hiding to nothing ...'

PHILIP PULLMAN: Absolutely.

DR ROWAN WILLIAMS: Well, that's a wonderful phrase, tremendously powerful. 'A hiding to nothing'. You at your impressive best! For me, it's a phrase that carries real emotional power. And of course, in a very real sense, the Christian pursuit of God – or whatever we want to call him! – is indeed a pursuit of nothing, in the sense that the divinity, or what-have-you, is *immaterial* and not of this earth. So the expression 'a hiding to nothing' very much sums up what the Christian Church should be aiming for. I think we're entirely at one on that, I must say.

PHILIP PULLMAN: Rowan, in my new book, *The Good Man Jesus and the Scoundrel Christ*, which you have so kindly agreed to help me publicise –

DR ROWAN WILLIAMS: Oh, it was the very least I could do …

PHILIP PULLMAN: … Very kind, nevertheless. In my new book, I attempt to show organised religion as a source of falsehood and wickedness. As a theologian, would you go along with this?

DR ROWAN WILLIAMS: Well, of course, it's a fascinating topic for conjecture, tremendously rich and intriguing, but, no, as the leader of an organised religion, on the whole I'm not sure I entirely buy into that. Frankly, I can see problems with it. Put it this way, Philip: it gives me pause.

PHILIP PULLMAN: Really, Rowan – it's so easy to be dismissive!

DR ROWAN WILLIAMS: I hope I wasn't dismissive. Perhaps I was, and if so, I can only apologise.

PHILIP PULLMAN: Apology accepted. So I think we can both agree that the established Church is a source of falsehood and wickedness. We have plenty of common ground.

DR ROWAN WILLIAMS: Well, though it's a profoundly interesting point, perhaps I wouldn't want to go quite as far as …

PHILIP PULLMAN: So we're entirely at one on that.

DR ROWAN WILLIAMS: I've always considered 'at one' an extraordinarily helpful phrase, and I must say it thrills me deeply to hear you use it, Philip. It reinforces my sense that, for all our surface differences, the two of us are really thinking along the same lines. Very much so.

PHILIP PULLMAN: And another point I make in my book is that any head of an organised religion is likely to torture and kill anyone who disagrees with him.

DR ROWAN WILLIAMS: That's a very striking point, Philip, though we may have one or two minor points of difference on the detail – for instance, as Archbishop of Canterbury, I would never seriously consider torturing or killing anyone just because they disagree with me, whatever we may mean by 'disagree'! But I think we are united in our search for human value, and that's the most important thing.

PHILIP PULLMAN: You say you won't torture or kill those of us who have the temerity to disagree with you! Well, if I've extracted that promise from you today, Rowan, then our discussion won't have been a complete waste of time! Now, I've got to rush to another speaking engagement, so I must go. Some of us have work to do! If you could just carry my bags to the taxi, Rowan, there's a good fellow.

DR ROWAN WILLIAMS: I'm frankly overwhelmed that a great author such as yourself thinks of me as a good fellow, Philip!

PHILIP PULLMAN: That's very literal of you, Rowan. Hurry up, now! Chip-chop!

PHILIP PULLMAN IN CONVERSATION WITH DR ROWAN WILLIAMS

January 26th

Have found a way of knotting my necktie using an extraordinary little gadget on my Swiss Army penknife. Its recommended use in the accompanying pamphlet is for taking the stones out of horses' hooves, but they keep these other uses quiet, don't they, just in case the ordinary decent people get to hear of them. Whereas tying my necktie used to take, ooh, a minute, with this handy gadget it can now take over fifteen minutes. I can't recommend it highly enough. Of course, the minute word gets out about it, it'll be dynamite, there'll be the most massive international cover-up involving all the powers the state has at its disposal. But that's what you'd expect of the feudal hierarchy under which we are forced to live, isn't it? Either that, or they make one out to be potty!

Unpeel a banana fruit and eat it, first throwing away the mushy white bit inside.

TONY BENN

I'm mad for the economic downturn! Mad for it! Mass unemployment is so sexy, hm? When the economic graph swoops down like that, like a curve from Fragonard, I think it is so gorgeous, so trendy! My new evening-wear range for Chanel is a wonderful homage to that curve, with all my clothes with downturns off the shoulders in dark, dark greys and delicious blacks.

KARL LAGERFELD

January 27th

On this day many, many years ago, I was introduced to Mr Gandhi at a party of Diana Cooper's.

I was perfectly frank. I informed him there was nothing very clever about parading around in a loincloth drinking one's own urine and generally acting the giddy goat.

As a result, he fell head over heels in love with me.

Men love to be told the truth, even when painful.

BARBARA CARTLAND

January 28th

I learn from the wireless that the American space 'shuttle' (horrid word) *Challenger* has exploded seconds after lift-off. Serves them jolly well right. When will these tenth-raters learn to place me in charge of their operations? Instead, they leave it to nincompoops and incompetents. Of course, these sissies at Mission Control are interested only in themselves. Their instinct is to engineer matters in such a way that their achievements catch up – surpass, perchance! – my own. What nonsense! Do they not realise that I am widely regarded as the foremost expert in the world on the vast majority of subjects? In a huff, they conceitedly disregard me and 'blast off' without so much as a by-your-leave. And look what happens! Will they never learn?

A.L. ROWSE

It's only this that motivates me to write about my father at all: this vexed question of masculinity, of what it is to be a man. An unutterably grey nimbus of brutality surrounded my parents. They fought to the death, brandishing decency, the nuclear weapon of the suburban bourgeoisie. On the crap terrace of our suburban semi, my mother would coldheartedly ask my father how his day had been. Shielding the blow, he would reply, viciously, that it had been fine – and with a final savage swipe he would then tell her to put her legs up, before threatening her with a 'nice' cup of tea. The two of them were a schizophrenic hermaphrodite, their marriage a screaming Procrustes, always stretched to breaking point – and beyond. I once overheard my mother say, 'How about a nice biscuit then, dear?' It was a dubiously interrogatory phrase designed to force upon the prostrate victim an all-out assault, or attack, that could be met only with the tiny porous shit-brown shield of the absent HobNob. When my father replied, 'Mmm … lovely,' I knew then that he had allowed his manhood to wither into a nothingness as weary, diminished and yet somehow sublimely totemic as a small mollusc stamped upon by an elephant before being subdivided with a pair of compasses by an aberrant algebraitician who is nursing a rare neurotic compulsive disorder that forces him to make things very small, or minuscule.

WILL SELF

January 29th

The Prime Minister of Korea is an exceptionally cultured man, a brilliant and congenial scholar and devoted public servant. We were indeed honoured to be able to entertain him to a finger buffet of a selection of finest cuts of British Spam at our Embassy, which has now been moved from the old mansion house to the more convenient and easy-to-clean lean-to just six miles further along the same road. He assured us that he found our new bring-a-bottle policy highly sensible, and was obviously delighted to meet Major Ronald Ferguson, who had agreed to come along to lend the necessary glamour and dignity to the event. The trade agreement went through very smoothly, with Korea agreeing to export millions of pounds of their manufactured goods to us and we, in turn, agreeing not to send any more of our awful stuff to them. Handshakes all round, leaving just enough time to prepare for a reasonably good dinner.

SIR NICHOLAS HENDERSON

Deep into my research for my mega-film *The Young Victoria*. Not many people these days have ever heard of Queen Victoria – and I'm determined to remedy that! I want the world to become aware of one marvellous little lady who went by the name of Queen Victoria – or Her Maj, as she preferred to be known!!!

So who exactly was the young Victoria? My intensive research tells me that not only did she climb her way up the greasy pole to become Queen of All England, but she was also far from the dowdy old boot-faced frump of popular imagination. The young Victoria was in fact a beautiful person with flowers in her hair, porcelain shoulders, great legs and truly galumptious boobs, a fun-loving chick who liked nothing better than hooting with laughter whilst flirting unashamedly with all the dishiest blokes in the room! She was one helluva young lady who adored going down to the local town square to literally stuff herself with barbecued bratwurst in a bun – and lots more ketchup for me, please, Albert!

SARAH, DUCHESS OF YORK

January 30th

My antecedents, seasoned aristocrats all, were the founders of what we are now pleased to describe, in our impishly ironic way, as the Land of the Free and the Home of the Brave.

My great-grandfather, Senator Bore Vidal of New York, the owner of 200,000 acres of prime farming land east of Buffalo, married my great-grandmother Edwina Crashing, the daughter of Amelia Crashing, whose father was one of the Wilds of Montana, giving birth to my grandfather, Senator Wild Crashing Bore, who in turn married Miss Gore Blimey from one of the most influential aristocratic families in London's gorgeously affluent Hackney East.

From their union sprang, with, I regret to say, more promptitude than pulchritude, the Hon. Mrs Bore V. Dull of Oklahoma, who then gave birth to a famously talented son, Gore V. Dull, later to become better known as Gore Vidal, now widely respected as the nation's foremost novelist, social commentator and historian.

On my father's side, I am related to Abraham Lincoln and Thomas Jefferson, neither of them inconsiderable figures in the political arena, though one must learn, I suppose, to overlook their deficiencies in the facial hair department. On the military side, my distinguished great-great-grandfather General Gore L. Vidal was at Custer's side at the Battle of the Little Big Horn. Many believe it to have been General Gore's personal message of encouragement to the troops ('TO THE FIRST MAN WHO GETS OUT OF HERE ALIVE, A FREE SHAMPOO AND SET') that swung the balance in that least dainty of skirmishes. In turn, General Gore's great-nephew, Sassoon Vidal, the founder of the first literary salon, emerged as the major poet of the First World War, no anthology complete without his moving lines: 'The shells burst all about us/Spraying mud o'er our uniforms/Clean on this bleak morn.'

My English critics have attempted to ignore the illustrious and influential pedigree from which I so deftly sprang. But then no one of any breeding cares any more about that inconsiderable little offshore isle, sinking beneath the weight of its own – how shall I put it? – snobbery.

GORE VIDAL

What is it about books that makes them so truly great to read? I think it's the way the words are printed on every page, the right way up and in just the right order.

This means you can start reading on the first page and then continue reading through the middle pages all the way to the last.

Here are some of my absolute favourite books to read.

War by Leo Tolstoy. A great read.

(And why not buy the two-volume edition which includes *Peace* by the same great author?)

Middlemarch by George Eliot. Another great read. Hundreds of pages of great words and punctuation, and all beautifully laid out.

Shakespeare by Shakespeare. He has so many great lines. 'Shall I compare thee to a summer's day?' 'Frankly, my dear, I don't give a damn.' 'I am the Walrus.' 'My heart will go on.'

They're part of the language.

Next week, I'm planning to learn how to peel an orange with a world expert fruit psychologist.

GWYNETH PALTROW

January 31st

JM* comes round. For half an hour, he holds my hand and whispers sweet nothings in my ear. 'Essentially,' he coos, 'these proposals for renewing the essential health of our domestic economy are the same as those I previously mentioned …'

I am overcome with desire. He is so sure of himself, so knowledgeable. I want to know more. 'Go on, go on!' I beg him.

'… and they represent,' he continues, a little breathlessly, 'a significant initiative in the formation of an important and imaginative element in our strategy to improve the supply performance of the economy …'

I am overwhelmed. At this point, he digs deep into his trousers and pulls out his pocket calculator. I've never seen one like it. 'Now, if we are talking about 3¼ per cent annual growth over a five-year fixed period, then that comes to …' he says, becoming very, very tactile, tapping all the right buttons with the dexterity of an expert.

---

*Name of bespectacled former Conservative Prime Minister initialised to protect identity.

After he has come out with a final figure, I dash to the BBC to record an interview on *Pebble Mill at One*. I dress as a crème caramel to launch our End That Fatty Diet initiative.

EDWINA CURRIE

Good morning, it's 5.15 a.m. and I have just scratched my right elbow as it was itching a bit. I sit at my desk, wondering what to write. I reflect that there is no reason at all not to start with my usual salute. So I write, Good morning, it's 5.15 a.m.

What next? I am in no mind to leave it there.

Fortuitously, I feel an itch on my right elbow. I scratch it. This gives me something potentially interesting to record, so I decide to insert the additional information that I have just scratched my right elbow as it was itching a bit.

A vista opens. I can now write about my decision to write about the fact that I scratched my right elbow, together with the reasons behind this impulsive action. So I put on record that a fresh vista has opened out, as I am now able to write about my decision to write about the fact that I scratched my right elbow, and the reasons behind that impulsive action.

NICHOLSON BAKER

February

February 1st

February is the month I devote to rearranging the cushions on the sofa in my dressing room, and I do so without any help whatsoever from our staff. As you might imagine, it is quite a job, there being no fewer than four cushions, each of a different colour. Thus one might choose to arrange the navy blue on one side, the pink on the other, with pale yellow and Lincoln green somewhere in the middle, only to find that, on second thoughts, it actually looks better to have the pink somewhere in the middle, with the pale yellow to the left, the navy blue to the right, leaving room for the Lincoln green to remain in the middle, only this time next to the pink and not to the pale yellow, unless of course it is between the pink and the pale yellow.

Whenever I have met them, I have found the British public extraordinarily ignorant of the demands and pressures with which we in the so-called 'upper classes' (how I hate all this 'class' nonsense!) are confronted day by day. I sometimes think that the 'ordinary' people, for all their immense pluck, fail to appreciate the many onerous tasks that befall the Stately Home owner, and I welcome this opportunity to 'put them in the picture'. Rearranging the cushions on the sofa in my dressing room is one such task, and the time and planning involved are not to be underestimated. First, I have one of our staff nip out to the local shops to buy me a range of excellent new French devices known as 'crayons', which are what we used to know as pencils, but with brightly coloured leads. I then spend a week or so measuring out on a piece of paper and colouring in four squares – pink, pale yellow, Lincoln green and navy blue – and a further week cutting them out. This leaves me just a fortnight to juggle these four coloured squares around this way and that, until I am perfectly satisfied that I have 'come up' with the best new arrangement. It all makes for a highly enjoyable topic of dinner conversation too, and come February our guests delight in spending an hour and a half or so over the soup arguing the pros and cons of, say, having the pink on the left or the pale yellow on the right, and thoroughly productive it is too.

ANDREW, DUKE OF DEVONSHIRE

February 2nd

What a decade the Sixties is turning out to be. It was tonight, in that steamy liberated atmosphere of sexual awakening, that I first set eyes on Harold Pinter. We were at a party. It was, as I recall, a fondue party. None of the usual rules applied. Knives, forks, spoons: who needed them? Cutlery was dismissed as conventional, and even serviettes had been discarded. Instead, we would – wildly, madly, crazily – dip pieces of bread just any-old-how into a hot cheesy sauce. Then we would toss them into our mouths as 'My Old Man's a Dustman' played suggestively in the background. The effect was electrifying.

Pinter and I went outside together. I said nothing. He said nothing. I said nothing back. He added nothing. Nothing would come between us. Pinter was already known for his pauses, but in those extraordinary moments he managed to stretch it from a slight pause to a mild hesitation and then, before we both knew it, to a full-blown silence.

Pinter was to become known as the master of the pause. He certainly couldn't keep his pause off me.

JOAN BAKEWELL

As I was being shaved yesterday morning, I found myself reflecting that no English monarch since the death of Edward III can be put quite in the first class, though Queen Elizabeth I was undoubtedly sound, and Queen Victoria was nearly Beta Plus.

And what of God? Though His mind is too eclectic to be considered truly first-rate, He may still be justly credited with one or two good ideas, the Rees-Mogg family being just one example. We stretch back twelve centuries to Ras Mag, the distinguished President of the Ancient Pict Chamber of Commerce, and a notably successful Vice-Chairman of the Woad Preservation Society. To Rees-Moggs, Windsor Castle is a comparatively modern, somewhat – dare I say it – *nouveau riche* building, as are its present tenants. But I still incline to the point of view that it should be rebuilt. Life itself is not unlike Windsor Castle: sturdy yet fragile, admitting visitors yet essentially private, permanent yet strangely temporary.

WILLIAM REES-MOGG

February 3rd

This morning, I moved to pour myself a cup of tea. As I sat stirring that cup, or, rather, the hard, strong tea within it, my elbow moved back and for'd, back and for'd in a movement that danced to a mysterious rhythm. I was nearing the end of my stirring, and weary, when as fate would have it my elbow inadvertently nudged the vase on the corner table. In consequence, the vase fell off the table, and the dampened daffodils within it were hurled onto the floor, causing our maid, previously young and carefree, to slip as she passed by. She fell headlong onto my prone body, so that a passer-by, unaware of the incidents that had preceded this tragic scene, might have surmised with good reason that she was nailed to me, like Jesus Christ on the cross.

Alas, that is not what the second Mrs Hardy surmised as she entered the room a few brief seconds later. Instead, she threw up her hands and hurled cruel epithets of abuse at myself and also at the maid, who had, when the caterwauling came to a stop, aged most visibly, her hair now wispy and grey, with furrows deep in her face like time-honour'd sheep-tracks over old familiar hills.

This afternoon, a fresh cup of tea was brought to me, this time by a fresh maid with an uncomely gait and the severest of squints. The second Mrs Hardy looked on with an air that betrayed contentment. I am left in a state of unknowing as to where our first maid has gone. I suspect it is somewhere far away and forsaken, and that our paths are never more to cross.

Why me?

THOMAS HARDY

February 4th

To an exhibition of driftwood jewellery at the Commonwealth Institute. I am waiting for Her Majesty in the company of Denis MacShane, MP, a junior Foreign Office Minister. He is still recovering from the excitement of playing host to Her Majesty three weeks ago.

'Have you noticed how she wears her hats so well?' he observes, respectfully. 'Always firmly on the head. And she's brilliant with gloves, too. She knows where to put every single finger, one in each slot. I've never seen her get it wrong.'

She arrives in lilac coat and matching hat. She approaches a figure holding a labrador on a lead.

'Ah,' she says. 'A dog.'

'She gets it right every time,' the Lord Lieutenant of the county whispers to me. 'Marvellous with animals.'

GYLES BRANDRETH

February 5th

JONATHAN ROSS: Fand-asdic! You look fablus! Cwoor! You look gwate! Just gwate! Darn she look fablus, laze and gennulmun? Fand-astic! Wooh! I twuly can't bleev you're here with me today! Unbleevbul!

Fancy a quickie? Fand-asdic! And you've also done all of us in this little countwy of ours the gwate honour of atchly coming to live amongst us!

MADONNA: Yes.

JONATHAN ROSS: Unbleevbaw. We all thank you fwom the bottom of our hearts for coming to live here. Jes thing of that laze and gennulmun – Madonna atchly living in England! Canyer bleev it? So er I guess you um must like it here?

MADONNA: Yes. Quite.

JONATHAN ROSS: Fand-asdic! Gwate! Thank you so much for answerwing that question! Hilawious! So now Madonna's gonna tweat us to a toadly genius new song! Let's hear it for Madonna, laze and gennulmun!

MADONNA:

Ah trahda stayur head, trahda stayon tarp
Trahda playapart, but somehow ahfugart
Ahdlark to spress my stream parnda view
Ahm not chrisjun nodda jew
Ooohweeoooweeoooh
This is American Lahf

JONATHAN ROSS: FABLUS! GWATE! FAND-ASDIC! Now, lez facey, you are the singaw biggest star in the histwy of the whirl of wall time ever. Thas quite an achievemun!

MADONNA: Wodever.

JONATHAN ROSS: Gwate! It must be litwully amazing being you! Tell us what you do on a nawmaw day?!

MADONNA: This and that.

JONATHAN ROSS: Fand-asdic! Gwate weply! Tellyawha, if I was Madonna, I'd get out of bed, stwip naked and just look at myself in the miwwor for hours on end!!! I mean, you've got the most FAND-ASDIC physique, you weally have! Gwate bweasts! Cwooor! If I were you, I'd just go STARKERS and look at them in the miwwor all day long – then I'd turn wownd and take a gander at that incwedibull bum! Is that what you do on a normal day, then? Is it?

MADONNA: No.

JONATHAN ROSS: Gwate! Um. So, Madonna, tell us about a day when you do somethin you weally want to do. Like, what would you do on a day when you do somethin you weally want to do – like, a day when you could do anything, so you decide to do not just anything but, like, somethin you weally want to do, f'rinstance?

MADONNA: Hmmm. A day when I do something I really wanna do. Hmmm.

JONATHAN ROSS: Yeah. I mean, like a day when you just wake up and you think, hey, I'm Madonna, I can do wodever I wanna do and what I wanna do today is to do, like, wodever I wanna do. Like, if I were you, I'd fondaw my bweasts all day, thas what I'd do! I mean, lez face it, you got twuly gwate tits, you weally have!

MADONNA: My husband and I might go to the movies. We read books. Go to a pub.

JONATHAN ROSS: Amazin! Laze and gennulmun, Madonna goes into our English pubs! Thank you so much, Madonna – you're a world superstar, but you are happy to go into an English pub! Thaz fand-asdic!

MADONNA: My husband and I go down to the Old Bull and Bush with Burlington Bertie to spend our bobs and quids on a pint of ale and eat fish and chips with brown sauce served by Pearly Kings and Queens. Chim chiminee, chim chiminee, chim-chim-cherooo. And then my husband and I jump aboard a double-decker bus and rabbit in cockney rhyming slang with Mrs Tiggywinkle and the cheery local bobbies.

JONATHAN ROSS: Fand-asdic! And do you let them feel your bweasts at all?

MADONNA: No.

JONATHAN ROSS: Shame! Ha ha ha! Let's have another bwilliand classic song. Les heawifaw Madonna, laze and gennulmun!

MADONNA:

Doan tellmedur staaarp
Tell the rain nodder draaarp
Tell the win nodder blow
Cos you said so
Tell meeee larvissun drew
Is jist somethin thad we do-oo-oo.

JONATHAN ROSS: Fand-asdic! Fab-lus! We are so deeply honoured to have you among us! Now, not only do you have the most fand-asdic physique – wiwya just look at that arse, laze and gennulmun – but you are a positive GENIUS at we-invention. Like, one moment you are, like wolling naked on the sand in just a wimple, then you toadly we-invent yourself and for the next album you've toadly we-invented yourself and this time you're wolling naked on the sand – in a cowboy hat! Bwilliand!

MADONNA: I don't stick to the programme. I reinvent myself.* I, like, play with the whole concept of adopting different personas as a means of, like, playing with the whole concept of different personas. By, like, reinventing myself. As a whole concept. Like, I wanted to wake people up to the whole notion that people get hurt in wars. By appearing naked in a gas mask I wanted to say, like, people wake up, war is such a negative concept.

JONATHAN ROSS: But then you withdwew the vidjo.

MADONNA: Sure. I withdrew the video because by then the war had started, and I wanted people to, like, get behind the whole concept of war, and wake them up to the more positive notion that war could actually stop more people getting hurt.

JONATHAN ROSS: Smashin'! Fand-asdic! Tellyawhat, that Guy Witchie's a lucky bloke! Fwankly, I wouldn't mind givin' you one in my dwessing woom later! Less heary for Madonna, laze and gennulmun – and the gwatest tits in the histwy of poplar music!

February 6th

Today, I almost lost count of the minutes I spent researching the story of Queen Victoria. I sat in the hushed atmosphere of the Royal Library for what seemed like an hour. A few minutes later I left with an over-

---

*Paul Morley writes: 'Madonna Ciccone burst onto the zeitgeist immediately after the post-war period but before 9/11, so she occupies a sublime mythic moment in modern – and post-modern – art, adding a complex mythical take on the zeitgeist, literally transforming myth into zeitgeist and back again in a manner so truly expressive that one can only describe it as a complex masterpiece. Or so it seems – literally – to me.'

whelming sense that the story of the young Victoria would make a wonderful film – a film she would undoubtedly have made herself if only she'd had the contacts.

The more I researched her, the more I became aware that poor Victoria had never once appeared on television or radio, had never agreed to guest on a chat show, and had never even attended a Royal film premiere! It's so easy to take these things for granted, but I wanted to truly understand what it felt like to be deprived of these necessities.

SARAH, DUCHESS OF YORK

I have two tape-recorders, one newer and more capable, the other older and more experienced. For security reasons, I never leave them in a room together, but I have often wondered how they have behaved when they are alone. So simply by way of experiment, I place the two of them together in my office having first – quite unknown to them – placed a third tape-recorder in an upper drawer of my desk with the 'Record' button pressed on.

The results are fascinating. For three hours, not a single murmur! Or were they tipped off by the third tape-recorder, as a result of some sort of nod-and-wink from the powers that be? I'll investigate further next week. A fourth tape-recorder may well be needed.

TONY BENN

February 7th

Poor, dear Hughie Trevor-Roper. I really couldn't feel more desperately sorry for him. One always held his scholarship in such high regard. But now his reputation has been smashed to smithereens by his over-hasty authentication of the so-called 'Hitler Diaries'. Oh, deary, deary me! It makes one want to weep!

On the other hand, what good would weeping do for poor, absurd, fallen Hughie? None whatsoever. Far better for him that we should all laugh out loud, and join in all the fun at witnessing a once-revered colleague falling flat on his silly face. It's what he would have wanted.

When the mirth has begun to subside, I pick up my pen and write a letter to poor old ruined Hughie, offering him whatever help I can give. 'I see that my local "branch" of Victoria Wine is advertising for a junior sales assistant, no experience necessary,' I venture. 'Do let me know whether this might be up your street – a friend in need, etc, etc.'

And with this, I help myself to another consoling glass of first-rate champagne. Infinitely agreeable.

A.L. ROWSE

February 8th

It had been a hugely successful tour. Once again, the Canadians had shown that they loved Queen Elizabeth and she had shown she loved Canada.

'I have never known anyone who could wave half as brilliantly as Queen Elizabeth the Queen Mother,' recalls a close aide. 'She had this extraordinary ability to hold her right hand up in the air and then – and this is where the real skill comes in – to move it, with amazing delicacy, very gently from side to side. And she really could do that for literally minutes at a time. I've honestly never seen anything like it.'

Another onlooker found himself entranced by her singular ability to combine this skill with another. 'I remember looking at her in her carriage. She was already performing that outstanding wave – it literally radiated sunbeams from its epicentre – when it suddenly struck me that she was also doing something else, equally remarkable. Yes, she was waving – but at one and the same time she was also smiling!'

And by all accounts, that smile was the most perfect smile the world had ever seen. 'I don't know how she does it,' one courtier confided to his diary, 'but it has something to do with her mouth. Somehow she manages to raise both ends at the same time. As if by magic, she creates a smile, and she then holds that smile for several seconds and turns her head, so that everyone can see it. I have never seen such selflessness and generosity. The effect is transcendent. In the shadow of that gracious smile, I have witnessed entire nations moved to tears of consummate joy, peace and understanding.'

By the time Queen Elizabeth arrived back from her tour of Canada, the Vietnam war had been brought to an end, world trade was prospering once more, thousands of patients had been cured of their illnesses, and Britain was enjoying a glorious heatwave.

Once again, Queen Elizabeth the Queen Mother had smiled her way into the hearts of the people. 'It's so very thrilling,' she confessed in a letter to Queen Mary. 'The little Canadians simply ADORE me!!!!'

WILLIAM SHAWCROSS*

Day 18,295 in the *Big Brother* house. 11.27 a.m.: Aisleyne and Imogen are in the kitchen.

AISLEYNE: How long we been in here then?
IMOGEN: Where?
AISLEYNE: Here?
IMOGEN: Here?
AISLEYNE: Yeah. Here.
IMOGEN: Fifty years, babes.
AISLEYNE: Fifty fuckin' years?
IMOGEN: Yeah.
AISLEYNE: Oh. Right. I gotta do something about these hair extensions.

February 9th

My father always said that one can never do without common sense in matters great as well as small. He never let anyone in his shop who had not first handed over their shoelaces to my mother at the door. In this way he sought to put an end to petty pilfering. 'No one can

---

*From *Most Beloved Ma'am: The Authorised Biography of Queen Elizabeth the Queen Mother.*

run far without their shoelaces,' he once said as an elderly lady crashed to the floor, a bag of stolen flour bursting beneath her arm. My father was a man of firm principles and firmer forefinger. Aged ten, I asked him why, when serving the smoked ham, he made a point of placing his right forefinger on the scales. He explained it was to give the customers better all-round service, by helping them pay that little bit extra for quality produce. 'A finger on the scales is a penny in the till,' he explained, and it is advice that I have treasured ever since.

MARGARET THATCHER

An actor must be a gazelle at a waterhole, a cabin bursting into flame, a bottle thrown into the ocean, a distant planet newly discovered by an astronomer whose wife has just left him for a younger guy who's into baseball.

And sometimes, just sometimes, all four at once.

BRAD PITT

February 10th

Odessa. I visit the Odessa Steps: lots and lots of steps, all named after Odessa. Odessa is one of the very few cities I can think of which begin with an 'O' – unless you count Orpington! Actually, it's rather like Orpington in a way: there are lots of buildings, and quite a few people, plus cars and so on. As cities go, Odessa is literally indescribable.

Before I came here, I had no idea how big Russia is. It really is very, very big indeed. The people here are very friendly. Today, after quite a comfortable night, it has been my privilege to meet a marvellous old character, a gentleman who speaks near-perfect English, dresses very smartly in suit and tie, has heard of the Pythons (always a help!) and is anxious to cooperate in any way he can. 'We must get him on film – he's a marvellous old character,' I say to my producer.

'He's our assistant director,' explains my producer.

Later, I rehearse the next day's script. 'I must say this view is simply stunning,' I say over and over again. Tomorrow, we will find a view to go with it.

MICHAEL PALIN

February 11th

Dreadfully distressed at this morning's news of the death of HRH Princess Margaret. She may have been the teensiest bit COMMON, bless her, but my goodness she had RAZZLE DAZZLE. In so many ways, Margaret personified the sheer devil-may-care spirit of the Sixties. I shall never forget a spectacular luncheon party she threw on the Isle of Mustique in August, 1969. Everyone who was anyone in the Sixties was there. Tripping around the exquisitely-mown lawn on my allotted golf-buggy before the serving of the Pina Coladas, I remember overtaking Gerry and the Pacemakers, all crammed into one little buggy, and Sir Gerald Nabarro, Frank Ifield and Freddy 'Parrot-Face' Davis having a whale of a time in another.

Luncheon was a delightful affair. One now forgets what the Princess was wearing, but I myself was wearing a crushed-velvet suit in the most beautiful deep purple, with a Burlington Bertie smock to match. Prompted by sheer JOIE DE VIVRE into perfectly SHAMEFUL indiscretions, I hugely amused the Princess with my running commentary on all the latest goings-on among the senior heads of department at the British Museum. The Princess sat fixed to her seat, her head cocked to one side, her eyes tight-shut, so as to soak it all in. It is greatly to her credit that she would surround herself with people far more intelligent than herself.

After a sumptuous luncheon, a vast cake was wheeled out by the most magnificent pair of coloured gentlemen. And then – PURE THEATRE! – Kathy Kirby and Norman Wisdom leapt out and proceeded to polka the afternoon away to the music of Burl Ives. MAGIC!

Margaret – who I will always remember as one of the most intensely musical figures of that era – clapped quite brilliantly in time, getting every other clap almost exactly right.

SIR ROY STRONG

I had an idea for these gloves today, and I was like, wow. I really want to be really, really creative and like really push ideas to their furthest creation. My fashion philosophy can be summed up as like, I want to take reality to the furthest reality, as part of the creative process. Because it's only by really pulling ideas into their furthest creative reality that you can find where you're gonna like push them.

I wanted these to be very, very stylish, very, very classic and very, very contemporary. That was my whole philosophy of them, my whole glove philosophy. But first I had all these different like THINGS to work out, cos I have always paid very, very close attention to detail, cos basically I'm a very-close-attention-to-detail kind of person, that's just the way I am. So first – how many fingers on each glove? I thought about this and like really studied the whole human thing, and eventually I thought like – wow! – yup, it's got to be four fingers and a thumb. And not just four fingers and a thumb on one glove, but four fingers and a thumb on both gloves. And that's not because I've got anything against thumbs. I was always brought up to really appreciate thumbs, and I'm dead against people who are, like, against thumbs. No – it's because if you look at the average human hand and count the fingers and thumbs, like I have, you'll find it's got four fingers and just one thumb, and that's what I wanted to, like, mirror, in my own gloves.

So I rang up my glovemaker and I'm like, a pair of gloves, four fingers and a thumb each, and I want it very, very stylish, very, very classic and very, very contemporary. And she transformed my own distinctive vision into reality. And that was like really really weird.

STELLA McCARTNEY

February 12th

There are always new characters to meet. This evening, I was placed next to Igor Stravinsky, the well-known composer. He is neither very tall nor very short, but if he had been it wouldn't have mattered as for most of the time we were both sitting down.

He held forth on the subject of music, to the exclusion of all else. After a good few minutes of this, I sought to change the subject.

'Would you agree with me that this lamb is a little overdone?' I inquired. I cannot remember his reply, so it can't have been interesting. He had no real conversation.

CLARISSA EDEN

The Hitch and I were in a burpfarty willybumcrack dive off the Portobello Road and drinking like men – one half of Skol leapfrogged swiftly by another, two packs of salt and vinegar, heavy on the salt, don't hold back on the vinegar, mush, then another half of Skol, this time with a slash of lime, followed by a Pepsi, all black, no ice – when I rasped that fuckitman, I preferred early Conrad to later James and middle Nabokov to either of them. The Hitch immediately puked into the pocket of a passing paediatrician and snorted vomitoriously that middle James could beat early James and late Nabokov hands down, ansdarn.

'Come outside and say that.' The words shinned out of my mouth like a nuclear siren signalling the decimation of a world boorishly encyclopaedic in its slavish variety. On the ashpuke streets wheezing with urine-drenched tramps, the Hitch and I squared up to one another, eyes unblinking, like men. I flexed my arms; the Hitch flexed his. GO! Hands working faster than the speed of travelling luminous energy, we began to trade smacks, all the while singing, 'A sailor went to sea sea sea to see what he could see see see and all that he could see see see was the bot –'

By this time, we were biffing our way through it full pelt. But I got to the end – 'bottom of the deep blue sea sea sea' – before him, and the

Hitch collapsed fighting for breath like a man fighting for breath, his defeat ameliorated by his knowledge that with his hands and his rhyme he had just participated in the tumescent whirligig of literary history in the late twentieth century.

MARTIN AMIS

February 13th

Anji Hunter was helpful. She said Campbell and Mandelson once had a shaky relationship, but it's much improved. 'These days, when Alastair pours the tea for Peter, it's into a cup,' she says.

LANCE PRICE

The second week of February is now virtually over, and I still haven't found time to assist poor Andrew with the uphill struggle he is having over the rearrangement of his cushions, so utterly hectic has my own life been, what with the frightful bother of trying to impose some semblance of order on my scarf drawer. 'Scarf' – that's an interesting word, and of course 'cushion' is another, and we discussed how interesting they were over dinner the night before last. Norman St John of Fawnsley pointed out that there is no other word in the English language spelt c-u-s-h-i-o-n, in that order, and when I pointed out that it is also the only word in English spelt exactly in that way meaning something you can sit on, darling Roy Strong got tremendously over-excited, clapping his hands together, and was kind enough to tell me how clever I was!! The two of them were such utter poppets that after they had finished their main courses I told them they could get off their knees for pudding and sit with us around the grown-ups' table.

DEBORAH, DUCHESS OF DEVONSHIRE

February 14th

If I am a master of the easy paradox, it is essentially because no paradox is easy to master. My prose style is the style of a pro(se). The clever effect is achieved by reversing the first half of a sentence so that the reversal achieves an effect of cleverness. This has gained me an international reputation for being smart, though I am not one to smart at the international reputation I have gained.

CLIVE JAMES

I told the Queen Mother how pretty she was looking and she said, 'I always try to put on something special in jewellery for you, Woodrow, because I know how much you like it.' At this point, I said, 'You are a poppet, Ma'am,' and placed my right hand on her upper back. I then began to rub it up and down in a soothing and strangely sensual manner. I may say she has the most sublime back of any of the Royal Family, up to and including Princess Michael. It was all I could do to restrain myself from sitting astride her on that sofa and licking it discreetly with my tongue.

Our talk turned to Nelson Mandela. She asked me if the rumours were true that he was black. I told her that, yes, they were. 'So does he play the trumpet?' she asked.

'I'm afraid not, Ma'am,' I replied.

'What a wicked waste,' she said, adding that Louis Armstrong had played the trumpet quite beautifully, and that he had never felt the need to waste time struggling against apartheid.

'It's just like the miners,' she added. 'They don't know how lucky they are to be able to spend their lives in a mine. Think how cosy it must be down there! Such fun! I do love black!'

She is one of the most politically astute women I have ever met. 'Might it not be a rather marvellous idea,' she said, signalling to her footman to unwrap me a Bittermint, 'were the good old Royal Air Force to bomb Liverpool? It would be like the war all over again, with everyone singing songs and pulling together. Such larks!'

I will suggest it to Margaret in the morning.*

WOODROW WYATT

February 15th

Watched something on TV about Florence Nightingale, poor love. I was a nurse in the Crimea, and believe me, it's no easy job walking around with your lamp, tending to all those brave soldiers with blood spurting out of them, hearing their last words, wrapping them up in bandages and that. So why are the media always going at poor Florence? She's just doing her bit, for God's sake, but they can't understand that, can they, so they try and make out she's only in it for the publicity. I don't tell people this, but when I came back from the Crimea, I founded Great Ormond Street Hospital for Sick Kiddies, but I don't go on about it, it's a secret.

HEATHER MILLS McCARTNEY

Gerry Adams is common, with that simply *ghastly* beard of his. But Ian Paisley is a poppet. One longs to put him in one's pocket and take him home, then have him bellow sweet nothings in one's ear! Heaven! I wonder if a very, very bold check tweed Biligorri two-piece might suit him? I saw Paisley (such a pretty name) last night on *Newsnight* arguing the toss with Jemima Paxman. Halfway through the interview, he turned to the camera and winked at me.

And him a Reverend!

Saucy boy.

NICHOLAS HASLAM

---

*His *Journals (1985–1997)* make it clear that Wyatt was largely responsible for all the key decisions taken by Margaret Thatcher during her time as his Prime Minister. He also provided a shoulder for many to cry on, including HM Queen Elizabeth the Queen Mother, President Reagan and Rupert Murdoch. Experts estimate that, among his contemporaries, the only person who exercised as much influence over the rich and the powerful, and was as well-loved by them, was Jeffrey Archer.

February 16th

Joni Mitchell song on the radio. 'I've looked at life from both sides now but clouds got in my way'? What's she on about? Why let a cloud get in your bloody way? It's only made of fluff or whatever. Just tell it to fuck the fuck off, that's what I say.

JANET STREET-PORTER

February 17th

For lunch, I eat some rice. Why am I the only person in the world who eats rice?

GERMAINE GREER

February 18th

Concomitantly, silence is, as I have pointed out in pioneering books and seminars, invariably quarried and pillaged by lesser minds (usually without acknowledgement and certainly without apology), golden.

Cities, towns, conurbations, large groups of buildings placed near or proximate to one another to form a definable whole, are both the conduits and the receptacles for noise, sound, clamour (*klamari* in Swahili, *calamari* in Italian, though I prefer the cannelloni). At regular time period intervals, I retreat to the French hillsides with my distinguished yet unspoken wife, to breathe in the silence, unloud and noiseless, that was once partaken by the by no means lesser minds of Flaubert and Racine.

Maritally, we sit in a fieldy meadow in an incipiently quiet time/space continuum observing the hush (*huss* in Somali) stretching far beneath us, down to the herd, team, group of cows below. 'Ah, silence!' I exclaim exclamatorily in simple wonderment. 'Silence – the silence that is with us now – a silence golden as James's Bowl, as

Apuleius' Ass, as Frazer's Bough, that silence blessed by my original study, now translated into fifteen languages, taken up yet still not acknowledged by those whose academic reputations fall sadly short of my own. Ah, silence! A void, a circumstantial gap, a vivid diaspora, the sound, rare and provocative, created when one's talk ceases. Silence, both metaphysical and actual, both concomitant and –'

'Moo!' enunciates a cow, bovine and cowlike, and the other cows follow suitly, 'Moo! Moo! Moo!'

My antennae, exceedingly alert, like a lieder by Schubert or a poem by Pound, inform me that this cuddish interruption is part of a Friesian conspiracy intent on placing in jeopardy my seminar on the nature of *la silencia*. These animals possess all the professional jealousy and unctuous mooishness of the Oxford-educated. They have been put up to their loutish intervention by those in the English faculty less honoured than myself.

'Shoo! Shoo! Shoo!' I interpolate.

'Moo! Moo! Moo!' they respond.

I seize the opportunity to point out to my unspoken wife that in the Oubanji language there are fifteen words meaning 'moo', only one of them in common use by cows. But she cannot hear me. She has her earplugs in (*arapluggi* in Cameroon), as she has done since 1974, still perversely intent upon listening to the mute, smothering silence that lies somewhere beyond words.

GEORGE STEINER

Michelangelo died today, in 1564. I used to think he was a great artist. But then I looked again at his work. To my horror, it showed no skill or originality whatsoever. I was so embarrassed on his account. The failure is extraordinary. It is not so surprising that since his death his reputation has been in free-fall.

V.S. NAIPAUL

February 19th, 1943

TO WINSTON CHURCHILL

Darling Winnie,

Just the briefest of scribbles to congratulate you on a superb tour of the front, so heroic and sweet and STIRRING. As always, you had our boys in the palm of your hand, and, I may add, looked quite gorgeous in your little khaki two-piece! Bravo! Forgive me, Winnie, but might I add the smallest of suggestions? It occurred to me that, after delivering an encouraging word to the troops, and just before conducting your inspection, you could do some marvellous 'stage business' with your handkerchief – perhaps dropping it casually on the ground before retrieving it with a flourish, or waving it to-and-fro with an air of infinite melancholy, or perhaps, with a few deft flicks of the wrist, folding it in such a manner as to create a snow-white swan. It is a little trick I have employed with notable success in my hugely successful run of *Tap-Dancing to Victory*, currently at the Albery. I am delighted to pass it on.

Ever Yours,

Johnny

JOHN GIELGUD

February 20th, 1943

TO NOËL COWARD

Darling Nolly,

There is no doubting Winston's brilliance, though I do wish he wouldn't slur his words so, and he is a trifle … BULLISH for my tastes. And MUST he wear that ghastly khaki two-piece? What DOES he think he looks like, the poor old pet?

His performance is undoubtedly strong – none of us would deny him that – but it seems to me he could make much more of his hankie, and rather less of that simply dreadful cigar.

Your own,

Johnny

JOHN GIELGUD

February 21st

Writers are territorial, and they resent intruders. My sister Susan (who prefers not to be reminded that her first name is Susan, though Susan it is, and who prefers to struggle along under the pen-name of A.S. Byatt rather than Susan, even though those of us in her family know all too well that the tell-tale 'S' definitely stands for Susan) said in an interview somewhere (I didn't read it myself, not having time to waste) that she was distressed when she found that I had written (many decades ago) about a particular tea set that our family possessed, because she had always wanted to use it herself. I had some sympathy with Sue, who felt I had appropriated something that was not mine, even though, as my lawyer pointed out, it was, strictly speaking, not exclusively hers either, and if she had really wanted to write about that tea set then why hadn't she done so when she had the opportunity, and not wait until she knew that I had done so before opening her big fat mouth and complaining that I had got there first?

I used the tea set in my novel *The Chest of Drawers*,* but employed the power of my imagination to change it from a tea set to a coffee set, in an attempt, sadly misguided, to prevent an indignant outburst from Sue. Incidentally, the 'chest of drawers' in the title was originally not a chest of drawers at all but a small occasional table, of the type common in the East Midlands immediately after the 2nd World War; I changed it from a small occasional table to a chest of drawers for reasons that I no longer remember, but which (knowing her!) may have had something to do with not wishing to upset my big sister Sue. For the purposes of fiction, in this particular novel I used my imagi-

---

*The novel's famous opening passage runs: 'The clouds parted ruthlessly as Liz left her tea set in the house and stepped out on to the pavement, cruelly disgorging a burden of rain.

'"Hello, Liz: how's James?"

'It was Charles, who had married Suzie on the rebound from Claudia. Liz had never forgiven Jemima after he had left Claudia, who had not recovered from divorcing Frank after his all-too-public affair with Araminta, abandoning Heriot to a lifetime of loneliness with Geoffrey. Still, life was like that.'

nation to transform Sue into a cut-price washing machine with an unreliable timing mechanism which the heroine, Meg, eventually throws away, for reasons I now forget.

MARGARET DRABBLE

February 22nd

One reason that people used to vote Tory was that Tory MPs always wore lovely tweed suits. And they respected them for it. But nowadays they see them in off-the-peg grey or black suits, many of them two-piece and without watch-chains, and consequently they have no one to look up to. And we wonder why so many unmarried teenagers have triplets and nose-rings!

CHARLES MOORE

PM very buoyant. 'The funny thing is that we are going to win the '79 election by over 100 seats,' he says. He adds that 'ordinary people have no time for Mrs Thatcher. She just doesn't understand them like we do. The last thing they want is to own their own homes, they much prefer them to be owned by us.' He tells Cabinet that once the North Sea oil revenue starts coming in, we'll be able to bury all those dead bodies everyone's going on about.

Denis Healey pipes up that the corpses have only got themselves to blame. 'Bloody layabouts,' he says.

Tony Benn puts forward a major new plan he has drawn up to allow corpses to form a union of their own – 'Something along the lines of The Union of the Recently Departed and Technically Deceased, or RDTD for short,' he says. Cabinet agree that if we allowed them to feel a vital part of the wider Labour movement then when it came to making a fuss they wouldn't have a leg to stand on.

The lovely Shirley Williams suggests that if the corpses are going to remain unburied, then it might be nice to decorate them, or wrap them in bright colours, so that ordinary, decent passers-by could feel better about themselves. The PM points out that Peter Jay thinks that corpses are good as a hedge against inflation. 'And let's face it, Peter's dreadfully clever, they tell me he knows all about money.'

Lovely dinner at Mon Plaisir with Harold Lever who advises me to invest in the development of technology to turn unburied corpses into fuel. Finish with a lovely crème brûlée over which he kindly suggests that I might care to be the next but one Governor of the Bank of England ('It would be very you, Bernard'), and taxi home by midnight.

BERNARD DONOUGHUE

February 23rd

Well, the Oscars are over for another year. Thousands of friends and well-wishers insist I was the belle of the ball on Oscar night, but I'd also like to pay tribute to the real efforts made by good friends Nicole Kidman and Angelina Jolie. They did their best, and that's good enough for me. We can't all be winners, girls!

Not many people know this – it's not something I go on about – but the Academy were pressing me to accept a Lifetime Special Achievement Oscar for all the amazing work I've done in the fields of cinema and music and the arts and worldwide peace and that. But I'm like, 'I was busy with my charity work, guys – and anyway my good friends lovely ladies Kate Winslet and Penelope Cruz need their egos massaged a bit more than I do!'

Close friends and total strangers have been coming up to me in the street ever since. 'I can't believe you didn't win an Oscar, Heather!' they all say. But my lips are sealed. When I saw my good friend the Pope for lunch today, I'm like, 'You know what, Ben? Some things are best kept to yourself.'

HEATHER MILLS McCARTNEY

February 24th

Dear Diary, It is February the 24th 1974 and I am seriously smitten. Martin Amis (or, as he styles himself, Martin: Amis) is everything I have ever wished for: moody, ironic, dishy, and, in his own characteristically brilliant words, 'f—ing clever'.

He is, again in his own words, a 'word-magician in velve' (a reference to his beloved velvet jacket, or 'jacky-jack' as he sometimes calls it). He has admitted me into his magical circle of brilliant intellectuals like legendary *écriviste* Anthony Holden, the funny, flirtatious Clive James (whose TV criticism is an art form in itself) and that doyen of wicked wordplay, Robert Robinson. Sometimes Cyril Fletcher, the *éminence grise* of television's fabled *That's Life*, graces us with his presence, and, urging us all to 'Pin back your lug 'oles,' brings the table to its feet with one of his immortal 'Odd Odes'.

Martin is working at the *TLS*, and sometimes sends me love letters he has written on *TLS* notepaper. 'I love you Martin' he once wrote. I remember mentioning that he must have left out a dash between the 'you' and the 'Martin', but he denied it. Is he in love with someone else?

JULIE KAVANAGH

I'm warming my slippers in front of the log fire when I turn to my wife. 'There's a funny sort of ringing in my ears,' I complain.

'It's the telephone, Dukey,' she explains.

She passes me the receiver. Someone is talking on the other end.

It's the Home Secretary. Douglas Hurd is my godson, and still runs the occasional errand for me.

'Oh, Dukey, how would you like to be in charge of the BBC?' he asks.

'BBC?' I say. '... Remind me.'

'Broadcasting. Radio, telly, that sort of hoodjamaflip.'

'To be perfectly frank, Douglas,' I say, 'I've got no use for a telly. I mean, where would one put it?'

'But you don't have to buy a television, Dukey – you just have to be in charge of it.'

'You've convinced me,' I say, and go to sleep.

MARMADUKE HUSSEY

February 25th

I'll never forget something the great Laurens van der Post* once told me. Things, he said, are as they are. Yet being what they are, they are also somehow different. And if things were not as they are, they could not continue to be what they both have been and will be. And consequently, they – the things in question – will always be not only what they might have been and what they are, but also what they will be. It is these simple truths that we are, I fear, in danger of losing.

HRH THE PRINCE OF WALES

February 26th

I am halfway through *Tess of the D'Urbervilles* when I throw it away in disgust. Thomas Hardy had no right – no right whatsoever – to write a book about me without my express permission. His presumption in this matter represents a total invasion of my rights to privacy. May I also point out that, like many a hack before him, he has got a startling number of the facts wrong.

FACT: I was born in Australia, not Wessex.

FACT: I was christened Germaine, not Tess, a name I have long despised.

Has the guy never considered checking his facts?

---

*In his second volume of autobiography, Sir Laurens van der Post recalls his days as a Jungian postman in the Kalahari, a time later immortalised, he claims, in the series of bestselling children's stories about the three-fingered South African philosopher Van Der Postman Pat.

FACT: I was never impregnated by a guy called Alec.

FACT: I have never – I repeat NEVER – been arrested and hanged.

GERMAINE GREER

February 27th

I peel the onion of my memory, first one layer, then another, and then assuredly another, when suddenly buried deep in it I espy the glint of something unexpected, namely something I had not expected to espy therein.

At first I can make out the shape distantly only, but then I realise that it is – oh yes! oh no! oh yes! oh no! – a hat, quite military, initialled with two distinctive letters, both the same. The first is S and so is the second. SS.

My goodness, the hat in question is undeniably an SS helmet, and at that moment I recall with a start that I was, unbeknownst to me, a member of the SS, an organisation that had done uncalled-for things but so very many years ago that it is most extremely hard to remember without forgetting.

GÜNTER GRASS

Picasso's attitude to boiled sweets has been the subject of much debate. His preference, some say, was for Barley Sugar, whilst others maintain he preferred the old-fashioned 'gob-stopper'.

One or two, including the meretricious Clive Bell, have even suggested he enjoyed Liquorice All-Sorts. Such a claim flies in the face of reason, since experts have proved that the Liquorice All-Sort has never counted as a boiled sweet. For one thing, it is far too chewy, but these stupid people – among them the pushy Clive Bell, who had no knowledge of boiled sweets whatsoever – couldn't be expected to know that.

Did Picasso ever include a boiled sweet in a painting? Received wisdom suggests that his *Weeping Woman II* (1936) is seeking comfort from a throat lozenge. Others point to the figure on the right in his *Bathers Outside a Beach Cabana* (1929) and say that her transparent sense of *Weltschmerz* is caused by the bubble-gum that may have enlodged itself in her tresses. And then there will always be those who maintain that the gentleman's erect member painted as a circle in *Seated Male Nude* (1927) is in fact a Polo Mint.

JOHN RICHARDSON*

News comes through of the death of Harold Acton. For me, no man was less like the area of London associated with his name. To be linked with that most unprepossessing part of West London must have been a matter of perpetual ignominy for poor, dear Harold.

DIANA MOSLEY

Today was the day of my funeral, which was so great. I came in a hearse ($154) in this beautiful open coffin in a black cashmere suit ($374) and sunglasses ($56) and the church was full of people like Diane von Furstenberg and Liza and Calvin Klein and Yoko and Bianca and Robert Mapplethorpe and just about everybody, they all showed up and everyone was saying how great I was looking and how I've never looked better which was really great, and my blood pressure's right down which is great. Liza's put on weight though, and I spotted Calvin's got a pimple on his nose and everyone could tell he was embarrassed about it. Afterwards, I was buried in Pittsburgh, so totally depressing.

ANDY WARHOL

*From *A Life of Picasso* by John Richardson, Volume XXVII: *It Takes All-Sorts.*

February 28th

One of the key things I've uncovered during my research is that Victoria became Queen of England at a very young age – and managed to remain Queen all the time until she died! And as a Duchess myself, I feel I have a duty to let the rest of the world into this truly extraordinary secret which has been kept undercover for a century, which is nearly a thousand years.

Instead of a childhood filled with the bestest kind of great big huggy-hugs, the young Victoria had to cope with a starchy, no-can-do, hands-off atmosphere of stuffy, po-faced courtiers telling her do this, don't do that: no, you can't get your rocks off with all the hunkiest blokes on the disco floor of Kensington Palace; no, you can't have a bit of fun going skinny-dipping in the Balmoral pond when there's a hoity-toity, tutty-tutty garden party in progress; no, you can't let it all out with a jolly good scream in the middle of a formal dinner party for the President of Snooty-Land, even if you are feeling stressed-up.

But Victoria wasn't the kind of girl to let a rulebook stand in her way. 'No way, José!' she exclaimed, 'I'm out to have fun!' One of my totally favorito scenes in my screenplay is when the young Victoria gets a fit of the absolute gigglies when her chewing-gum shoots out of her mouth while she's talking to the Archbishop of Canterbury, a very senior vicar at that time! And the next minute, she's standing up to the German Prime Minister Adolf Hitler, telling him straight up that no way is he going to invade England, not while she's Queen. It's that kind of period detail – fun and laughter, yes, but also quite a few tears – that'll make the whole film such an emotional roller-coaster!

SARAH, DUCHESS OF YORK

Henry James died today, in 1916. He was the worst writer in the world. He never went out. He never rolled up his sleeves and put his arm up the backside of a cow. He never slapped a woman about the face to teach her a lesson. He never lived. It is an absence which shows in his 'novels'.

V.S. NAIPAUL

March

March 1st

Harold a little peeved over dinner at L'Artiste Assoiffé when the under-waiter fails to congratulate him on the truly splendid production of *The Caretaker* that is presently running to 'packed houses' (theatrical speak for 'full up'!) at the Shaw Theatre. I don't think anyone else around the table notices, but I can always tell when Harold is a bit 'put out' because he tends to smash the plates with his fists.

But otherwise an evening of great jollity, with the best intervention coming from David Hare who expatiated on how we must all strive to help liberate the 'working class'. (How I hate that term – it implies that some of us aren't workers, even though we may work fearfully hard on a biography of Marie Antoinette for absolutely years and years!!) When the aforementioned waiter comes over and asks whether everything was all right for us, Harold interjects – brilliantly – that it's a damn fool question.

We end by ordering a bottle of Château d'Yquem on behalf of the sugar-plantation workers of East Timor.

LADY ANTONIA FRASER

Buy new fuckin house for a load of bread, but at least it has a brilliant swimmin pool for the car.

KEITH RICHARDS

March 2nd

Lady Diana Cooper was a lifelong beauty, famous for wearing impossibly large hats. I once asked her why she wore such big hats. Her reply was delightful.

In response to another question I put to her some years later, she told me that the answer was yes – but only in some respects!

I now forget what the question was. Dickie Mountbatten may have been in the room at the time. Dickie was very proud of his suede riding boots, and rightly so.

CLARISSA EDEN

March 3rd

The full history of Picasso and his vexed relations with boiled sweets must, alas, wait for a future volume, *Picasso: The Too Good to Hurry Years*. For the moment, let it suffice to say that he was rarely, if ever, observed sucking on a boiled sweet whilst painting, and since, when offered a Lemon Sherbet by the rich, spoiled homosexual narcissist Jean Cocteau, whose family money, incidentally, came from dry-cleaning, of all things, and whose coarse, unsophisticated father sported a singularly ill-fitting toupée, Picasso declined, saying thank you, but he had just had luncheon. Three days later he painted *Woman in an Armchair*, now hanging in the Musée Picasso, and some have detected a suggestion of Lemon Sherbet in the distinct yellow oval just above the woman's right eyebrow.

JOHN RICHARDSON

March 4th

The sight of a fresh spring daffodil bursting forth into the dappled sunlight fills me with disgust and despair. What sort of a world have we created for ourselves that allows these yellowy, sickly, foul-smelling, so-called 'flowers' to shove their misshapen and elongated necks through the Lord's earth and then lets their vomit-coloured petals infringe the sanctity of our own old and very dear English countryside? What have we as a nation in, I fear, a deep and irreversible decline, busily wallowing in our post-colonial cowardice, puffing our chest up and then wheezing like some bronchial old colonel, what have we as a nation come to when we allow these daffodils, these malevolent globules of terminal jaundice, all yellow, yellow, yellow, to poke their noses through our ground and into our private lives?

DENNIS POTTER

Find corpse of chick in swimmin pool. Downer. Sell house.

KEITH RICHARDS

March 5th

The anniversary: of the death of Iosif Stalin. Beast and Monster. Mass-murderer. What do we need to call him? What is it necessary to call him? Stalin is too simple: too simperbubble. In considering our selection of an appropriate word, I must first contend that the simple word 'Stalin' does nothing to convey the guy's sheer horrid horridity. Let's think again: let's reinvent the language to form a noose around his head.

Mister Walrus Whiskers. That just about does the trick. I can candidly argue that, following a great deal of research, I know he wouldn't want to be called Mr W-W: not one little bit. Or what about 'Starling'? No way, José Feliciano. It sounds too like a bird: and a bird he was most certainly not.

The guy hated flying: hated it. Nor can we call him by his matey primonomenclaturalition, which is, of course, Iosif: Iosif is no mate of mine.

And why, pray, is it necessary to point out at this post-millennial juncture that Iosif Stalin – or Starling – is no mate of this fifty-two-year-old male novelist? Or, to put it another way: Novelist male old year fifty-two this of mate no is – Starling or – Stalin Iosif that juncture this at out point to necessary it is, pray, why and?

It can here be stated, boldly and fearlessly: Iosif Stalin was a very bad man. And my contention goes further, and can herein be tersely stated: he wasn't nice at all.

MARTIN AMIS

March 6th

Buy new house with lovely clean swimmin pool. Build new upstairs room for throwin TVs out of.

KEITH RICHARDS

Women divide into two categories. The kind who does what you tell her to. And the kind who doesn't. Frankly, I've got a hell of a lot of time for them both. But one or two I can't abide.

Not long ago, I had lunch with Mother Teresa at Wilton's. She was no bigger than the partridge on my plate. In fact, I was half-tempted to pour my remaining gravy over her. I could have downed her in a couple of mouthfuls and still had room for a decent rice pudding.

God helps those who help themselves, I advised her. You're frankly barking up the wrong tree grubbing around the backstreets of Calcutta. No one goes there. They're not what I'd call serious players.

Sadly, she chose not to take my advice. Small wonder she died with barely a penny to her name. With her reputation and connections, she could have expected – what? – 250, 300K?

No one likes a little person, be it man or woman. If you're going to be a hard-hitter, you've got to be over 5ft 2ins. And let's not imagine that slogging around in a grubby habit gets you anywhere, either. For all her undoubted domestic virtues, Mother Teresa would never have made the position of Sub-Editor on a national newspaper.

MAX HASTINGS

The X-Factor. Don't get me started! When those lovely young men come on stage in their tight little trousers and sing their hearts out for Sharon, my heart melts. I truly care about every single one of them, I really do, and the public senses that, and that's why they love me.

Just yesterday, I was being driven along by my chauffeur in our $463,000 limousine. I was in the back with my plastic surgeon Roger, who was just putting the finishing touches to my new toes (sorry, but you've got to have six on each foot these days if you want to be noticed). Suddenly, we hear this fucking yell from the river. A boat had capsized, and there's five people in the water struggling for their fucking lives, bless 'em!

Call me a great big softy, but I couldn't just leave them to drown, I'm sorry, that's not the kind of person I am! So I get the chauffeur to park near the river, and I get out the old mirror and make sure I'm looking fan-tastic – I'd never let the fans down, they want to see me at my best – then I squeeze into my $3,000 stilettos and walk ever so sexily down to the riverside, where there's just the one lifebelt to throw them.

The five of them are still thrashing about in the river, all fucking soggy and that, hair all over the place, only now there's only four, bless, because one's gone under! 'Sorry guys, I can only rescue the one of you!' I announce, as sweetly as possible, because I truly care about them all, and I'd dearly love to be able to save each and every one of them from drowning.

'So which of you lovely young people is it going to be?' I ask them. They look so adorable, all shivery and panicky and cuddly, thrashing about in the river and that. By now, they're all so desperate, they're screaming for help at the very tops of their super voices, they really are! Yes, they love me!

'Decisions, decisions!' I say, flashing my trademark smile. 'I only wish I could save you all, you're all so truly fabulous!'

By now another one's gone under, and there's just the three left – but it doesn't make my choice any easier! 'Ho-hum!' I say. 'This is one of the toughest decisions of my life. It's truly momentous! You know what, guys? Sharon's going to have to have herself a little sit-me-down before deciding.'

You could almost feel the tension in that river! So I have's myself my little sit-me-down, and check on my make-up – but when I get up again, the last three have disappeared below the water!

Yes – I'd left it too late! Story of my life! I'll never forget those young people's faces. I'd made their day! They looked so thrilled to have met Sharon Osbourne before they drowned. I walked back to the limousine with a lovely warm feeling in my heart. See, when you're in my position, you've got to put something back, you really have.

SHARON OSBOURNE

I hate pineapple. It should be banned.

GERMAINE GREER

March 7th

A hectic week ahead. After church, Mr Lucian Freud, who is a painter, arrives to paint another portrait.

He is quite old.

When I ask if he likes corgis, he tells me he does.

Good, I say. I ask him if he has been painting long.

He tells me he has.

How interesting, I say.

He doesn't reply.

Otherwise precious little small talk. He tells me he paints pictures, mainly. A lovely hobby, I say.

I might have asked him if he wouldn't be awfully kind and paint over that crack on the bathroom ceiling, but I forgot. They tell me he can be desperately expensive, so I think we got off lightly!

Freud: not a name you hear very often.

HM QUEEN ELIZABETH II

Let's face it – we are at a watershed in world history. And like all watersheds, it's full not only of sheds, but of water too. Yup, this shed is full of water – and we've got to do something. So let's be brutally honest. You can't store all that water in a shed without something dreadful happening. First of all, the water could spill out through the gaps in the walls. Look, I don't pretend to be an expert in watersheds, or how they're constructed. I'm an artist. But what I do know is this. If there's too much water in the shed, then it doesn't matter how many people you've got guarding it, or trying to plug the holes. That shed is going to burst.

And then we'll all get soaking wet.

Our clothes will be ruined. Our hair will go all flat. And there's no point even talking about highlights in a situation like that. It'll all be totally unmanageable.

And that scares the shit out of me.

GEORGE MICHAEL

March 8th

8 March 1960: Happy Birthday Dear Me! Twelve today! The Headmaster approaches me personally and wishes me Many Happy Returns of The Day!! I tell him how simply WONDERFUL he's looking, and insist ('There's nothing in the world I'd like more, Headmaster!') on walking with him. He is understandably overjoyed, but says he'd rather walk alone. Poor old fellow – no one likes to be outshone!! Onwards and upwards!

GYLES BRANDRETH

8 March 1970: Happy Birthday Dear Me! Twenty-two today!! That's twenty-two years of fun and laughter and all-round entertainment for all my family and friends! I've had the most MARVELLOUS year with literally billions of achievements to my name! I've built a full-size traction engine (*The Gyles Brandreth*) out of 5,734,297 matches, I've

written, directed and starred in my own musical (*Gyles: The Musical*), I've published *The Gyles Brandreth Book of Irish Knock-Knock Jokes*, I've become the first ever person to sing 'Yes We Have No Bananas' backwards on Radio Luxembourg, I've made best friends with Fanny Cradock, Gilbert Harding and Mr Pastry, I've climbed the world's smallest hill, and I haven't even mentioned my exciting new range of brightly-coloured pom-poms to brighten up your dowdy old oven gloves! Next stop: I plan to ascend Mount Everest!

GYLES BRANDRETH

8 March 1980: Happy Birthday Dear Me! Thirty-two today!!! I may not yet have quite managed to climb Mount Everest – the offer from the gentlemen's mountainwear sponsors simply wasn't jolly enough, financially! – but I did manage to break the world record for playing twenty-four different songs on the spoons in under two minutes while standing on one foot on a lilo dressed as a nun!

Yesterday, I attended a formal dinner for all us former Presidents of the Oxford Union. Frankly, I stood out from the others. I was the only one who came as Little Bo Peep.

This year I wrote thirty-two books, including the bestselling *501 Uses for a Daffodil*, I ghost-wrote the *Simply Fantastic Michael Miles Quiz Book*, I was paid nearly £17,542 for telling my ten best John Gielgud Bloopers at 167 luncheons, I continued to present my own daily mid-morning phone-in programme on Radio Solent, I masterminded the Potty Putty Museum in Bradford-on-Avon and I helped market a splendid new keep-fit machine which lets you run flat-out without getting anywhere! All this and my new best friend Jeffrey Archer has assured me that if ever I feel like becoming an MP he'll see to it that I'm Chief Secretary to the Treasury before the year's out!

Next aim: to climb Mount Snowdon!

GYLES BRANDRETH

8 March 1990: Happy Birthday Dear Me! Forty-two today!!! I never quite managed to climb Mount Snowdon – but at least I've done the next best thing, which is to make the world's second largest sherry trifle!!

Other noteworthy achievements over this most tremendous of all years: I sucked my way through fifty-eight delicious fruit pastilles in under four minutes on the marvellous Radio Stoke-on-Trent, I was appointed Vice President of the Yo-Yo Club of Great Britain, I was runner-up in the Tie Wearer of the Year semi-final, I launched Betamax, a revolutionary new videotape that's set to take the world by storm, I became best friends with Monty Modlyn, Captain Mark Phillips and all three Beverley Sisters, and I've just handed in my fantastic tome, *Absolutely the Best: 100 Years of Asbestos!*.

We arranged a tremendous birthday dinner, with guests Mr and Mrs Charlie Drake, Larry Grayson, Magnus Pyke, the Tim Rices, the Lionel Blairs, the Jeffrey Archers and the Krankies. Larry told a truly classic anecdote about John Gielgud – apparently, in a fit of madness he once mistook Eileen Atkins for Maggie Smith!!! Cue the sound of clangers dropping!

Promise to self: in the next five years I shall certainly climb the Eiffel Tower!

GYLES BRANDRETH

8 March 2000: Happy Birthday Dear Me! Fifty-two today!!!!

I still haven't got round to climbing the Eiffel Tower, but at least I have spoken on the art of plate-spinning to the Epsom and Ewell Back Pain Association Annual Dinner!!

Today I finish my *Illustrated History of the Novelty Pullover*, tomorrow I write my *Life of William Shakespeare* (now they'll HAVE to take me seriously), the next day I get going on *Gyles Brandreth's Great Big Book of Fun Party Games Involving Balloons* and over the weekend I'm ghosting *The Michael Barrymore Book of Totally Impossible Brain-Teasers*. Meanwhile, plans for my National Museum of Cocktail Party Umbrellas in Rottingdean are coming on apace.

GYLES BRANDRETH

March 9th

My uncle Stiffy, who lived for a lightly-poached tongue, had strong views on food. 'Never remove the gunk from a trotter before boiling it,' he would say, whilst tending to a particularly troublesome toenail with a fine sixteenth-century silver corkscrew. 'There's oodles of nutrition in filth.'

At Chatsworth, we take care to remember Uncle Stiffy's maxim whenever we boil a trotter. This is what makes this receipt so particularly tasty.

TROTTER ON HORSEBACK

1 pig's trotter
2 onions
2 pts water
2 slices Mother's Pride

Do make sure your pig is completely dead before removing its trotter. Great Aunt Squinty forgot, and lost an eye as a consequence. Thankfully, the eye boiled up well, and made an interesting addition to the fruit salad we served on Coronation Day. Waste not, want not, as our old Governess used to say. If ever she came across a dead insect – a bluebottle or wasp – she would never dream of throwing it away. After all, what is a Lemon Curd without insects?

First, discard the onions. You will not be needing them for this receipt.

Now boil the trotter in the water for 10–15 minutes, but not a second longer. It should remain nice and chewy, with that delicious trottery flavour.

Wrap it in the two slices of Mother's Pride, buttered to taste. Serve warm-ish. Ideal for a late breakfast, or perchance as that 'little something extra' for afternoon tea.

DEBORAH, DUCHESS OF DEVONSHIRE

I'm five years bloody old. My parents and me have nothing in common, no conversation, no small talk, nothing. Now I find they've booked me into a primary school. How bloody dare they? Don't they know who I am?

The school is rotten. The uniform is a total turn-off, the teachers are middle-aged with no like sense of style and the service is truly appalling.

JANET STREET-PORTER

March 10th

England in March! What a horrid, class-ridden, snobbish nation, packed with the most ghastly common little low-brows.

Today I am forced to suffer a disgracefully expensive five-course luncheon at the Savoy with Arnold Wesker, who, I regret to say, certainly isn't up to much, intellectually speaking: I ask him to name five plays I had personally directed in the past three years – and he doesn't even know!

But we agree on the burning need for a truly savage and satirical film that skewers the fat-cats in our overblown, moribund, post-imperial society.

Suddenly, an impertinent suburban waiter interrupts us to ask if we would care for a sweet.

'"Care for a sweet"?' I complain bitterly. '"Care for a sweet"?!! What sort of a country are we living in when a functionary interrupts a highly serious discussion to ask if one would "care for a sweet"! Very well, I'll have the Black Forest Gâteau – but only as a symbol of our overblown and tasteless age.'

Outside the Savoy, a pompous hotel functionary in a top hat and braid asks if he can hail me a cab.

I tell him in no uncertain terms that, as an anarchist, I am perfectly well equipped to hail one for myself. But the first cab drives straight past me with someone else in the back. I have never known such a kick in the teeth. I have been suppressed and disregarded in this country for decades – and now this! It's really too much.

LINDSAY ANDERSON

I crave simplicity. What could be more satisfying than a simple boiled egg? Ever since, as a young man, I became the first Englishman to visit Europe, I have pursued a love affair with the boiled egg. A boiled egg is a feast for all the senses: the eyes amazed by the deep rich yellow contrasted with the stark, translucent, almost virginal white; the ears alive to the gentle knock-knock-knock on the warmly curvaceous and softly yielding shell; the mouth teased by expectations of the flowing yolk softly easing its way along the salivating contours of the tongue, and down, down, down into the throat; the penis quivering in readiness to be used as a spoon, diving deep, deep, deep, deep into the very nub and hollow of the ovoid, then rising up once more, now drenched in the brightest yellow. And it's also very pleasant with toast.

SIR TERENCE CONRAN

March 11th

The young Victoria's life, it seems to me, really begins the moment she sees the super-sexy Prince Albert in his skin-tight figure-hugging uniform and thinks to herself, 'Hmmm, tasty! You know what? I want some of that!'

The couple fall head-over-heels in love, and simply adore driving around the little country lanes near Windsor in his fast car on hot summer days. They love each other totally, and uncovering that really was revelatory for me. The more I read about her – and in the end I finished an entire biography, non-swanks! – I couldn't believe how their love was so exactly like my own love for Andrew.

As couples, we were like peas in the proverbial iPod. Victoria and Albert used to eat meals together – and so did me and Andrew. Victoria and Albert used to sometimes go out together – and so did us. Victoria and Albert stayed married until the day he died – and so did me and Andrew, or nearly. Victoria wrestled the whole of her life with weight issues bound up with a lack of self-confidence – and so did me. And, just like I, Victoria eventually went to live in the United States of America, where the people respected her honesty, admired her for her amazing work with WeightWatchers and literally took her to their hearts. The list goes on and on.

SARAH, DUCHESS OF YORK

Albert Einstein. Let's face it, the guy didn't know the first thing about science.

GERMAINE GREER

March 12th

Violet and I attended pre-luncheon drinks with the Somersets at Gloucester. Then on to the Gloucesters in Somerset. The Devonshires had brought Kent along. Halfway through the luncheon, the butler informed us that Lady Avon was at the door. 'Tell her to join us!' said Gloucester, drawing up a chair for her. She sat down and was halfway through her main course (medaillons de veau, pommes Lyonnaises, épinards à la crème – all perfectly eatable), entertaining us with fulsome praise for a new lemon-scented shower gel, whatever that may be, when it emerged that the butler had misheard. She was not Lady Avon at all, but the Avon Lady.

ANTHONY POWELL

In the operations room at Downing Street, the telephone rings. Prime Ministerial aides sigh knowingly. They know from long experience that when a phone rings, there is sure to be someone on the other end of the line.

It is a call for the Prime Minister from someone very important, perhaps even a VIP. According to seasoned observers, Tony Blair has matured in office. He is now very adept, very professional with a telephone. And today is no exception. He takes the telephone receiver in his right hand, and places it to his ear. This way, he can not only hear what is being said, but speak himself, knowing he will be heard down the other end.

'Hello. It is good to speak to you,' he says in a clear voice into the telephone receiver. Whoever it is on the other end will probably have heard him, loud and clear. By saying, 'Hello. It is good to speak to you,' he is signalling to the other person not only that he is now on the 'other end of the line', but also that he is pleased to be able to speak to him. A born diplomat, this morning he is also proving himself a highly skilled politician.

SIR PETER STOTHARD*

March 13th

Riding into New York I was struck, not for the first time, by how busy it is, and how many skyscrapers there are: it's the city that never sleeps, a bit like Beijing or Vladivostok. Dublin's quite like that too.

CHARLEY BOORMAN

March 14th, 1960

TO HAROLD MACMILLAN

Darling H,

You were such an absolute poppet last night in Downing Street listening to silly me rambling on about Larry's deceit – and you so dreadfully, dreadfully busy, too! But if Larry hadn't promised, absolutely promised, me the role, and then reneged on that promise, I would never have burdened you with my worries, particularly when you were so busy trying to sort out your little Balance of Payments.

I can't tell you how much I value your friendship – your powers of oratory, your command of politics, your urbane manner, those

---

*From his book *Eyewitness to History: Thirty Minutes in the Hallway of Blair's Downing Street* (2004).

splendidly coarse yet effortlessly elegant tweed suits and, perhaps above all, your magnificent moustaches. Promise me you'll never shave them off. They look so very becoming on you – and one dreads to contemplate what lies beneath. My best love to your darling Dorothy, too. She looked so very lovely in that pretty floral dress last night.

Your dearest,

Johnny

JOHN GIELGUD

TO DADIE RYLANDS

Dearest Darling Dadie,

One feels so dreadfully sorry for them both. Harold, perfectly hideous in tweeds, is now something desperately important in politics. He does go on so. I fear that moustache of his has gone to his head. He asks my advice on the Balance of Payments. I tell him that Tony Quayle would be excellent in the lead, with Peggy as second fiddle, but he pays no heed. These politicians are so one-track minded.

Dorothy M was clad from top to toe in the most hideous fabric, poor darling. Had I not known better, I would have taken her for a large pair of curtains and attempted to draw her shut.

Big kiss, Johnny

JOHN GIELGUD

March 15th

Mauritius in March, so many years ago. I was wearing a rather low-cut bathing suit which displayed my bosom to maximum advantage! It was unconventional in those days to wear a rather low-cut bathing suit to a formal dinner party! But then I have always been a rather unconventional sort of woman!

Needless to say, the eyes of the men at the table were literally glued to my cleavage!* So I decided to divert their attention by insisting on a round of silly games!

'I know what!' I shrieked, delightedly. 'Let's play hunt the thimble!' And with that I withdrew into the sitting room, and got darling Mrs Stokes, who once cooked her perfect sherry trifle for Adolf Eichmann, to place a thimble down what many have been kind enough to describe as my remarkable cleavage!

'Hunt the thimble – ready, steady, go!' I whooped as I returned to the dining room! In fact, I tried to make it easier for them by pointing at the likely area! But sadly not one of the gentlemen looked up, thank you very much!

On closer investigation, I discovered they were otherwise engaged in plopping their 'members' (how I hate that word!) on the table to see whose was the largest!

Then they all got out their felt-tips, painted funny faces on them and re-enacted the Battle of Omdurman! 'I know when I'm not wanted, gents!' I exclaimed, good-heartedly dipping into my own bosom for my thimble and retreating upstairs for an early night with something milky and a copy of the latest *Vogue*!

LADY ANNABEL GOLDSMITH

Find corpse in upstairs guest bathroom. Freak out. Sell house.

KEITH RICHARDS

*The friends referred to in this passage include Nicholas Van Hoogstraaten ('Hogey is an absolute scream! A lot of people don't realise how devoted he is to his adorable Pekingese, Spot'), C. Montgomery Burns ('Monty has a passionate love for the environment') and Dr Hannibal Lecter ('a gifted raconteur and gourmet').

March 16th

Oh Jasus. Oh Jasus oh Jasus oh Jasus. Oh Jasus. Will you look at that? asks Dad. I look down at me plate. Oh Jasus, he asks, was there ever a child like him for the greed and the gluttony, the gluttony and the greed? And now the others are staring at me plate, and they'd take a pitchfork to me head out of jealousy if we hadn't sold the pitchfork to Ma McGubbins to pay for the last season's hay which they needed to feed the donkey to pull the peat to buy another pitchfork to replace the one they'd sold to old Ma McGubbins.

How's he get to have two peas? says Malachy. Oh Jasus, is tis birthday? Dad snatches one of me peas and cuts it in half, snatching half for himself and placing the other half in his top pocket for safekeeping, alongside last year's moth. Malachy caught the moth in his sock and Dad said he'd keep it for our St Patrick's Day fry-up, moths cook beautiful in batter he said though their wings can prove a mite chewy, it's all that flying they do, Jasus who'd be a moth in this day and age? Malachy says moths are Protestant, ye've never seen a moth with a rosary, now have you, he says, but Mam says they're good Catholics, and all that flitterfluttering is them making the sign of the cross to the good Lord, is it not.

So I'm cutting me remainin' pea into four and spreading the quarters round the plate to give an impression of quantity when there's a swoosh from the chimney and Great Grandma McCourt emerges covered in soot, her false teeth close behind. She's been out whorin' agin, whispers Alphie. Jasus, how can ye tell? I hiss back. She's suckin' on a cough-drop, says Alphie, they always pay her in cough-drops. But is it not a mortal sin? I ask. Will she not be condemning her soul to eternal damnation?

Not for a cough-drop, snaps Mam. Maybe for a sherbet lemon or two toffees, now shaddup and eat your pea or you won't be getting your mouse-tail for puddin'.

FRANK McCOURT*

---

*From the first volume of his memoirs of an Irish childhood, *Tings Can't Git Much Worse* (1996). This was followed in 1999 by the concluding volume, *Wrong Again*.

The trouble with staying in places like Windsor Castle is that you so rarely meet anyone of interest. Bumped into the Reagans as I was going up the stairs. Dull little couple. He's making a goodish stab of being President of the USA, she has a reasonable figure but eyes too far apart. Feel sorry for the pair of them. Should I put him on the board of the Tote? Might give him something to do.

WOODROW WYATT

March 17th

I have always found the look and smell of a bottle of Heinz tomato ketchup powerfully erotic, in that noble word's original sense of 'tasting slightly of tomatoes'. In the contemporary sense of the word, it is not erotic at all, or at any rate not nearly as erotic as a can of tinned peaches in heavy syrup, one of which I remember taking to the opera and courting successfully in the spring of '48, only to be turned down when it came to bed because it had become suspicious of my infatuation with a beautifully ripe pineapple. All full-blooded Englishmen, particularly those of Irish descent, have found sexual desire within their loins for the suppurating convexities and soft, skeiny protuberances of the fruit (originally 'froo-it', owing to the fact that, if it had an unrelenting central core, it was hard to bite froo it), and this explains why the Establishment has never allowed a law to be placed on the statute books forbidding full intercourse with any type of fruit.

ANTHONY BURGESS

I collar Reagan over a brandy and give him some advice. 'A lot of people tend to forget,' I say, 'that America's a very big country.' He is very grateful.

WOODROW WYATT

March 18th

My God, I despair of women sometimes. My whole life and my every breath has been informed with the imprint of my love and respect, admiration indeed, of women. But for Christ's sake, they sometimes let me down. If there is one type of woman I hate it is the very thin type of woman. And if there is another type of woman who gets up my nose it's the fatty. And what about those detestable in-betweenies, those spineless wretches who don't have the guts to be one thing or the other? They frankly get on my wick. Not until woman can truly be herself – neither fat nor thin nor in-between – can our sisterhood hope to save this doomed planet.

GERMAINE GREER

Time to leave Windsor Castle. I worry over a point of etiquette. How much should one tip the Queen?

WOODROW WYATT

March 19th

You are wrong, I am right.
I am right, you are wrong.
You are Ron, I am Reg.
But who is he?

EDWARD DE BONO*

*Author of *Lateral Thinking* (1967), *Parallel Thinking* (1973), *Diagonal Thinking* (1976), *Downhill Thinking* (1977), *Thinking as it is Thought* (1978), *Think, Thinking, Thinked, Thunk* (1980), *Think Estate* (1982), *What to do if Your Boat Starts Thinking* (1983), *Kitchen Think* (1985), *From Fat to Think: Dieting the de Bono Way* (1988), *Stretching Yourself Think* (1989) and many other titles.

Pair of Siamese twins knocks on my door, lovely couple of ladies, joined at the hip or wherever, they say we need the media attention, one of us has a tragic terminal illness, the other's struggling with a tragic drugs problem, we want to strike while the iron's hot, Max, so how can you help us?

As luck would have it, this very morning my client and good friend Simon Cowell of *X-Factor* fame had been on the old mobile asking if I knew a pair of Siamese twins he could perform his magic on, so, swings and roundabouts, to cut a long story short I put Simon and the tragic Siameses in touch at a mutually agreed venue of my choice and Bob's your uncle, the twins are lined up for a major role on next season's *X-Factor*, followed by an episode of their own on *Celebrity Surgery*, I can't tell you any more at this moment in time but believe me it'll be dynamite, and between ourselves one of them's enjoying something of a fling with one of Stephen Lawrence's young killers, so that can't be bad, especially if a marriage results, *Hello* are interested, so's UK Living TV, you name it, sweetheart, we're talking mega-bucks. Yes, it's nice to be able to put something back.

MAX CLIFFORD

March 20th

We invaderate Iraq. Thanks to our courageous actions, today our world is a safer place than it will ever be.

GEORGE W. BUSH

March 21st

I have often heard it said, and sometimes within earshot of the upper echelons of respectable society, that two and two make four. Yet this is quite plainly not the case. How could two and two possibly make four when it is so obvious to one and all that they make six? To put it simply, if I have two snuff boxes in my left hand, and two snuff boxes in my right hand, the total number of snuff boxes I have in both hands is six. Or to translate the same truth into the characteristically modish and inelegant language of numbers favoured by the more churlish mathematicians:

$$2 + 2 = 6$$

Point proven. Yet our present system of egalitarian government, by which is really meant totalitarian rule by the proletarian hordes (many if not most of whom have dandruff), has convinced generations of citizens (their shoes in grave need of a polish) that the equation 2 + 2 = 4 can somehow be made to hold water. Down this path lies madness. Next, they will be telling us that one and one makes two!!!

This grave mathematical deception, from which floweth the depraved and decadent condition of England today, must needs rightly be placed at the feet of Harold Wilson, who, far from being an aristocrat, was the product of inferior breeding, misusing the adverb hopefully and never learning to hold his pipe in a manner befitting a gentleman.

And, forsooth, how much has changed! When I first joined *The Times* as an apprentice leader-writer in 1950, all journalists on that newspaper were expected, quite rightly, to don top hat and tails at all times. Nor were we permitted to write our own articles, for it was considered an activity unfit for a gentleman. Instead, the necessary pieces were written for us by uniformed parlour maids, whom we would tip generously (sixpence ha'penny every Christmas) for their troubles. Never let it be said that there was a jot or tittle of snobbery about this. Like slavery, it was valued equally on both sides, allowing them to look up to us and, at one and the same time, us to look down on them.

Nowadays, to my certain knowledge, *The Times* is staffed almost exclusively by common people, many bussed in from the East End in boilersuits. Even Lord Rees-Mogg is obliged to adopt a flat cap, grubby overalls and a cockney accent before reporting for work. And a certain coarseness has crept into the prose. For instance, leading articles on the situation in Iraq invariably begin with the lamentable phraseology, Fuck this for a game of soldiers. It all goes to show that equality may be a good thing in theory, but, like mathematics, it never works in practice.

SIR PEREGRINE WORSTHORNE

March 22nd

Nelson Mandela is one bloke I hugely admire. I can't imagine being locked up in a cell for literally days on end without a personal assistant or even face-cream. I wrote a song about Nelly's time in prison – 'It's Those Little Things I Miss So Bad' – and I was privileged to sing it at a concert in his honour:

Larked up in jay-ul
Cos my skin's not pay-ul
Yit's those lit-tul thungs I myiss swooo bad –
Thwose lit-tul things
That Santa brings
Like dia-mond riiiings
An' pure gold wiiiings
An' thwose pearl yearrings I once had

When I finished singing this soulful tribute, I glanced over at the great man. The guy was in tears.

Afterwards, I attended a ceremony at which Nelson Mandela was going to give a bit back to society by presenting yours truly with an honorary degree. It was a marvellous moment as I received my degree from Little Miss Mandela, truly a legend in her own lifetime.

SIR ELTON JOHN

Now I hear that the brave firefighters, lovely, decent lads, are going on strike to try and stop this whole ghastly business of the government's secret time-changes.

I pop into the local home furnishings store, march up to the bedding counter and ask for some Polos. They say they sell pillows, not Polos, and they show me one. 'Well, I'll never be able to fit something that size in my ear!' I exclaim. What a bunch of proper Charlies!

Eventually, I locate some Polo mints at the sweet shop next door. 'Do they come with batteries?' I ask, but it turns out these are extra, like so many things these days. So blow me down if they haven't even privatised Polo mints! I have no wish to bring personalities into it, that's not my style, never has been, never will be, but I place the blame fairly and squarely on that smarmy, self-satisfied, grinning lickspittle Tony Blair.

TONY BENN

March 23rd

Buy new house. Find it's in France. Fuckin drag. Have to sell it.

KEITH RICHARDS

March 24th

TO BERNARD BERENSON

My dear BB,

I must apologise, inter alia, for my tiresome silence. I have now emerged from les horreurs de la term, a pleasing respite, and one that allows me time to devote a generous portion of my thankfully not inconsiderable intellect to the service of this, our most deliciously civilised correspondence.

It was whilst walking round the Christ Church Meadow, and pondering on the complicated subtleties of St Augustine's theological system, which I had long tried to take seriously, though to little avail (for St Augustine was, frankly, a second-rater, perhaps even a third-rater), that the undoubted truth came upon me that my erstwhile colleague A.L. Rowse is singularly ill-suited to the teaching or writing of history, being dwarfish and plebeian. There is neither breadth nor depth to him, and precious little width or height.

On my return to my study, I set in motion a plot to discredit the oikish Cornish charlatan. Creeping along the corridor on tip-toe, I eased open his door the merest half-inch, deftly placing an open bottle of black ink of the darkest hue on its uppermost surface before tip-toeing back down the corridor again. The entire operation was o'er in something less than a minute.

Within seconds of the dinner-bell sounding, I awaited the tell-tale creak of Rowse's door with the keenest anticipation. Sure enough, when it came it was accompanied by a high-pitched – almost feminine – howl of quasi-scholarly anguish. I counted to ten before nipping out into the corridor. 'My dear Leslie!' I exclaimed, surveying this woebegone figure, covered from head to foot in the blackest ink. 'The true scholar always guards against the overloading of his fountain pen!'

Needless to say, the sight of poor little drenched Leslie at luncheon convinced my colleagues that it would be highly inappropriate for him to be granted a Fellowship, from which those of the Negro persuasion are sadly disbarred. C'est, as the untrustworthy French have it, la vie. Discussing the episode later with three of Oxford's keenest intellects, we found ourselves in complete agreement that Rowse had brought it on himself. 'If one insists on pushing open doors upon which ink has previously been placed, one must surely be obliged to make an accommodation with the consequences,' I observed, sagely. 'St Augustine may have been an undistinguished boulevardier, but he at least taught us that much.'

I visited France last week: a disappointing country, with nothing and no one to detain one for more than a few minutes.

HUGH TREVOR-ROPER,
LETTER TO BERNARD BERENSON

'I Wandered Lonely as a Cloud'

I wandered lonely as a cloud
That floats on high o'er vales and hills
When all at once I saw a crowd,
A host, of golden daffodils
And I said, come on, Lady Antonia,
Get your coat on, I'm not standing
For any more of this fucking nonsense
Those fucking daffodils have got it in for us
It's free speech they can't abide.

HAROLD PINTER

March 25th

How am I approaching playing Hamlet? Puerto Rican, with a crewcut. Either that, or Irish with a fringe.

When I approach a role, I channel all the pain I've ever felt in my life. Like, when I was ten years old, I was told I had to wait an hour before I could have a candy, and man, that truly hurt. I used that experience in *Fight Club*. Another time I felt real searing agony was once when I was at the Golden Globes and like I looked across the room at my fellow actors and I knew deep inside we were all aching in the same way – we were horribly isolated from the rest of humanity by our fame and our money and our looks, and, Jeez, were we hurting, and we were all so involved in the search for self. And that's how I made Achilles such a very vulnerable figure, I could really draw on that, there's a real isolation in the guy.

Like there's this real telling line when he says, 'Take that, you bastard!' and he puts his sword clean through his enemy, and the way I read it, in some sense he was just trying to express his hurt, his pain, his vulnerability in the face of so much fame. And in those days of ancient Rome they didn't have much television, least not so much as we have now, so I guess it's got a lot worse since for the rest of us like celebrities.

BRAD PITT

Put an ad in *Country Life*. 'Bloody great French mansion for sale. No corpses. Bargain.'

KEITH RICHARDS

March 26th

HM Queen Elizabeth the Queen Mother invites one over for a drink.

'You have never looked so positively *radiant*, Ma'am! I don't know how you do it!' I exclaim as she greets us. In fact, she looks like an overweight hippopotamus – and an ill-bred hippopotamus at that – and I know perfectly well how she does it: by pigging out on chocolate *bon-bons* and knocking back cheap house champagne from dawn til dusk. She may indeed look radiant, but then so too did Hiroshima in its day.

'Cecil, will you sit next to The Queen?' she says. I had high expectations, but once again I was dreadfully let down. Alas, The Queen is no beauty. Far from it. A card-carrying midget, of course – she surrounds herself with corgis to lend her height – and she is not improved by that hair, which is got up to look like Mrs Mopp. It does rather rankle that she makes so little effort when one 'drops round'. She obviously sees herself as fearfully 'important' – all superior smiles and hoity-toity gestures – yet she has *zero* sex appeal, and would be better suited to serving behind the haberdashery counter at *Maison Woolworth*. Her *embonpoint*, too, is crudely obtrusive and tiresomely invasive, so that for one's personal safety one is forced to duck every time she turns round.

'What a marvellous complexion Her Majesty has!' I purr sympathetically to Louis Mountbatten (raddled old mascara'ed *buggeriste* got up like a pantomime admiral, all over-shone epaulettes and hideous buttons) upon adjourning to the withdrawing room. 'And such natural grace and dignity!' Manners are so desperately important in this coarse and vulgar age.

CECIL BEATON

March 27th

In our end is our beginning, and in my bottom is my worth.

Today, I met Sven.

It was at a very sophisticated party full of very, very important men, men of wisdom and experience, and their sadly resentful wives, who, behind their cold smiles, desperately yearned for the attention to fall upon them, not upon me.

Like a bolt from the sword of Thor, I felt those ice-blue Nordic eyes land on me from across the room. I was wearing a distinguished miniskirt, with a tight open-top blouse overflowing with the grace and wisdom of my forebears.

I turned to see this brilliant, important man with the hard, thrusting spectacles of a Greek god.

I knew, as only a beautiful woman can, that in that split-second he was transfixed with a desire verging on obsession.

'How do you do?' he said. 'My name is Sven.'

At this point, sex was out of the question. Am I not already happily married to someone else – a venerable old man with an extensive property portfolio?

But we must all follow our hearts, and where our heart leads us, sex will follow.

The man who called himself Sven put out his hand. Call it intuition, call it what you will, but I knew at that moment that what he desired most in the world was to shake mine. And so I let him hold my hand and move it rhythmically up and down for seconds – seconds that to him must have seemed like hours.

I touched his hand. His hand touched mine.

Together we shook and shook and shook, until we could shake no more.

'May I be having the number of your telephone please for so as to contact you?' said Sven.

I could not hold back my tears!

This was madness!

But looking at Sven I could see that under that neat grey suit, a volcano was ready to erupt.

Without thinking, I wrote down my name on a piece of paper. As I did so, I noticed Sven's eyes following another woman – a woman dressed in a vulgar, attention-grabbing mini-skirt, anxious to sell her story for a vast amount of money – around the room. I had just finished writing my number when I heard Sven whisper to her:

'May I be having the number of your telephone please for so as to contact you?'

In that moment, my world is turned upside down. How can my Sven do this to me? My blood runs hot and cold.

NANCY DELL'OLIO

I am proud that our country remains the scourge of the oppressed. Freedom is once again on the march, as the good people of America join together to wave it goodbye.

GEORGE W. BUSH

Quite terrifying, really. I am woken by my wireless alarm clock, only to discover from the so-called newscaster that while I was asleep the Government has altered the time by an hour or more. Now they expect us to believe that 8 is really 7, that 6 is really 5, and so on.

It makes me absolutely sick. What an untrustworthy man Blair really is. Of course, the Establishment have always wanted it darker in the night, just so's ordinary decent working people will lose their bearings and trip up on kerbs, or walk slap into walls.

I expect the candle manufacturers put them up to it. And the more candles we have, the more likelihood there is of fire, causing a great many homes to burn down. Don't try and tell me the big guns of the construction industry haven't put Blair up to it.

TONY BENN

March 28th

New novel out – so huge and jam-packed full of lovely, super characters that it might be best described as long a-weight-ed!!!

It's all set in the fabulous world of Fine Art – and that includes the Hon. Amelia Wiggle-Worthy, the twenty-something Fine Tart (!!) with skin-tight leather trousers cheekbones as high as a really high building and smouldering breasts to match.

Dearest Darling Diary, something tells me you're hooked already! That's so sweet of you, it really is, I almost feel like blubbing my eyes out, I really do, you're so impossibly kind, you really are. Anyway, the Hon. Amelia Wiggle-Worthy, is the highly-sexed and hugely successful auctioneer at top Fine Art auction house Smotherby's, and Amelia has fallen passionately head-over-heels in lust with hugely successful lothario dark-eyed sixteenth-century Italian porcelain expert Lord Guy Bigge-Crotch, whose muscles are as full of ripples as the Bay of Naples, where he first seduced moist-lipped, full-breasted, twin-legged Cordelia Van Pert-Bottom whose lovely gorgeous super adorable mongrel puppy Rachmaninov has just been run over and killed in an incredibly sad-making moment as a wicked act of revenge by hugely successful and irresistibly attractive but cold-hearted and ruthless but well-endowed and hugely wealthy but sadistic and really rather beastly entrepreneur aristocrat Viscount Conrad Nasty-Mann.

Little did I realise before I undertook five years of intensive research guided by my lovely friend the utterly adorable and hugely successful ex-head of the VandA Sir Roy Strong (on whom the madly attractive and stunningly seductive bronzed Museum Director Sir Roy Heathcliff is based) on a tour of Christie's, quite how much frantic, thrusting, really super sex they go in for in the orgasmic world of antique porcelain.

Take this extract, in which Lord Guy Bigge-Crotch escorts the to-die-for Amelia through his priceless well-researched collection of sixteenth-century Sèvres vases for the very first time:

> 'And this,' said Guy, picking up another priceless exhibit, his eyes still fixed on Amelia's full, high, incredibly springy breasts – soft and yield-

ing, yes, but also ruthlessly ambitious and thrusting – 'is one of my finest pieces of hand-crafted antique china. It's from the sixteenth century, which of course actually means it was made sometime in the 1700s.'

Amelia noticed Lord Guy's long, long, really very long fingers clutching the priceless Sèvres vase. How she wished they were even now unbuttoning her expensive wet-look silk blouse which cost £375 from Prada in London's impossibly glamorous New Bond Street. 'I love him,' she sobbed to herself in a frenzy of despair whilst maintaining a look of deepest composure on her face, covered as it was with a layer of perfect spot-free skin.

'Oh, hang it – who cares about bloody china!' sighed Lord Guy impatiently, as with a manly swing he threw the priceless Sèvres vase over his rippling, feverishly sweating left shoulder. 'All I want, Amelia, you hugely successful but nonetheless strangely insecure international beauty, is to bury myself deep inside your smouldering breasts.'

Amelia swooned. 'Mon Dieu!' she gasped, as she watched her breasts smoulder in his hugely successful hands. At moments of passion, the hot, red, moist French blood of her mother, the impossibly glamorous but desperately unhappy Comtesse Madeleine de Villefranche, seemed to course through her tongue.

At that moment, the priceless sixteenth-century Sèvres vase shattered against the priceless fifteenth-century Ming serving dish and both fell headlong onto a priceless thirty-six-piece Louis XIV dinner service, smashing it into hundreds of little pieces.

'Whoops! Don't MING us, we'll MING you!' said Lord Guy, bringing out his impossibly long and hugely successful manhood which glistened like the moist nose on a healthy pedigree Labrador puppy.

Amelia clutched her sides with laughter at his brilliant pun. 'SÈVRES you jolly well right!' she quipped in response, her smouldering breasts springing up and down like excited dachshunds at dinner time. 'Bonjour!' she added, once again her passionate French blood seeming to take control of her body as she raced headlong onto the field of passion.

JILLY COOPER

I hear of the death of Anthony Powell. This is not an easy entry for me to write. I was the man's friend for many years. But now that he is dead I find he has nothing more to say to me.

V.S. NAIPAUL

I order a cab. 'Hello,' I say as I get in, 'I'm Tony Benn.'

The driver looks me in the face. The penny drops. 'Golly gosh,' he says, 'you're Mr Tony Benn! Blow me down!' Without any sort of prompting, he has recognised me. I am tickled pink.

We engage in a tremendously stimulating discussion. He tells me that the junction of Kensington High Street and Kensington Church Street has been blocked for three weeks now, due to roadworks. 'I don't know what this country's coming to,' he concludes.

I explain that the Establishment doesn't want the traffic to go any faster, because that would totally undermine the Government's secret time-changes the day before yesterday, which were designed to remove an hour from ordinary people's lives.

'You can tell MI5 are behind most of these so-called "roadworks",' I explain. 'You can recognise them by their shiny yellow jackets and hard helmets.'

'You should be Prime Minister,' he says as I pay the fare. What a fascinating discussion we have had, offering me much food for thought.

I take out a Polo mint and put it in my ear. But I can't get a signal. Frankly, I'm beginning to suspect it is being deliberately jammed.

TONY BENN

March 29th

Michelle asks, do I want an egg?

In my life, Michelle, I say, I have learned that eggs may be found in unlikely places; that though eggs may come from chickens, they rarely remain with chickens. No: they spread themselves far and wide, often to end up on the great breakfast plates of America.

Eggs or flakes? sighs Michelle.

I tell you this, Michelle. We reject as false the choice between our eggs, howsoever they may be served, and our flakes, from whichsoever packet they may be poured. We will not falter until we have harnessed our eggs and our flakes, and, with eyes fixed on the horizon, those two ingredients will combine to produce a great American breakfast of which our grandchildren may yet be proud.

BARACK OBAMA

There is no doubt that to talk to Sibyl Colefax is very depressing. She mews and mows. Wont speak out; complains with one breath, asks pity but cant be induced to say what is on her mind. Perhaps there is very little there. She makes ones soul flop. Today she came half an hour late in her tiara and white fur & we had it out. After the usual patter, I managed to thrust in first & grabbed her tiara & hurled it thro' the window. Her defences crumpled: she flushed & quickened. I seized my chance to give her a quick jab between the ribs & she buckled and fell. She sat on the floor & pulled down some white undergarment which had become creased. And she started twittering out how I had really hurt her & how her tiara was worth a small fortune & I said, Even smaller now.

Stupidly, I turned away & in that second Sibyl was back up on her feet pummelling me again & again with those cruel diamond-studded fists, all the while shouting that I was insensitive to her upsets & heartless & interested only in myself. Happily, a large frying pan was close to hand & I so grabbed it & managed to land it on her head so she went down once again on the floor bleating and mewling.

Cry baby! I goaded her as she lay sprawled on the floor Cry baby Cry baby Cry baby!

Dont you dare call me that I'm not I'm not I'm not she yelled back & I said ha! That just proves that you are – so bad luck, Cry baby!

As she lay there straggled across the floor and twitching like a moth I took the opportunity to pour a jug of tomato sauce over her white fur but at that point Leonard put his head around the door & asked if everything was all right. Very much so, I said. Sibyl has just popped around hoping to continue our debate, as you can see it is all very agreeable, all very civilised.

VIRGINIA WOOLF

March 30th

So. The Queen Mother has died.

Will someone answer me this?

Why is it the old who always die first?

First top soccer commentator Kenneth Wolstenholme.

Then Spike Milligan.

And now the Queen Mum.

Evil monster Adolf Hitler once called her his most deadly foe.

And this was a man who knew a thing or two about deadly foes.

Adolf reckoned that if ever it came down to a showdown between the two of 'em in a dark alleyway, the Queen Mum would have him in an armlock and be jabbing out his eyes with a well-sharpened pencil before he could gurgle, '*Achtung! Schweinhund!*'

She was a lady with bottle.

When everyone else deserted London, she was the one who stayed, catching those doodle-bugs in her arms and single-handedly flinging them back at the Hun.

That took guts. That took nerve.

That took bottle.

In the middle of the Blitz, she'd be down the East End every night with her Ack-Ack gun, giving Jerry all she'd got.

And never a hair out of place.

They say the best die young. Agreed. And the old die young. True.

But in her case the old died old. And that's all for the best.

TONY PARSONS

At long last, the Queen Mother has popped off. Wasn't she marvellous? Well, no, actually, since you ask, she wasn't marvellous at all. In fact, her death marks the end of an anti-democratic era of deference and armchair fascism.

She was billed as the Last Empress of India, but when she kicked off her purpose-built shoes she was only 3 foot 11 inches high. Yet this didn't stop this card-carrying dwarf having the hots for Oswald Mosley, and strutting round the East End arm in arm with the old monster screaming anti-Semitic abuse through a haze of pink gin.

That's something they don't tell us in the history books. And for some reason they also forget to mention her role in the notorious Watergate break-in, taking orders direct from Howard Hunt. And there are still many questions to be answered about exactly what part she played in the Irish Potato Famine, and just how she came to be in Scotland when Pan Am Flight 103 crashed at Lockerbie.

In her private life, she was rarely seen without a fag and a bottle, and spent her rat-arsed days propping up the bar, spouting exaggerated opinions on topics of which she knew very little and cared even less. Drunk, pampered, carefree, louche, burp, I feel a bit queasy actually. Who are you calling louche, you arsehole? Come outside and say that. Whoops, now you've made me spill it all down my trousers.

CHRISTOPHER HITCHENS

The news comes over that Queen Elizabeth the Queen Mother has finally pulled stumps after making a decent century. We encountered one another five or six years ago. Over an expensive banquet at the Palace, I got the cut of her jib pretty damned quick. She was sitting next to me, short and buxom with far too much make-up. Not my type, but there we go. 'So what d'you reckon the silver on this table is worth, Ma'am?' I said, putting her at her ease. '500K? 600K? Bloody hell! That's nearly two years' salary!'

Let's not beat about the bush: the Queen Mother was a woman. Nothing wrong with that, of course. It remains my undiminished belief that the female of the species is more reliable, professional and idealistic than men, particularly when it comes to cooking and needlework. But something told me that it affected her judgement.

'Have you come far?' she asked me.

'Bloody daft question!' I replied with an engaging chuckle. With a deft stab born of many years in waders, I speared my smoked trout starter and shoved it with a single thrust into my mouth. 'Frankly, Ma'am, I don't know why we pay you such a vast amount if you can't come up with something better to say than that!'

My jovial remark broke the ice superbly. From that point on, the old lady wisely shut her trap while I gave her the benefit of my experience. 'With the greatest possible respect, Ma'am,' I began, in deference to her historic position, 'your whole family would win first prize in the World Class Nouveau Whingeing Stakes. What a bloody shower of second-rate bloody shits!'

My off-the-cuff comments helped clear the air. Just as importantly, they also gave the QM a first-rate view of what the nation was thinking. She responded magnificently, staring down at her plate, thinking seriously about what I had said.

'And pardon me, Ma'am,' I added, 'but you really shouldn't toy with your food like that. It's common as muck. Either put up or shut up. If you can't manage any more, then place your knife and fork together and be done with it. No good blubbing. For God's sake, woman, don't act like something the cat's brought in!'

I then felt it judicious to clear the air. 'What are you on these days?' I asked sympathetically. '400K? 500K?'

MAX HASTINGS

In 1973, 1974, 1981 and twice in 1992, I experienced violent orgasms as Queen Elizabeth the Queen Mother walked into the room. I was not alone. Her Private Secretary, Sir Martin Gilliat, would make a point of always being at hand with a box of luxury paper tissues as she entered any roomful of admirers. Sir Roy Strong was heard gasping, 'Yes, yes, YES!' before collapsing in an exhausted heap as the

Queen Mother arrived at the National Portrait Gallery to view a newly-acquired miniature by Holbein in June, 1972.

HUGO VICKERS*

March 31st

They talk of green shoots of recovery! How disgusting! Green shoots are so ugly, so *passé*. When I see a green shoot in my garden, I have my gardener to get rid of it. I tell him, 'I have no time for the Spring, it is the most vulgar and pretentious season.' Hope and optimism? So Nineties. So *démodé*.

KARL LAGERFELD

*From *After You, Ma'am: The Gracious Life of HM Queen Elizabeth the Queen Mother*.

April

April 1st

On his back, Beckham has a tattooed angel, whose arms reach out in a crucified posture along his shoulder blades. The angel's body is aligned with his spine; it wears a coy loin cloth, although it appears – perhaps it's the effect of gravity – to be exceedingly well hung. Like his own guardian angel, Beckham extends sheltering wings over the world ... Although his face is everywhere, his mystique becomes invisible. He is what we see when we close our eyes. Inside our heads, he is as mutable as his hair, a creature of infinite plasticity and demographic universality ... He is available for interactive fantasising, like your other half during phone sex; that is the deal the celebrity makes with us, and Beckham solemnises the transaction with that shy, dazed, long-suffering smile of his – a promise of surrender, compliance, infinite availability. He bends the ball, and we bend him like the ball.

PETER CONRAD

Paul Gascoigne was a highly-charged spectacle on the field of play: fierce and comic, formidable and vulnerable, urchin-like and waif-like, a strong head and torso with comparatively frail-looking breakable legs, strange-eyed, pink-faced, fair-haired, tense and upright, a priapic monolith in the Mediterranean sun.

PROFESSOR KARL MILLER

Tony Crosland said, 'I expect you have heard, Chairman Mao is dead.' Somehow I did feel that Mao merited a moment of reflection in the British Cabinet. In my opinion, he will undoubtedly be regarded as one of the greatest – if not the greatest – figures of the twentieth century ... Whether history will just put him among the emperors or whether he will be seen as having a quality distinct from them, I do not know, but he certainly towers above any other twentieth-century figure I can think of in his philosophical contribution and his military genius.

TONY BENN

Why would the Queen be scared of me? ... After a gruelling six-hour drive from Wales I found myself in a line at Buckingham Palace to meet the Queen at her historic buffet lunch for 150 or so of Britain's top female achievers. The first problem was getting a drink – not that HRH ever has this dilemma. A couple of surly footmen tried to palm me off with orange or apple juice – sod that – but a mini JSP strop soon ensured that Kate Moss, Sam Taylor-Wood, Vivienne Westwood and I were downing bubbly and marvelling at the ancient one-bar electric heaters in the fireplaces under the Rembrandts. These gadgets screamed 'economy' and seemed more suitable for a council house in Peterlee circa 1955 than a gallery packed with Old Masters.

As I approached the Queen in my black Christian Dior man's suit and white T-shirt, a momentary panic seemed to flit across her face – it must be a bit of a strain meeting females who actually work for a living when your daughter-in-law, Sophie, has proved herself such a turkey at PR.

JANET STREET-PORTER

I have slowly come to realise, and somewhat unwillingly, that I will have a crack at the leadership as soon as I can. Partly because I am in touch with real people, partly because I can offer some leadership and view of the future. I look at rivals like David Mellor and I like me better.

EDWINA CURRIE

The front-page photos after John had announced his new ministerial team brought home to me exactly what he had done: put the women he wanted in the Cabinet, those he finds no threat.

Mostly I was cross about Gillian Shephard. I like her, but what has she done, ever? Where were the achievements that make her a suitable candidate for the highest posts in the land? When has she stuck her neck out, made a great speech, made her mark on the nation?

Answer: she hasn't, and isn't likely to, and that is why she has advanced so smoothly, because she looks (a little) like me, but with none of the risks my appointment would cause.

She went round during the election introducing herself as 'the one who looks like Edwina Currie'. Never seems to have occurred to her that that's bloody hurtful to the original model still in circulation and makes her appointment an insult, a real slap in the face. I'm not cross with her, but with John.

EDWINA CURRIE*

April 2nd

Rhodes. I must say, this view is simply stunning. This is a truly magical place, a city full of almost Pythonesque contrasts: very colourful and full of real character, very much like some English towns, in some ways more so and in some ways rather less so! Strolling around Rhodes – which incidentally has rather fewer 'roads' than Birmingham! – I breathe in its character: truly magical, and full of – almost Pythonesque! – contrasts.

---

*Entries for April 1st should be treated with suspicion, as an ill-judged joke. They have recently been verified as authentic.

Always on the look-out for humour, I bump into one old boy who quite literally can't speak a word of English, and has no idea who I am! We get the camera crew assembled, and sure enough he makes a great interviewee, not understanding a word I say, thus allowing me to do a variety of funny faces to camera!

Before I arrived here, I had no idea how big Rhodes was. I must say, upon further investigation its actual size is really quite surprising. But why, I wondered, does it have that mysterious 'h' in its name? No one could tell me!

MICHAEL PALIN

I have never been attracted to men with facial hair. Which is not to say that they have not been attracted to me!

Quite the opposite! Before my marriage, I received proposals from over twenty-nine men with moustaches, seventeen of them sporting beards as well.

The gifted novelist Anthony Trollope once asked me to marry him, and so too did the famous Benjamin Disraeli, just one of eight Prime Ministers who have fallen head-over-heels in love with me.

The famous scientist Charles Darwin, the highly respected composer Johannes Brahms and the tireless philanthropist Father Christmas all begged me to accept their hands in marriage.

But I thought they could all do with a jolly good shave.

So under a star-filled sky, with the moon as bright as can be, I waved them goodbye to the distant music of Cole Porter.

BARBARA CARTLAND

April 3rd

Ronald Reagan is a man who walks tall, and, walking tall, the free world looks up to him. Looking up to him, the free world walks tall, walks as tall as Ronald Reagan. Ronald Reagan may walk tall, but he also talks walls. The Berlin Wall was also a Burly Wall when Ronald

Reagan came to the Presidency of the United States of America, but by the time he left office it was a Hurly-Burly Wall, not a tall wall at all but a short wall which had just had a shortfall.

My questions were carefully judged to be hard-hitting without hitting hard, forceful without being full of force. In this manner, Reagan ended up getting more out of me than many a more aggressive interviewer. Of course, many of the most interesting answers were never screened. For instance, when Reagan said, 'Did you come far?' I replied with a brief but mercilessly funny résumé of my biography. I began with an anecdote concerning the condition of my donger after I had plonked it once too often in the sheepdip. I then talked him through the lighter side of the notably incautious acne I experienced throughout a prolonged adolescence. I spoke movingly of the moment as a wide-eyed and gifted Cambridge undergraduate when I first realised that I was not only wide-eyed but gifted. I spoke as briefly as humility would allow of my television reviews from the early '70s, with extracts from my classic '*Game for a Laugh*? Game for a Bath, More Like!' review (since reprinted in many anthologies). I wound up by telling the great man that I was now proud to dine out on a regular basis with the Duke and Duchess of York. 'So, yes, Mr President,' I concluded, 'I think you could indeed say I've come far!!' And, under that gently slumbering exterior, I think I detected a chuckle.

CLIVE JAMES

April 4th

I have been Chairman of the BBC for some weeks now, and am settling into the job. I have already mastered the essentials of television. It comes on when you press the little button on the bottom left, and you switch 'channels' by pressing the little buttons to the right. To hear the sound, one looks to the button marked 'vol' – but this is purely voluntary, as the name implies.

MARMADUKE HUSSEY

April 5th

Has anyone solved the problem of what to do when you reach the end of the right-hand page when reading a book? It really is an awful chore to attempt to what is now known as 'turn the page over'. Often the pages turn two, or even three, at a time, so that one loses one's place and misses some major event that may or may not have happened in those two or three pages, and, even if one does manage to turn just the one page, one still encounters the problem of having to reorganise one's fingers and hands so as to incorporate the freshly-turned page. Of course, during the daytime, one can call for a highly-skilled member of one's staff to perform the necessary feat – and they do so with great dexterity, I might add – but while reading in bed at night, for instance, it really is too tiresome to have to ring one's bell so that some poor fellow has to come running in his nightshirt. One solution, of course, if the book consists of two-hundred-odd pages, is to buy two-hundred-odd copies of the book, and to ask the bookseller politely if he will pre-open each book to a fresh page, but I imagine this solution may present some storage disadvantages for those living in the more modest stately homes, 'bungalows', and so forth. Incidentally, I am at present reading, and greatly enjoying, a booklet called *Rearranging Your Upstairs Cushions*, available through the National Trust, as I may or may not have told you that February is the month I devote to rearranging the cushions on the sofa in my dressing room – quite a chore as it turns out!!

ANDREW, DUKE OF DEVONSHIRE

April 6th

Over the next four weeks I'll be out in the battlebus taking the fight to the electoral. We've got the Tories on the run and that's for sure!

I'll be campaigning 7/24 on the doorsteps knocking up ordinary people!

But it's a day mixed with sadness. I'm departuring the House after forty years that's forty years bringing equation to the ordinary hardworking people of this country but there's no denying I've a lifetime of achievements to look forward to!

I entered the Commons determining to go into battle with the ordinary working people of this country. And today I'm proof of a battle not lost but won. I've a six-bedroom house two very nice saloon cars a well-earned nest-egg for my wife and myself a handful of profitable consultatationcies and the chance to don the old ermine and take the battle for social equality right to the very heart of the House of Lords it's not for me it's for Pauline.

JOHN PRESCOTT

'War is over if you want it.' When John and I first sang those historic words, the Second World War was still fighting and many people die. But luckily Winston and Adolf hearing our song on the radio, and they straightaway agree to lay down their arms and hug each other. A great big beautiful hug. A lovely tender moment, like first dewdrop of spring. So thanks, Winston and Adolf. You truly great guys. Yoko so proud of you!

YOKO ONO

April 7th

I'm also researching Victoria's little-known husband, Prince Albert. He wasn't just a mega-heart-throb – the Robbie Williams of his day – he was also a literally amazing scientist, the inventor of all sorts of things to which he lent his name, like the Albert Bridge, the Royal Festival Hall and Alberto Balsam shampoo for problem hair.

From the very beginning, this film has been so close to my heart. But now I discover that being a co-producerer is not an easy job! Far from it: it involves slogging your way through the script, or as much as you can of it, time permitting, and then, what seems like years later, making it to the World Premiere bang on time. But it'll be worth the sweat just to be on that red carpet, ready to pay tribute to that poor, misunderstood young lady who the world called Her Majesty but who for me will always be just Vicky, the lovable little scamp with the great mop of red hair who kept putting her great big foot in it!

Welcome to Planet Victoria!

SARAH, DUCHESS OF YORK

Over the years, I have learnt that there is no point in being in charge of an organisation like the BBC if you can't fire someone. But who? The BBC is a self-indulgent organisation, filled with employees entertaining friends and family at the licence-payers' expense. I needed some top-class advice on how to improve matters, so today I invited my son-in-law, my wife, my nephew, my godson and my old nanny (who is now Chancellor to the Duchy of Lancaster) out to a really first-rate lunch at the BBC table at Claridge's.

By the end of this magnificent repast, we are at our wits' end over who to fire. 'I know,' says the head waiter, a marvellous old character with a great deal of wisdom in that head of his, 'why not fire the Director-General?'

I leave the fellow a handsome tip, not forgetting to ask for a receipt.

I return to the BBC knowing what I have to do. The Director-General has taken me for an utter fool. Little does he realise that this is a cunning ploy. I have always enjoyed being thought an utter fool. It is a brilliant double-bluff: I am in fact far more stupid than they think.

MARMADUKE HUSSEY

First stop Carlisle. Grab some breakfast before boarding the battlebus then make a pitstop outside Watford so I grab a bit of breakfast manage a bacon sarnie very tasty before we grab a quick pie somewhere round Liverpool ready for early lunch when we reach our destiny.

I get out the old loudspeaker. 'We got the Tories on the runs!' I tell the shoppers gathered round the Primark, 'so let's stop them fat cats for a fourth time!'

The local Labour candidate is delighted at my presence. He waves at me across the square before rushing off to an urgent meeting. No time for a chat even with a very senior figure, not when there's a battle to be winning!

Over sandwiches in the toilet, I reflectivate on how the campaign's gone so far. A bloke of my experience has the experience it's what comes of experience in my experience.

The electoral are sick and tired of Mr David so-called toffee-nosed Cameron they want normal people like Gordon and me.

One more heave!

Flush the toilet for a second time just to make sure and move on.

JOHN PRESCOTT

April 8th

Gentleman's Relish is common. Anything with anchovy is desperately common. Bronchitis is common, and so is Arthritis. Anything ending in 'tis', in fact, except for clematis. Sore throats are dreadfully common. Athlete's foot is not common. In fact, it's gloriously *distingué*. I'm having some artificial fungus painted on to my left foot tomorrow, in beautiful pinks and violets.

NICHOLAS HASLAM

My mother was quite a saver. She would encourage us to take long steps to chapel so as to save on shoe leather. She kept the house at North Parade immaculately clean. She achieved this by making my sister wear a feather duster on her head. I would be deputed to 'wheelbarrow' her around the house every evening. Nowadays, television and the wireless provide instant entertainment, but I sometimes wonder whether it provides a fraction of the pleasure.

MARGARET THATCHER

April 9th

Today, we recorded another session with the distinguished rock singer and composer Michael George. He told me afterwards that my questions on the war in Iraq had gone further than any interviewer had ever gone before.

MELVYN: Your song, 'Hey, Hump Me, Hump Me, Baby, I'm Your Kinda Guy' was written as a response to the invasion of Iraq.

GEORGE: I was that livid, I really was, Melvyn. It was when I heard that Tony was going to invision Iraq. Honestly, that guy had no business to, I don't care if he is Prime Minister or whatever! As a sexually active gay man, I felt that no one should put up with this kind of invasion, I mean, how would YOU feel if one morning there was a ding-dong on your doorbell and all sorts of soldiers and what-not just sort of marched their way in uninvited and without their VIP passes or anything? I mean, it all comes back to human nature, doesn't it, Melvyn? So I thought, I'm not having this, this calls for a protest, and so I thought I'd show my anger against the whole war thing in a very very smooth, very very protesty, very very sexy sort of song, and I'd like to sing it for you all now.

MELVYN: Zzzzzz. Sorry?

GEORGE: I'd love to sing it for you all now.

MELVYN: Sing what?

GEORGE: My protesty song, silly!

MELVYN: That would be tremendous. So would it be true to say that what you are saying is that it would be true to say that you are a um singer as well as a signwriter?

GEORGE: Yes, silly!

MELVYN: That's extraordinary. You certainly kept that quiet!

GEORGE (singing):

> Oooooh!
> Hey, hump me, hump me, hump me, baby!
> I'm your kinda guy!
> And if you go and invade Iraq again

You'll only make me cry!
Ooooh! Hump me! Ooooh! Ooooh!

MELVYN BRAGG

What is the – to my mind – almost mystical allure of soccer? It is at one and the same time geometry transposed into music, architecture mobilised by synchronicity, astronomy reconfigured as ballet. My edition of Chambers Dictionary defines soccer as 'a short knitted covering for the foot, usually not reaching the knee', and that definition stands, as far as it goes. But to my mind it is something much more than that, something very different, something that possesses both inner and outer meanings that somehow evade definition.

Football is, above all, a meta-text. I find one can read a game of soccer just as one would read a novel by Cervantes or Dickens, picking it up and putting it down, and placing a bookmark carefully between ball and pitch, so that one may recommence one's perusals later.

A.S. BYATT*

April 10th

Take to reminiscing about the Eighties. They all came to my restaurant back then, all the celebrities, and not just any old celebrities: former Bond Girl Fiona Fullerton, top pop duet Bros, former glove puppet Basil Brush. It was the place to see and be seen.

A lot of these famous names became very special people in my life. Gerald Harper. The thin one off *Casualty*. Vanessa Feltz. The lot.

Michael Winner became a firm friend. I cooked a five-course meal for him at the unveiling of the plaque for top dead celebrity policewoman WPC Yvonne Fletcher, and he came back for seconds, with an extra dollop of jelly.

---

*From *Back of the Meta-Text!: David Beckham, Balls and Me* by A.S. Byatt (OUP, 2006).

Michael regularly ate at my restaurant in the Eighties. He appreciated the way I would always make sure two of my staff came to the table with his own monogrammed potty, then wipe his bottom afterwards, saving him the bother of a trip to the toilet.

MARCO PIERRE WHITE

The Queen Mother had the unique ability to say the right thing at the right time. On one memorable occasion, Osbert Sitwell asked her if she would care for another glass of champagne. In an instant, she held out her champagne flute and exclaimed, 'Fill her up!' Her fellow guests remain convinced that this was not a 'prepared' remark, but a genuine 'ad lib'.

'With just three short words, she managed to transform that room!' recalled Norman Hartnell. 'It was the most perfect display of wit and grace any of us had ever witnessed.'

Barely fifteen minutes later, possibly aided by the champagne, the Queen Mother broke wind. 'The most wonderful thing about it was that she "blew off" to the tune of "Land of Hope and Glory", which of course set us all at our ease,' recalled the Duchess of Albemarle.

Others present recall an intense perfume of lavender and hibiscus filling the room at that moment. 'It was the most perfect display of breaking wind any of us had ever witnessed,' wrote Ruth, Lady Fermoy in a letter to the author.*

HUGO VICKERS

---

*On another memorable occasion, she summoned the authors and poets of the day to Clarence House, bidding them take part in a Christmas pantomime to delight an audience composed of her and her old friend Ruth, Lady Fermoy. The poet T.S. Eliot took the role of Buttons, with W. Somerset Maugham and Osbert Sitwell as the Ugly Sisters and Edith Sitwell as Cinderella, whilst the noted art historians Sir Kenneth Clark and Bernard Berenson played respectively the front and back halves of Dobbin, the faithful horse. H.V.

April 11th

ANDY FROM KENT: I had double wooden front doors, which I have replaced with new fibreglass doors. These were stained with a maple wipe-on stain and finished with a clear finish. Our home is brick and the shutters are grey. Some of my friends have suggested that the doors would be more attractive painted as opposed to stained. What do you think?

GORDON BROWN: Well, Andy from Kent, first of all let me congratulate you on your double wooden front doors. And let me make one thing quite clear. It's not my doors that matter – it's yours. I am serious about your doors, and I understand your concerns.

DAVID CAMERON: There's something you need to know about me, Andy. I believe in doors. I believe that there is no point in having a room unless it has a door through which you can enter, and, just as important in the long run, exit. That's true in good times and in difficult times. And if a room hasn't got a door, I'm sorry but I have to say this: the system simply isn't working.

NICK CLEGG: There they go again! This is the old-style advice on doors! We've heard it all before! One thing's for sure, Andy, whether you're going to stain them or paint them, we as a country urgently need a whole new approach to doors. So I'll be frank with you, Andy. I want to change doors. I want to see fundamental change in the whole way this country goes through doors. Under the old-style politics, 90 per cent of ordinary, decent people who had accidents going through doors were going through them forwards. So let's grasp the nettle. Let's take a different approach. What we propose is that everyone starts going through doors backwards. It's just simple common sense.

FIRST EVER TELEVISED LEADERS' HOME DECORATION DEBATE, 2010

We had that remarkable novelist and veritable wordsmith Graham Greene on the show tonight with George Best, in my book undoubtedly the greatest footballer of this or indeed of any age. It was truly fascinating to hear Graham listing his ten greatest goals of all time and George discussing the future of the English novel. Lovely moment when both these giants agreed that at least being famous got you the best table in a restaurant! The music was provided by the ever-lovely Lulu, or was it the legendary Clodagh Rodgers? There's only one word for it. Pure magic.

MICHAEL PARKINSON

April 12th

I re-examine the *oeuvre* of my dear cousin Polly James. Polly is not just a bird: she is a Liver Bird. The most important situation comedy of its generation, *The Liver Birds* was always more than just a comedy of situations. *The Liver Bird Annual 1971* remains the third best book for the student to read on the subject, and should have a place in every library. I managed to acquire it in the rare Swiss edition, and taught myself Swiss in order fully to appreciate its nuances, many of which yield their richest nuance only after being rewritten as epic verse, and that only by one fully versed in the epic.

> 'Eee, Sandra – ah don't 'alf fancy 'im'
> – Polly James, 1969

To fancy another is the lot of many: and for many it is a lot of others who they fancy. Like Picasso and Hemingway, I too have fancied many women. Which of the two Liver Birds I myself fancied must remain a matter for intellectual conjecture. But what no one can deny – the Norwegians have a word for it: *benekte* – is that there was one hell of a lot of fancying going on in my household once the distinctive theme tune – reminiscent of one of Schubert's minor sonatas – of *The Liver Birds* had proceeded.

CLIVE JAMES

Can I really make a difference? That's what I wonder to myself when I have my assistants put on my diamond bustier and oil my buttocks before each show. Can I really make a difference to this world in which we live by starting my show with my legs astride this giant gold phallus with a ninety-foot purple crucifix in the background and singing my latest hit, 'What is the Like Meaning of This Life?'

Look around, everywhere you go
All you need's a bit of class!
To bring this world some peace and love
You need the firmest tits and ass!
CHORUS: The only way I'm gonna eliminate
This war and hurt!
Is to keep movin' my butt
So it stays nice and smooth and pert!
Hey, I don't know if I can make a difference.
But I sure as hell can try.*

MADONNA

In the early 1950s I married Anthony Eden, a politician of above average height, with a prominent moustache. Anthony was not an intellectual by any means, nor was he an inspiring writer or orator, but he was an immaculate dresser and very much looked the part.

When, a year or two later, my husband became Prime Minister, it was a feather in his cap, but he would often complain within my hearing that Colonel Nasser was being most frightfully tiresome.

'I wish the infernal fellow would stop trying to get his hands on the Suez Canal. It simply isn't his to take,' Anthony would grumble. If Nasser had known how upset the whole business made Anthony I'm sure he wouldn't have persisted in his mischief. Eventually, we were

---

*The show concluded with a medley consisting of 'I Can't Get Enough of Your Love', 'I've Had You' and 'I've Had Enough, Get Off Me Love'.

forced to send in our warships, an absolute bother, though they were a very pretty silvery-grey in colour, with the barest hint of pink.

CLARISSA EDEN

April 13th

Dear Diary, I cook dinner while Martin (Amis – silly!) sits nearby, chuckling away as he rereads his own prose. While I knock up a coq au vin with creamed potatoes and broccoli, he sits there, splitting his sides over one of his most brilliant word-inventions. He is a master of language. 'Rig' means penis, 'metal motorway' means zip ('Ouch! I've caught my rig in my metal motorway!' exclaims his character Fred Fucker, immortally, in his early novel *Phlegmy Cushions*), 'sock' means house, 'bra' means bar, 'bar' means car, 'car' means bra, and 'baa' is the noise a sheep makes.

Friday lunch is always spent with his circle, each sparring to outwit the others with their brilliant *mots justes* (in fact, he's planning on writing a dystopian novel called *Stalin's Hitler* with a walk-on Nazi character who's called Mo Juice). Christopher Hitchens – universally known as 'The Hitch' (he explained to me that this was a reference to the first syllable of his surname) – is also there. He says Martin is always the centre of attention. 'He does a genius imitation of Frank Spencer, the neo-Beckettian anti-hero of *Some Mothers Do 'Ave 'Em*,' he tells me, excitedly. 'He places this beret low down on his forehead, and then says in his expertly-modulated, brilliantly high-pitched voice, "Oooh, Betty!" Needless to say, we all fall about.'

This is what it must have been like to have been around the table in Magny's Restaurant in 1860s Paris, with Turgenev, Flaubert and Zola. Some of the conversations they had today are still imprinted on my mind. Talk ranged from Shakespeare's Globe (which Martin referred to, memorably, as 'Shagspeer's Gob') to passionate and informed condemnations of Adolf Hitler ('The guy was a bloody Nazi').

JULIE KAVANAGH

I've not like told anyone this before now because it's like private and you've got to like respect people's privates but the whole thing about secrets is you've got to tell them to everyone so they're no longer like secrets because once you've told someone then a secret's not a secret anymore so you can't really still call it a secret because then it's not in which case you're allowed to tell it let's get real.

KATIE PRICE

April 14th

The State of Britain, Part Three: I've tried to bring out the symptoms of our national decline in my new play *An Absence of Interest* which is currently being staged at the National Theatre. *An Absence of Interest* seeks to analyse the system whereby the ruling classes use the money gained from the working classes to finance other members of the ruling classes to write a trilogy about how they take money from the working classes to finance their systems, a trilogy which will be visited, I hope, not only by other members of the ruling classes but by a few representatives of the working class as well. It is a tremendously strong piece, devastating in its indictment of the inherent hypocrisy of those involved in its creation.

SIR* DAVID HARE

*In his formal acceptance speech for his knighthood – later staged by the author as a one-man show at the Cottesloe Theatre from April to September 1998 – Hare stated that he was 'accepting this great honour on behalf of women, and the working classes, and all oppressed people throughout the world. I speak for them, so they certainly have no excuse to interrupt.'

April 15th, 1941

TO BINKIE BEAUMONT

Darling Binks,

This war is really most disagreeable. The incessant explosions play havoc with one's delivery. I feel like writing to that dreadful little Adolf H. I would sum up everything I had to say in just two little words: 'Must you?'

Eternally yours,

Johnny

JOHN GIELGUD

Thoroughly enjoyabled today's rally in Humberside. The local candidate meant to be meeting me least that's what I thought but she's nowhere to be seen must have more important things to do than welcome the former Deputy Prime Minister I wish I had her sense of confidence I really do.

So I pay a call on the local primary school and knock on the door offer to have a word with the kiddies be photographed doing sums playing with crayons and that but they say they're up to their necks so I drive to the nearest supermarket but the manager says if I'm not planning to buy any items then I should move along calls himself a manager but he doesn't even recognise the former Deputy Prime Minister let's see what his bosses say about that!

Jumbo sausage roll lovely pastry just right goes down nice then it's off to the local Labour Q.H. for a moral-boosting talk to all the helpers but when I ring the bell and again a second time then a third there's still no reply. So I look through the slats in the blinds and a couple of heads appear from behind a desk they must of been searching the floor for something urgent.

So I shout, 'Open up it's John Prescott come to rally the troops!' but they shout back they'd love to help but they're snowed under so I grab myself a meat pasty with a side-order of chips and sit on a bench in the park putting the finishing touchities to my campaign strategy.

JOHN PRESCOTT

What the Seventies were to the Sixties, the Eighties were to the Nineties. Just as the Sixties were to the Nineties what the Seventies were to the Eighties. And from where I'm sitting in the Nineties, the Sixties were basically the Eighties, or an Eighties version of the Fifties, but with the Seventies in the middle.

It's as simple as that.

JULIE BURCHILL

April 16th

TO A.L. ROWSE

Dear Leslie,

One cannot live for twenty years on & off in such delightfully close proximity to someone as wonderful and unique as, if you'll let me say so, you are and not develop a strong and permanent bond. I cannot tell you how enormously grateful I am, and shall, I am sure, forever remain, for your characteristically generous invitation to join you & the other Fellows for dinner with HRH Princess Margaret on the 25th April, an invitation, I am genuinely honoured & delighted to have been given, and, I am pleased to report, for which I have experienced no hesitation before accepting.

Yours ever, Isaiah

ISAIAH BERLIN,
LETTER TO A.L. ROWSE

TO THE WARDEN OF ALL SOULS

Dear John,

Poor Leslie Rowse continues to pester me to attend his little dinner for Princess Margaret. Leslie is of course marvellous in every way, but he is, on reflection, in many other ways in some curious sense a figure of the most consummate absurdity, socially ambitious, insensitive to all but his own needs, bitterly resentful of those of us who have, through our own efforts or talents, risen higher in what I suppose one must call 'society' than he has so far managed himself. I have perforce accepted his invitation – loyalty has long been my spur – but, to be very indiscreet, as the day approaches, a dreadful sinking feeling enters deeper into my being. The prospect of sitting next to Princess Margaret alas holds little charm for me, I'm afraid, though I have long been a close friend of her mother.

Yours ever, Isaiah

ISAIAH BERLIN,
LETTER TO JOHN SPARROW

April 17th

It's the dawn of the Sixties and after just three months it's lined up to be so totally a happening decade. For starters, there's super-trendy alternative music with Tommy Steele and Frank Ifield. I met Frank Ifield down the Roxy and might have given him a shag but got bored after a few minutes and he settled for a hand-job.

Then there's cutting-edge comedy with Arthur Askey and Cyril Fletcher. I didn't half fancy a shag with little Arthur Askey, but even though I was totally besotted he kept telling me yet bloody more of his tedious jokes so I got bored shitless and dumped him. And the Black and White Minstrels aren't much better at shagging either, but that's another story. Would I like to ride in their beautiful, their beautiful ballooooooon? No I bloody wouldn't, guys, so why not fuck the fuck off.

JANET STREET-PORTER

Heed well the wisdom of our ancestors, my sons and daughters, for it is rough-hewn by time. 'The birdy does not sit on the tree; it is the tree that sits on the birdy.' The wise man will recognise this as correct in all its essentials. And another old African saying also proves as true today as ever it was: 'He travels furthest who never leaves his homestead.' For the human heart is a rock containing much water and bundles of sweet fruits; a rock that can soar in the air, flying higher than the steepest lakes. And before it comes to rest, this rock will gallop as fast as a speckled hen, eager to rest its head on the distant murmur of soft glades. So heed ye well the wisdom of our ancestors.

And learn.

MAYA ANGELOU*

April 18th

Some annoying things encountered too often at present: bicyclists who insist on pedalling slowly uphill and then sue the poor drivers who are thereby forced to run them over; politicians who puff themselves up by declaring that there is something intrinsically 'wrong' about poor people starving but who never stop to worry about wealthy people who are afflicted with indigestion; discrimination in our so-called 'public' services against those educated at public school (when was the last time you bumped into a railway ticket-collector with a public school education?); men and women who work in the City but who nevertheless modishly refuse to wear bowler hats and wing collars; bus drivers who refuse to go just a little out of their way to deliver you to your front door, preferring to suit themselves by dropping you at a Maoist 'bus stop'; characters in soap operas who forget

---

*Lift up your face, America, you have a piercing need
To breathe awhile as you kneel before your President
In gratitude. And now open wide your lips, America,
To accommodate the hard-pressed vessel
Heading fast towards its port in these storm-toss'd times.
For his bright new morning glory is dawning just for you
And, if faced with courage, its passion spent, need not be
Faced again until the dawn. Good morning, America!

From 'Lift Up Your Face, America', poem composed by Maya Angelou for the inauguration of President Bill Clinton.

to say 'Good morning' or 'Good afternoon' before addressing one another; Gordon Brown's churlish refusal to wear a kilt and sporran whilst simultaneously affecting a Scottish accent; the conspiracy by BBC radio to limit the airtime given to Lord Rockingham's XI. Where will it end?

CHARLES MOORE

Kangaroos. They can't hop for toffee.

GERMAINE GREER

KATE FROM SWINDON: I have to paint a small room with a slanted ceiling. How do I make the room look more spacious? Should I paint the whole room the same colour?

DAVID CAMERON: You know, Kate, yesterday I met a thirty-year-old man from Wolverhampton, and he told me how important painting his small room had been to him. So let me make this quite clear. We are not going to prevent anyone in this great country from painting their small room if they want to. That's not why I came into politics. In fact, I want to see a situation where anyone who wants to paint a small room is able to do so.

NICK CLEGG: Kate – first may I congratulate you on your small room with its slanted ceiling. It sounds tremendous. And now let's face facts. Your small room needs change. On the one hand, it's not a big or medium-sized room. On the other hand, it's not a tiny room. It's a small room, and that's something to be very proud of. What David Cameron and Gordon Brown are proposing – the old-style redecoration! – would, I'm sorry to say, simply make it fall to pieces.

GORDON BROWN: I come from an ordinary family, Kate, and we had a small room much like yours. And what my father always taught me was that a small room was a good thing, and should be cherished. And so I still have a small room, where I very much enjoy playing with my two children – that's when I can find the time! And that's why I think it's simply UNFAIR and IMMORAL for David Cameron to suggest that there's anything wrong with having a small room. I say to him: look at the facts. If you paint 65 per cent of the total wall surface of 73 per cent of small rooms, excluding ceilings, then between 42 per cent and 61 per cent of visitors will express 83 per cent satisfaction with the results. And that is a change worth making.

SECOND TELEVISED LEADERS' HOME DECORATION DEBATE, 2010

April 19th

The past is long, and top-quality TV is long-past. It may have looked simple, but its simplicity was highly complex, and it was a complex that was by no means inferior. Inferior decoration is not the same as interior decoration. The two words have many letters in common, but they mean something different. My programmes may have been interior, but they were never inferior. Sadly, the days are over when one could talk to Norman Mailer about Henry Miller on BBC television while being massaged by a young lady with bazonkers the size of *War and Peace*, Leo Tolstoy's magisterial masterpiece, which I myself have read in the original Russian nearly all the way through. The cult of celebrity has changed all that.

CLIVE JAMES

For all our belief in thrift and service, there was always much joy in our home. Every night, my father would let us hear a new saying he had picked up during the day. 'Watch the pennies,' he would say, 'and the pounds will look after themselves.' Then he would throw the topic open to discussion, and the evening would come to a happy conclusion after we had all voiced our agreement. It was from my father that I learnt the value in consensus. 'There's no value in consensus,' he would say, and we would all agree.

MARGARET THATCHER

April 20th

I find the whole processing of food – slicing, grating, cutting, stirring, nibbling, masticating, imbibing, savouring, swallowing, digesting, expelling, wiping, flushing and then slicing again – enormously satisfying. I take enormous pride from the fact that in the 1950s, I became the first Briton to visit France. In those days, the avocado, the tomato and the potato were quite unheard of in Britain. I take enormous pleasure in having introduced them to this country, where they now form part of our everyday lives.

SIR TERENCE CONRAN

Moscow is just so much fun. I went with Lee Radziwill to a party for Roy Cohn given by Steve Rubell for Diana Vreeland and Martina Navratilova to honour Yuri Andropov in Barry Diller's apartment on Red Square.

Yuri was just so great, he's fat with grey hair, he was wearing all these shiny medals, I was so filled with envy, he just loves being President of the USSR, he's crazy for it. Afterwards, Halston said and he swears it's true that Yuri told him in secret he's never even met Bianca though obviously he's heard of her. You'd think if you were President of the USSR you'd somehow be able to get to meet Bianca but that just shows how backward they are here, I suppose.

Bob says Yuri would look great with a crew cut. Pia Zadora was there too, which was great.

ANDY WARHOL

April 21st

JABBERJABBERJABBERJABBER. When actors get together, we YAK. WOOOOO-FUCKING-WHEEEEE, don't we yak! I guess it has something to do with the strain and TENSION of being someone other all the time. So we talk ourselves back into real life, comparing combat notes like 1st World War soldiers coming back from the trenches, tough and urgent.

'Loved your *Withnail*,' says John Malkovich.

'Thanx,' I say. 'Loved your *Liaisons*.'

'Thanx,' he says. 'Loved your *Withnail*.'

'Thanx,' I say. 'Loved your *Liaisons*.'

'*Withnail*,' he says, changing the subject. 'I just loved you in that.'

We jabber on like this for hours, getting to KNOW one another, blood brothers in fantasy.

RICHARD E. GRANT

The birthday of Queen Elizabeth II. She has ruthlessly pursued the path of fame and fortune. Sadly her reputation remains low. You can see the disappointment etched in her face. The last time I met her, she asked me if I had come far. It was the sort of mean, embittered comment for which she has become known.

V.S. NAIPAUL

April 22nd

I spend a producted afternoon in Nantwich collaring with ordinary decentrified people in the park to highlight the interminal damage the Tories would do this country if they got in again and this government's achievements at Kyoto the problems are global we need change let's have more change there's not enough climate change so you got to get out there and bloody vote. After an hour the park attendant tells me to move on says I'm scaring the kids, typical Tory dirty tricks, so I grab myself a double bacon sandwich plus king-size Galaxy, three for the price of two washed down with strawberry milkshake just the job.

JOHN PRESCOTT

Rushed off my feet with my new book, which is going to be completely different and awfully artistic, set in lovely snowy Norway at the turn of the century, with lots of friendly huskies and really smashing reindeer and super cuddly polar bears.

The plot is going to be very, very Norwegian – 'Nor-way' to treat a lady, you might say! – with our hero, Sven Lloyd-Johnson, impossibly handsome, chasing after all the married women in the little Norwegian community of Cosytown-on-Fjord, but eventually falling absolutely madly in love with the lovely heroine, Brigitte, or Brigie for short, who's always a bit of a mess and can't stop bursting into absolute fits of giggles at all the wrong moments but has an insatiable passion for mongrels and a pet moose called 'Moose at Ten'(!) and is blessed with an utterly blissful heart of gold.

Of course, there's simply oodles of the most super sex in the book, very passionate and deliciously steamy and very, very Norwegian. In this opening passage, Sven has it off with Hedda, or Heddie, on the tundra he has just had laid – at the most frightful expense – outside his £2,000,000 mansion. Quite a turn-on – or 'tundra-on'(!):

> Sven was like the most amazingly bouncy energetic dog when it came to sex. He insisted on eating minced morsels out of a bowl on the floor before leaping onto his latest love.
>
> When he leapt at last, Heddie, super, adorable, kind-hearted Heddie, who looked rather like the lovely, brilliant Anne Diamond when she became a TV superstar in Britain a full eight years later, lovely Heddie was waiting for him like an obedient Spaniel, her ears flapping over the sides of the pillows.
>
> There followed three hours of deliriously passionate love-making, absolutely super and hardly messy at all. For Heddie, it was like nothing she had ever imagined before: like winning all the rosettes at the very best gymkhana and seeing the most fabulous film and being awfully naughty and stealing some chocolate mousse from the fridge and having a jolly good giggle and all at the same time! It was super to be a sexy girl in Norway at the turn of the century, she thought.

When it was all over, Sven picked up his nineteenth-century Norwegian mobile phone and forcefully tapped out a number with his wildly masculine forefinger. 'Hello!' he barked, setting the scene. 'This is ruthless but irresistible Sven calling from Norway. The time is 1901, just one year into the new century.'

Suddenly, Sven felt the utterly overwhelming urge to make a Norwegian pun. 'Let me inform you that there hasn't been much sunshine here. Also, thank goodness I'm not a soldier outside Buckingham Palace,' he said, a smile lighting up his heart-stoppingly fanciable face, 'or otherwise it wouldn't be so much "the turn of the century" as "the tan of the sentry"!!!' From the other end came simply gales of merriment. No one in Norway had ever made a joke before, and this was simply the best ever!'

JILLY COOPER

Shit.
That's not a word you're comfortable with?
You're not comfortable with that word?
You're not comfortable with that shit?
Well I don't give a shit.
So shit, shit, shit, shit.
And shit.

I wrote the above poem, which I called 'Shit', while being driven in my courtesy limousine from Heathrow to Campden Square. Such was my fury that I had completed a final draft before we had left the airport precincts. I later retitled the poem 'Utter Shit', giving it extra force.

Recognising it at once as a very important piece of work, I biked it round to the editor of the *Observer* for immediate publication.

In that Sunday's *Observer*: nothing.

In the next Sunday's *Observer*: nothing.

I got put through to the editor: 'Oh dear, Harold,' he said, 'it's obviously a very striking poem but …'

'Don't "Oh dear, Harold" me, chum. I thought you were a serious newspaper,' I said. 'Can't you see it's about what the Americans are doing? If you don't print it, the war will continue and you'll have blood on your hands. It's up to you, chum.'

At this point, my wife, Lady Antonia, came in bearing a plate of fairy cakes. I took one and stuffed it into my mouth. Then another. And another. I like fairy cakes. Fairy cakes are what I like.

'Personally, I love the poem, Harold, but I feel our readers might not ...' said the editor.

At this point, I exploded. Fairy cake shot out of my mouth like a hundred bombs from a nuclear arsenal, hitting random civilian targets – the smoked-glass coffee table, the porcelain figures on the mantelpiece, the carriage clock, the sleeping Pekingese, Antonia's new frock, clean on that morning – without a thought for human life.

HAROLD PINTER

April 23rd

Today, I wrote an open letter to the Prime Minister of this country:

> Dear Mr Blair,
>
> I enclose a copy of my most recent poem. It is 'Utter Shit'. I believe that, if we are to divert a disaster, you should give it sober thought.
>
> It was written to express my feelings of revulsion at the way the Americans are blowing the shit out of Kosovo and fucking it up the arse before wiping their noses with the soiled toilet paper and tossing it on the ground to be sniffed over by dogs. A more mature attitude is needed.
>
> My wife, Lady Antonia, and I agree that this is a situation which cannot be allowed to go on. The US elephant must be stopped. It has trumpeted too long, keeping its neighbours up at night. First we must shoot it. Dead. Then we must cut off its tusks. With wire wool, we must then grind those tusks down. So we can sell the powder as an aphrodisiac to underprivileged nations. Then they can fuck the

dead corpse of America just like America fucked the shit out of them. I believe this to be the only feasible solution to the appalling state of affairs developing in Eastern Europe at the present time.

OK, chum?

HAROLD PINTER

William Shakespeare died today, in 1616. He was a minor playwright. By common consent, his plays do not stand the test of time. As a young man, I quite admired his overlong play called *Hamlet.* Struggling to read it again recently, I was struck by how dated it now seems. In time, the self-consciously 'universal' can seem desperately parochial.

V.S. NAIPAUL

April 24th

The Duchess of Windsor has died. It has been erroneously suggested that the Queen Mother held the Duchess of Windsor in low regard. Nothing could be further from the truth. She always took a Christian view of the Duchess, regarding her as the woman taken in adultery. In a characteristic gesture, she even went so far as to send her a small packet of supermarket own-brand digestive biscuits as a token of her good wishes in the December following the Duke's death. 'A joint Christmas and birthday present,' read the inscription, written personally by an aide. 'Invoice enclosed.'

'It was the most perfect display of generosity I ever witnessed,' recalls a close friend of the Queen Mother. She could have given her chocolates, but she knew how the Duchess kept a close eye on her figure, so she ate them all herself. 'Always such a treat!' she exclaimed delightedly, tearing away the crinkly dividing paper to reveal the layer beneath.

Her relationship with biscuits was occasionally fraught. Aged ninety-three, the Queen Mother choked on a Chocolate Bath Oliver, purchased specially for the occasion, at the author's own home, also purchased specially for the occasion. The author cupped his hands and bade the Queen Mother cough up the Bath Oliver into them. Happily, a major crisis was averted, and the evening's entertainment – the author – was allowed to go ahead as planned. To this day, the author maintains the coughed-up remnants of the Bath Oliver at a fixed temperature on a pedestal in his hallway. 'It was the most perfect display of regurgitation I ever witnessed,' recalls a fellow guest.

HUGO VICKERS

TO A.L. ROWSE

Dear Leslie,

The Warden of All Souls is cock-a-hoop at having received an invitation to the Princess Margaret dinner tomorrow. I am delighted, &, I must admit, not a little surprised that you have been good enough to invite Warden Sparrow, but his invitation bears testament once again to your extreme kindness and tolerance towards those whom nature, in her wisdom, has not, at least for the moment, seen fit to bless.

Might I offer a word of well-intentioned advice? I know the Princess's mother intimately, &, from what she tells me, the Princess would, in some sense, feel more 'at home' sitting next to one of her mother's dearest friends – I leave it to you to choose which – than next to a complete stranger, & a potentially very troublesome stranger at that. And – *entre nous* – Sparrow has long experienced trouble with his bowels, which are not, I regret to say, as efficient as one might have hoped. For this reason, it would be doing him a very great kindness – a kindness amounting, in a very real way, to moral splendour – to place him down the very far end of the table, ready to effect a swift exit unnoticed.

Yours ever,

Isaiah

ISAIAH BERLIN,
LETTER TO A.L. ROWSE

April 25th

TO THE WARDEN OF ALL SOULS

Dear John,

I have just spoken to Sibyl Colefax, and she had no hesitation in expressing her horror when I told her how very far you were placed down the table from the Princess this evening, & so cruelly close to that draughty doorway, especially after all the immense intrigue and negotiations that it took to get you invited in the first place. Much as I admire Leslie Rowse, he in some curious sense lacks both empathy and intelligence in roughly equal proportions. To like him is difficult, perhaps even to respect him, but in a curious way one can remain fascinated by his abiding self-love, which is outmatched only by his almost grotesque yet surely not unadmirable capacity for envy.

ISAIAH BERLIN,
LETTER TO JOHN SPARROW

TO THE MASTER OF PETERHOUSE

Dear Hughie,

I was so bitterly disappointed not to see you at Rowse's dinner for HRH Princess Margaret this evening. That you were summoned at the last moment to urgent business elsewhere is, I feel, the sole explanation, for I feel sure that, in normal circumstances, you would have been the first, or, if not the first, at any rate, not the last, to be vouchsafed an invitation.

You will be glad to hear that the Princess was in fine form, delighting in the opportunity to renew our acquaintance & expressing the very keenest interest in everything I told her. She has, I think, an, in some sense, intuitive intelligence. She is far from empty, yet in a curious sense not remotely full either. That having been said, I can confirm that we both, Her Royal Highness and I, kept our discretion intact: despite my most earnest promptings, she never once mentioned you, nor any of your books. It was almost as though she had never heard of you(!).

Yours ever,

Isaiah

ISAIAH BERLIN,
LETTER TO HUGH TREVOR-ROPER

GEOFF FROM HUNTINGDON: I want to decorate my four-year-old's room with brighter colours, but can't afford it. Any suggestions?

NICK CLEGG: Let's move away from trying to score old-style party political points. If you can't afford to paint your son's room, Geoff, then, let's face it, there's only one fair and sensible solution. You must paint your son – but only if the economic conditions are right. It's just simple common sense.

GORDON BROWN: I truly believe that home decorators are our unsung heroes. They are angels in overalls. So when I hear Nick Clegg and David Cameron attacking them, I simply have to speak out. When I last spoke to him, President Obama agreed with me that there is only one effective way of brightening a four-year-old's room, and that is by painting it with brighter colours.

DAVID CAMERON: Well, Geoff, I believe if you work hard and you save your money, then it's the most natural human instinct of all to want to decorate your four-year-old's room with brighter colours. Yesterday, I met a thirty-year-old woman in Shepton Mallet who told me about a twenty-year-old man in Staines who had just repainted his four-year-old's room in a very nice shade of green – and apparently he was absolutely delighted with the result, no matter what Gordon and Nick may have us believe.

THIRD TELEVISED LEADERS' HOME
DECORATION DEBATE, 2010

April 26th

I must stop dwelling on them but I've had my share of hardships. It wasn't much fun coming face to face on that dark, stormy night with the Loch Ness Monster armed only with a pencil and an elastic band, I can tell you. And the day I went up to Saddam Hussein, looked him straight in the eye and said, 'You've got to let some love into your world' – believe me, that took some nerve. By the way, after just ten minutes he asked me to marry him, begged me, just like every other guy, but I was married to Paul, right, and that's not the kind of person I am. But I sometimes think that if I'd said yes, perhaps there wouldn't be all this sort of tension in the world, which is a shame really.

HEATHER MILLS McCARTNEY

The time I spent as an undergraduate at Cambridge was by no means uninteresting, not to say seldom dull. Those who have read memoirs of the time will have grown used to seeing me in group portraits, my head always clearly circled. From the start, I had worn a hula-hoop around my head for all group portraits. In this way, I would be ready-circled when the photograph was developed, so that all could marvel at such a mark of destiny on one so young.*

By repeated use of the hula-hoop, I soon rose to committee level on the Cambridge University Conservative Association. Ours was an outstanding generation, with a shared vision of Britain's future in the world. 'By the time I leave politics,' John Nott announced one day, 'I want this country to be very similar to when I went in.' And the motion was passed without further ado.

I was never a flashy politician, never one to go for the crowd-pulling gesticulation, the unneeded 'quip', the interesting 'remark' or the original 'opinion'. Even now, come Christmas, I can walk into my own

---

*From *The Fowler Years* (1990).

home, packed with family and friends, and still pass unrecognised through the merry throng. This, I need hardly add, remains a source of quiet pride.

SIR NORMAN FOWLER

April 27th

Still no reply to my letter to Blair of the 23rd. Just the usual piss – The Prime Minister thanks you for your 'Utter Shit', and was interested to hear your etcetera etcetera.

But it doesn't end there. This afternoon, a man in his forties appears at the door. In uniform. Says he'd come to read the meter.

'What meter? We don't have any meter,' I say, barring his way. I experience an overwhelming urge to wrestle him to the ground and spit my spittiest spit in his face.

'Yes we do, darling. The electricity meter, just outside the servants' sitting room in the basement,' says my wife, Lady Antonia, a woman in her sixties. She is wearing a fresh frock, clean on.

'You'd better come in then,' I say. I want to smack him in the bollocks. Hard.

Something about the man alerts me to the fact that he is actually a senior Cabinet minister. I know instinctively that he has been sent by the Blair regime at Downing Street to flush me out. I am a dissident. 'They want to flush dissidents down the toilet,' I whisper to Lady Antonia.

Antonia agrees but with reservations. 'Lavatory,' she says.

'All done,' says the so-called meter man in his forties.

'Now clear bloody off,' I say.

'Harold says thank you so much for coming,' repeats Antonia. 'I'll show you out.'

'Yes,' I say. 'Antonia will show you the bloody door, matey. And tell your chums in Downing Street that I'm not going to take it up the arse any longer.'

On the evening news, I hear they have dropped another lot of bombs on Belgrade. The regime must have thought it would teach me a lesson. Well, you've got another think coming, Mr Tony Bloody Blair. You can send a meter man round and attach electrical cables to my genitals whenever you like, but you're still not going to silence me, chum.

HAROLD PINTER

All abroad the Prescott Express! Down to Exeter where there's a great crowd well into double figures give or take a few turns out to hear me talk environmentals and global warnings and such.

I've always been good at the oratoricals ask anyone. 'We need every vote out to ensure Labour keeps delivering for hardworking people and stop the Tories turning the clock back to the Eighties when we saw interest rates of 70 per cent and three million unemployed and the Tory fat cats with their noses in the trough doing ten million workers out of jobs and little kids of just eight or nine years of age being sent up the chimneys and down the mines to catching asbestosis while our senior citizens were thrown on the scrapheap by Lord Ashcroft and fat-cat tax-avoiding cronies from Belsize Park Gordon's the man to do it.'

That'll showed 'em! Tell it like it is, Prescott! There was a lot of press interest in Exeter too – guy from local CB radio, the lot. They just can't leave me in peace! 'If the so-called Gentlemen of the Press could just stop harrassing me for one moment so's I can talk to ordinary decent hardworking people!' I said, telling the reptile from the Exeter talking newspaper for the blind where he could shove it. I don't want to find myself in a Princess Diana-style tragic type death situation, thanks very much, not when I'm about to become Lord Prescott (not my choice – blame the wife!)

JOHN PRESCOTT

April 28th

The Dalai Lama is a prize shit, oily and loathsome little runt of the first order, awful churchy holier-than-thou air about him.

'What's your game, then, baldie?' I asked him when we met at a parliamentary reception today.

'Velly nice meety you,' he replied.

'Cut the cackle,' I said. 'Just tell me why you insist on poncing about like a prize ninny in those simply ghastly robes. Who do you think you are? Mrs Gertrude Shilling?'

'Solly no understandy.'

What a sanctimonious little charlatan, all smiles and deep bows and sweaty hands clasped together in prayer, spouting non-stop balls. Nouve, too: no gentleman ever wears orange. I could see through him a mile off.

'I can see YOU never went to Eton!' I said. That saw him off pretty damn quick.

ALAN CLARK

JOHN: One thing I've always wanted to know, Robin, is why intelligent people – comedians and so forth – often like to talk about themselves in public: their problems, their innermost thoughts, their feelings about themselves, and so on?

ROBIN: Good point, John. In layman's terms, this is what we call 'talking about yourself in public', often to the exclusion of all other people. Broadly speaking, the world is divided up into two groups of people: people who always talk about themselves and people who never talk about themselves. Research shows that though quite a few people talk about themselves, and about the same number never talk about themselves, most of us are in a third group, somewhere in the middle, of people who occasionally talk about themselves, but certainly not all the time.

JOHN: So what you're really saying, if I've understood you correctly, is that the vast majority of people occasionally talk about themselves, but certainly not all the time?

ROBIN: Correct.

JOHN: Yes, I know what you mean. I used to talk about myself all the time – my 'problems', my 'innermost thoughts', my 'feelings about myself', and so on, but, thanks to psychotherapy, I now find that I talk about myself in public only very occasionally –

ROBIN: And another thing worth mentioning is –

JOHN: I'm sorry, if I could just finish, Robin – I was just saying that, speaking personally, I now find that psychotherapy has helped me 'come to terms with' my past need to 'talk about myself', and that I can now be much more objective, showing an interest in other people. What do you think about me and the way I've overcome this solipsism, for instance?

ROBIN: I –

JOHN: Because, speaking personally for a second, I feel that I have somehow 'got out of myself', and can now concentrate on spiritual, psychological and philosophical matters outside my own little world. 'Me', if you like, is now less important than 'You'.

ROBIN: I –

JOHN: But, forgive me, I'd like to hear what you have to say for a second. How would you describe me, for instance, to someone who had never met me?

JOHN CLEESE AND ROBIN SKINNER

April 29th

This morning, another man calls. He represents himself as a postman. Cap, uniform, the lot. He has an electricity bill. They want to charge us for our electricity. The same electricity that goes into making those planes that have fucked the shit out of Belgrade. Now they are trying to force us to pay for their crap. Antonia and I are dissidents – dissi-bloody-dents – in our own land. Next they'll lock a ball and chain round Antonia's ankles and gag her so that she won't be able to read an extract from her latest work, *Darling Duchesses: A Celebration*, at the Waterstone's wine-and-cheese evening. Bastards.

And all because they were so shit-scared by my latest poem. In a rage, I write to the *Guardian*:

> Sir: US foreign policy can be defined as follows: 'Kiss my arse or I'll kick your head in.' Their level of intelligence is infantile. And Clinton is the shittiest shit who ever shat shit.
>
> Yours ever, Harold
>
> P.S. Lady Antonia sends her regards.

And they print it. That's the way they stifle dissent in this country. They print what you write. But it won't work, Tony, old chum. Not while I'm alive to arm-wrestle you to the ground and suffocate you with my bare fist, it won't.

HAROLD PINTER

I was intrigued to learn recently that there is now a product on the market which can turn bread into 'toast', without any need for all the palaver of toasting fork, fire, butler and so forth. This splendidly ingenious contraption is called a 'toaster', comes in a variety of colours and can be obtained from many leading shops. What on earth will they think of next? Andrew and I now spend many a happy hour making toast, by simply placing a slice of bread (which now comes 'ready-sliced', would you believe?) into the slot in the 'toaster', pressing the button down, and waiting a minute or two before it 'pops up'. If one wants a second slice, one simply buys another toaster and repeats exactly the same moves again. Buttering the toast is another matter, which we feel safest leaving to our excellent cook. Isn't it about time someone invented a contraption so that buttering, too, became the proverbial 'piece of cake'? How well I remember in the old days my sisters Pecca,[*] Becca,[†] Recca,[‡] Necca[§] and I[¶] all having an absolute whale of a time attempting to butter a piece of bread by holding the

---

*Pecca Mitford, anorexic.

†Becca Mitford, Wimbledon tennis champion.

‡Recca Mitford, anarchist terrorist.

§Necca Mitford, nymphomaniac.

¶Decca Mitford, record producer.

bread in our hands and passing it roughly over the wodge of butter, but we met with little success, so – with typically delightful aristocratic eccentricity! – we simply threw the butter out of an upstairs window for all the simply marvellous little servants to enjoy! I wonder what happened to that concept of fun, or is it now considered 'old-fashioned' or – worse – 'square' …?

DEBORAH, DUCHESS OF DEVONSHIRE

TO A.L. ROWSE

Dear Leslie,

I think I let poor Hughie down as gently as possible. He is at heart if not quite trusting, then at least in some sense gullible, so will, I imagine, never suspect that you did not invite him, nor that, for all his very special qualities, the Princess hadn't the foggiest who he is.

Yours ever,

Isaiah

ISAIAH BERLIN,
LETTER TO A.L. ROWSE

TO HRH PRINCESS MARGARET

Your Royal Highness,

It was, indeed, one of the most profoundly affecting experiences of my life to find myself placed beside you at dinner on April 25th. I cannot tell you how moved, deeply & permanently moved, I was by this placement. As a philosopher, I was, I might add, quite overwhelmed by your extraordinarily intuitive observations that a) 'One thing leads to another' and, furthermore, that b) 'It never rains but it pours.' I am embarrassed by the depth of my own feelings of admiration & must not go on for fear of going on & on: but I seize this opportunity to go on nevertheless, for if I did not begin to go on & on, I might not continue to go on & on. From observation b), I am at present developing a valuable theory that philosophers may be divided up between those who 'rain' and those who 'pour', so that, if your Royal Highness would graciously permit me to dedicate the ensuing lecture to you, then I would be forever in your wise and generous debt.

ISAIAH BERLIN,
LETTER TO HRH PRINCESS MARGARET

April 30th

In the dying embers of the April of 2001, as the world entered its final phase of destruction and, looking down at my feet, I began to notice that the hole in my sock was becoming each day ever larger, like the mouth of a shark, its teeth numerous and sharp as the spire of Chichester Cathedral, though more plentiful, stretching wider and wider so as to swallow its intended victim, though unlike a shark in that it was made of wool, when my eyes, bruised with despair, caught sight of a photograph, both timely yet untimely, present yet strangely absent, of Nigella Lawson, whom I had once watched, with the fateful glare of a tawny owl, its wings flapping as if in desperate mourning while it remains wholly still, sighting something – a gatepost, a leaf, a cigarette packet abandoned and discarded – to which it remains wholly indifferent, but when I looked a second time I realised in a sudden horrific grotesque flash that Nigella had altered the colour of her hair, or hairs (for there were many of them) from brown to blonde, a transformation that was, like the muddy tread of the bootwear of the decrepit Scandinavian philanthropist Santa Claus on a newly-vacuumed carpet, both menacing and reassuring, so that I now had no inkling as to whether Nigella was still the brunette I had always imagined her to be, a question that haunted me as I took to wandering the streets in the early hours of the morning, that period in time that arrives, like the excelsior pike in the North Sea, before afternoon yet after evening, when the shadow of night is drawn like a black veil across the earth, all the while agonising over whether hair that was once brown but is now blonde can be said to be in essence brown, or whether the colour superimposed has now become the reality of the hairstyle, that word – HAIRSTYLE – snarling at me like a wounded leopard.

W.G. SEBALD

Tomorrow sees the General Election. In every important respect, this year, 1997, is the same as 1723 – a fact ignored by the so-called commentators, who have no sense of history. My own prediction? John Major will scrape back in. Blair will stand down to make way for someone with the popular touch (probably Gerald Kaufman, clearing the way for a triumphant return by Jim Callaghan). Today's instant political punditry lacks this sort of broad historical sweep. Incidentally, I remain supremely confident that the SDP under David Owen will emerge as by far the most powerful second party.

LORD RUNCIMAN

May

May 1st

I hate it when people say 'It's only fashion,' really hate it. To me, fashion is intrinsically concerned with morality and politics and changing society and the evidence for this is obvious if you know your history. The downfall of President Nixon came in 1974, the very same year in which the Tank-Top took America by storm. End of argument.

Let's look at some other major historical events, forged by my own direct influence as a fashion designer:

1978: The Vivienne Westwood Paris collection displays for the very first time my revolutionary pink stretch velour shoulder seams on a crenellated pinafore-style rubber bustier embroidered with *fin-de-siècle* Beardsley-style hand-stitched prints. Less than six months later, the Shah of Iran is driven into exile by supporters of the Ayatollah and the Islamic revolution has begun.

1982: I exclusively reveal my velvet Tudor bloomers with appliqué stitching in bright orange, purple and mauve. General Galtieri invades the Falkland Islands. In an unexpected move, I bring forward my new collection of Diane Arbus-inspired straitjacket undergarments for an immediate launch. On June 14th 1982, the Argentineans surrender.

1989: My outrageous bondage-style evening-wear collection, 'I Think Therefore I Is', with safety-pin-style navel decoration accessories and matching earrings, is launched in London to universal acclaim. Overnight, the Berlin Wall comes down.

1994: I attract worldwide attention and acclaim when I appear in a see-through evening dress to dinner at Kensington Palace. Just six weeks later, Nelson Mandela is elected President of South Africa in the first-ever democratic elections in that divided country.

Yet still they continue to say: 'It's only fashion.'

VIVIENNE WESTWOOD

On this day, Joseph passed away, all those yonks ago. Dr Goebbels, as so many knew him, was clever, good company and very well-read. Alas, the pressure of his life got too much for him in the end, and he felt obliged to take his own life, and the lives of his beloved children. But I feel sure that he and his stalwart little wife Magda took the trouble to tell them all a splendid joke before slipping those cyanide pills into their well-brought-up little mouths. Perhaps he told them they were tasty boiled sweets! Joseph always adored what we used to call a 'leg-pull'!

DIANA MOSLEY

May 2nd

What is the challenge? This is the challenge. The challenge is this. The challenge is our challenge. And it is up to each of us to meet that challenge. And challenge that challenge. And to say to that challenge: yes, you are a challenge. And that's a challenge. But you are challenge worth taking.

TONY BLAIR, ELECTION SPEECH, 2005

May 3rd

The so-called London Eye may be very 'relevant' and 'contemporary', as the so-called experts(!) insist on telling us, but why on earth could it not have been constructed out of traditional materials, and in a form that has deeper roots in our nation's historic past? Our obsession with 'the modern' can be so dreadfully soul-destroying. A classical square rather than a modish circle would have been far more appropriate, and I would have preferred each of the 'pods' designed as a perfect replica of a delightful Georgian pavilion. And I can't say this too often: was there really any need to make the whole contraption spin round and round in that mad frenzy? I sometimes feel 'in my bones' that we as a nation stand in very grave danger of losing sight of the immense virtue in sitting still.

HRH THE PRINCE OF WALES

I take a ride on the so-called London Eye!

It's that bloody great circular thing – monstrosity, more like! – that sits by the River Thames in London like a huge great wheel – which is basically what it is.

I went on it the other day, for my sins. Talk about rubbish. Queued up for what seemed like hours, even if it was just a few minutes. Then the uniformed officials – uniformed Nazis more like! – pointed me in the direction of a glass capsule.

'Sorry mate!' says I. 'I'm not being cooped up in there! I'm a bloke! I value my freedom! If I wanted to travel inside a pod, I'd grow my own broad beans!!! Which means, I'll be riding outside, on the top!'

But guess what? You've got it. No can do. The deal was this: either you ride inside the pod or not at all. Welcome, my friends, to the wonderful world of the fascist state.

So you go into the pod, give a cursory nod to your passengers – many of them our foreign friends, I regret to say – and make your way to the driving seat. Wrong again! Guess what? There's no driving seat.

Zilch. Some bugger's stolen it – and not only that but he's made off with the steering wheel, too.

What kind of vehicle is this, when it's at home? It crawls along at less than two miles an hour, you can't change direction, and there's no sound system on which to play your classic Phil Collins tracks at full blast. Not only that, but twenty minutes after you've set off you're back in exactly the same place you started!

For crying out loud, I'd have had more fun talking to a Dane and a German over a Nigerian cocktail in a Spanish-run hotel on a wet Sunday in Belgium! So the next time someone suggests riding on the London Eye, you know what I'll say? Not bloody likely, mate – not until someone fits my pod up with a 1200cc engine, a pair of thermodynamic wings, Best Bitter on tap, a rocket booster and a selection of halfway decent porn-mags!

JEREMY CLARKSON

Oh, bottoms. Bottoms, bottoms, bottoms. Bots. BOTTOMS. B-O-T-T-O-M-S. BOT-TOMS. Botty-botty-botty-tom-tom-tom-toms. Bbbbooooootttoommmmsss. Botties. And, once again, bottoms. Bottoms, bottoms, bottoms.

What a lovely yummy word BOTTOMS is, all lovely and cuddly and generally pretty bottomy. And how infinitely the very weave and fabric of our national life would benefit from the enforced repetition of that delightful noun 'bottom' at least twice an hour by all public servants, not least the present Cabinet. Botty-botty-BOTTOMS! I count it as an obscenity that anyone in the latter half of the twentieth century should be shocked by that most innocent and excellent and singularly buttocksome of words. Not until we as a nation can shout the word 'BOTTOM' freely will we be able to consider ourselves truly sophisticated, truly grown-up, truly capable of entering our post-colonial phase with our heads – and let's not forget botties! – held high.

STEPHEN FRY

May 4th

Where next for the Prescott Battlebus? Newport Pagnall here we come! Between breakfast and elevenses, the old tum starts to rumble. I could murder a Chinese so we stop at a little place I know off the M1 set dinner for six plus all the prawn crackers you can eat all in for £12.95 not bad at all. But it repeats all the way to Newport, and when I step out the Battlebus I'm burping like a drain and it seems to put them off 'Oi! You! Come back here or I'll hit you!' I say to the electorals but still they don't stop. Yes, the fat-cat Tories are on the run! Mission accomplivated!

JOHN PRESCOTT

The Sixties. Streuth! That was a decade and a half. London was alive with a new, hungry classless generation, overturning the citadels of the tired old aristos. By the end of that amazing decade, the so-called toffs had been forced to let us in to their restaurants, their clubs, their posh Ascot enclosures – and even into their stately homes. I count myself lucky to have played a leading role in that revolution.

How long ago that seems now, mate. Blimey, you only have to look at this country to see that it's going to the bow-wows. These days, they're letting anyone into the restaurants, the clubs are full of riff-raff and the enclosures at Ascot are jammed with blokes who don't have the foggiest how to behave. And you can't be a private guest in a stately home no more without every Tom, Dick and Harry paying his two quid to take a gander. Whatever happened to the old standards, I ask myself.

MICHAEL CAINE

May 5th

My Aunt Phyl was a larger-than-life character. Some of my happiest moments as a child, and, later, as a teenager, and, later still, as a young woman, and, some years on, as a middle-aged person, were spent watching Aunt Phyl eating her beloved digestive biscuits, one after the other, straight out of the packet. In my novel *The Empty Box* (1983), the second in my state-of-the-nation 'Articles of Furniture' series, chronicling the greedy Thatcher years, I imaginatively turned those original digestive biscuits into garibaldi biscuits, using them as a symbol of something, I now forget what, though I now recall that Aunt Phyl had entertained little enthusiasm for raisins or dates, always preferring what she would call, in her inimitable way, 'a nice plain biscuit'.

Many an enjoyable evening spent with Aunt Phyl we fruitfully occupied in debating the pros and cons of the digestive biscuit over the garibaldi. There were, of course, arguments on both sides. Those who like dried fruit in their biscuits would probably opt for the garibaldi, while those who like a less eventful biscuit would no doubt go for the plain digestive. To add extra interest to our evenings (we both disapproved of the television set, though I am now fully prepared to watch serious documentaries of an educational nature) I once broke a packet of digestive biscuits (in those days available for three shillings and sixpence from the local store, Mannings of Stradbroke, if I remember correctly, and served, more often than not, by a man whose name I now forget, if ever I knew it) into irregular pieces, thus giving us hour upon hour of splendid diversion for six or more evenings as we pitted our wits against biscuits and attempted to reassemble them as a jigsaw, though, more often than not, with little success, regrettably.

MARGARET DRABBLE

May 6th

'Aren't those daffodils lovely?' Her Majesty confides in me as we tour the Wiltshire countryside.

'Funny you should say that, Ma'am,' I tell her, setting her at her ease. 'The daffodil is one of my very favourite flowers, so I know a fair amount about it. Typically yellow, with a fair bit of green foliage, and most plentiful in this country, particularly in the spring. The tulip, on the other hand, is generally red, or at any rate red-ish, and is, I believe, one of the most successful exports of the Netherlands, where they speak Dutch, fend off the sea and ride bicycles.'

Looking down, I note Her Majesty has removed her gloves to place one forefinger in her left ear, the other in her right ear. She is humming to herself. Delightful! She took piano lessons from an early age, and was, I believe, a hugely gifted young pupil. Blessed with a musical ear, I pick up the tune and hum along.

GYLES BRANDRETH

Too many cooks spoil the broth.

Or did the broth always need to be spoilt, so as to attract too many cooks?

ADAM PHILLIPS

May 7th

Am I merely snobbish in thinking that the lower classes have no aptitude or instinct for great literature or indeed literature of any kind? This morning I went into the kitchen & found Nelly sitting down reading a cookery book. How will you ever improve your lower-class mind if you spend your days simply reading receipts? I asked her, kindly.

Her reply was intolerable. She said that she was reading her cookery book for my benefit & if I did not want her to read it then fine, she would gladly seek employment elsewhere among people who would appreciate her & would not seek to undermine her every move, & do not call me lower class when I am lower middle class thank you very much – and you are not much higher if truth be told.

I could take no more & so lashed out at her with a tea-towel, flipping it again & again & again in her odious fat face screaming at her, You have made me the most miserable person in the whole of Sussex and I shall not forgive you for it.

Unbeknownst to me, Nelly was carrying her own tea-towel about her unduly bulging person as plump as a ptarmigan & as I paused to regain my breath she whipped it out from its hiding place & struck me with it once twice three no four times in quick & brutal succession. She persists; prods; brutally tramples. I asked myself: am I forever doomed to let every worry, spite, irritation & obsession scratch and claw at my brain?

It was at this point that I recalled the disciplines taught so fortuitously at the unarmed combat course at Rodmell village hall in which Vita & I enrolled last year. I set my fingers in a V and, leaping up from the kitchen floor, I poked them into Nelly's ill-formed, damp & porcine eyes. She howled her lower-class howl & fell to the ground, begging for a mercy which, in my present state, I had little inclination to offer. I remarked upon how underbred, illiterate, insistent, raw & ultimately nauseating she was before retiring from the room to my bed, therewith to restore myself with a little George Eliot.

VIRGINIA WOOLF

May 8th

Typical! The third-rate nincompoops who compose the judging panel have once again turned down my application for the Nobel Prize for Literature. I hate the guts of this modern world, with its oafish ignorance of true value. Instead, they have awarded the prize to, of all things, a bald Russian with a beard.

He has, it seems, spent two decades in the Gulag. Well so jolly what? He can spend another two decades there, for all I care. The only book of his I have managed to plough through – *A Day in the Life of Ivan Hoodjamaflip* – is dreary, dreary, dreary, though I suppose one must be thankful the Day did not extend to the full Weekend.

What must one do to have one's worth recognised in this shiftless, tasteless, trivial modern age? It seems that nowadays, all one has to do to win a prize is clip a beard on, book into the Gulag for a few days and scowl for the cameras. Not only is Solzhenitsyn worthless but one couldn't help notice he has fat legs too. He now takes his place among a gallery of overrated Russians including Pasternak (wholly lacks that great Cornish quality of sympathy), Count Tolstoy (wordy! wordy! wordy!), and Dostoevsky (oh, do stop all that snivelling, Fyodor!).

A.L. ROWSE

Arrived at Downing Street, going in the back door so as not to be seen. I was ushered straight through to the Prime Minister's study. I was just trying out his chair when Tony came in. He was wearing a rather fetching open-necked check shirt. He looks great in jeans. I was not afraid to tell him so.

T.B.: I must tell you this. I am thinking of moving the goalposts.

P.A.: Thank you for telling me this. I think it is important not to beat about the bush so I may as well say that, bluntly, if you pursue this course of action, you are in danger of scoring an own goal.

T.B.: My attitude has always been, for God's sake, let's kick the ball around a bit before the final whistle blows.

P.A.: I am in full agreement. But where does this leave electoral reform?

T.B.: Eh? Who said anything about electoral reform? I was talking about the kids' new football pitch. It's great!

I came away deeply depressed.

PADDY ASHDOWN

May 9th

After an excellent dinner for the Plumbs and their forty guests – seafood consommé, lobster, cheese, crème brûlée, with an excellent Pouilly-Fumé – the conversation turns to news from home. It is irredeemably bad: economic decline, rising unemployment, inflation, rising discontent, and goodness knows what else. As the brandy and mints are taken around by the staff, complaints continue to crop up about our 'something-for-nothing' society, with its roots in British indolence and greed. By this time, we have all taken the weight off our feet in order to enjoy some first-rate brandy snaps with our liqueurs. 'Can nothing really be done to halt the decline of this once great country of ours?' asks an immensely distinguished visiting statesman. It is generally agreed that only a renewed sense of vigour and national pride could spur our pitiful old country out of its present torpor. But by this time we are all feeling sleepy so, after another brandy or two, we make our separate ways to bed.

SIR NICHOLAS HENDERSON

May 10th

The Duke and Duchess of Windsor are great adornments to one's dinner table. For a small extra fee, the Duchess is prepared to sit in the middle, gargling like a swan.

The Duke of Windsor is unmistakably Royal. No one who ever observed him in that much-loved baseball cap stamped with the words 'I WAS KING' could ever think him otherwise.

The Windsors are the most tremendous fun-lovers. Their favourite game is to assemble all the guests into a line to form a 'human xylophone'. They then tell each of them to open their mouths and then they hit each in turn on the head with a spoon, tapping out the tune of 'God Save the King'.

The Duchess is a lady of infinite wisdom. 'A woman,' she tells me before departing, 'can never be too thin.' She then slithers out without opening the door. In exile, the two of them never forget that they are Royalty, behaving with true dignity at all times. Summering at Cap d'Antibes, the Duke always insists on water-skiing in his Coronation robes.

ALEXIS, BARON DE REDE

The way that man treated poor Edwina, well, it makes my blood boil. I was an MP myself once, and it's no secret that every Prime Minister tried his best to seduce me, but I wasn't having any of it, that's not the sort of girl I am. But that John Major forced himself upon Edwina, he wouldn't take no for an answer, he said, 'I'm Prime Minister and it's the law,' and there was nothing she could do, nothing. And after he's had his way with her, he just swans off to some international banquet for world statesmen, leaving her there, all sobbing and distraught while he tucks into an innocent lamb or a little baby chicken.

HEATHER MILLS McCARTNEY

May 11th

A whale has been found in the Thames. Quite terrifying, really, when you come to think about it. Needless to say, it was the arms manufacturers who put the whale up to it, in league with the multi-nationals and the whale leaders. The Establishment have always wanted a whale in the Thames. That way, they hope that ordinary decent working people will have their minds on other things, so won't start asking awkward questions.

They must think we're all proper Charlies. Don't tell me that whale wasn't controlled by MI5. Blair would have called him in, sat him down, perhaps offered him a knighthood or a peerage, and told him that they urgently needed a diversion from the whole Iraq fiasco, so couldn't he be an awfully good fellow and swim up and down the Thames.

Then they got scared, didn't they? The intelligence services couldn't afford to have this undercover whale blubbering his mouth off, so they made sure he never came back. If you looked carefully, you could see it was the Home Secretary who was driving that barge, with George Bush in his sou'wester at the helm. Quite frankly, it makes my blood boil.

TONY BENN

To a finger-supper with the blessed Sir Harold Acton at La Pietra. Tony Snowdon in a lime-green blouson with high-standing sleeves, tightly waisted matelot jacket and sky-blue brushed silk pantaloons. Dicky Buckle collars me and says that Binkie Beaumont really hates Cecil Beaton. Later, Binkie Beaumont shepherds me into a corner to tell me that Cecil Beaton really hates Dicky Buckle. As brandy is served (certainly not five-star) Cecil asks if he can have a word. Apparently, Dicky Buckle really hates Binkie Beaumont. And they all really hate Harold.

A divine evening of friendship and warmth in the company of angels.

ROY STRONG

May 12th

9.15 A.M.: John Smith dies of a heart attack.

9.16 A.M.: Brief period of private mourning.

9.17 A.M.: Breakfast meeting at my flat. Tony, Robin, John, Margaret and Gordon agree that, as a mark of respect to the late leader, they will not discuss the succession issue with the press until early afternoon, or possibly late morning, so as to make the lunchtime news.

9.45 A.M.: Walking across College Green, I bump into Peter Mandelson. He says he's considering backing Gordon Blair. Is he hedging his bets?

PHILIP GOULD

May 13th

What's it like growing up the daughter of Paul McCartney? Why do people always ask that? Is it just because I'm the daughter of Paul McCartney?

STELLA McCARTNEY

To luncheon with William Hague and his equally unremarkable wife Ffion. What did I think of them? A superb couple, absolutely superb. Anyone who knows me knows that I would never call them unremarkable.

Unremarkable is not a word I use.

Sadly, Ffion struck me as unremarkable. Ffion! That's not the way I would have chosen to spell it.

'You should do something about that hair,' I advise her, taking her to one side over a small glass of Scotch. 'You don't want it like that! It's far too thin to wear that long! You must get it cut, my dear!'

After another small Scotch, I see it as my duty to reach into my bag and pull out a decent pair of strong British-made household scissors, just right for the job in hand. Only last week, I used them to improve the Ancrams' curtains before setting sail on the unnecessary tassels on their cushions.

'Stand still!' I tell Ffion. 'I'll see to it!'

But the silly girl has darted off to the other corner of the room. Frit! The girl is frit! So after another small Scotch I chase after her, scissors snapping in readiness.

'Anything the matter, Margaret?' It is William, standing in my way. 'Out of the way, little fellow! I have a job to do!' I advise, drinking another small Scotch. Why on earth do one's junior ministers never let one finish the job in hand? Isn't it high time the little fellow realised that after twenty very enjoyable years as Prime Minister, I know what needs to be done with a pair of scissors?

If you'll just let me finish!

MARGARET THATCHER

May 14th

On this crisp May morning, I pay a visit to Totteridge and Whetstone for 'background' to my new book, *Twelve Tube Stations*. I first saw Totteridge and Whetstone when I was, I fancy, but fifteen years of age. I cannot claim, in all honesty, ever to have been back. He would be a saint who could place it among the first rank of London underground stations, and I make no claim to sanctity, though over the years I have enjoyed close, though seldom intimate, acquaintance with no fewer than six Popes and seventeen Cardinals. I was never a Cardinal myself, though I cannot claim this omission causes me a very great deal of regret. In the late 1950s, I was for a short while Archbishop of Verona, but, for all its splendid sartorial opportunities, I found the post in the main tiresome, and communication with the Lord Almighty for the most part haphazard and tiresomely one-way.

Nevertheless, Totteridge and Whetstone has remained vivid in my mind. I make no claim for it as a rival to, say, the sheer magnificence of the Place Vendôme in Paris, or, for that matter, the extravagant Neo-Gothic of the Plaza de Colón in Madrid. It is set, a trifle clumsily, in surroundings that are not, one must confess, greatly conducive to the pleasures of the table or, indeed, the amenities of social intercourse. Neither High Barnet, its more northerly neighbour, on the far from undistinguished Northern Line, nor Woodside Park, its somewhat less trumpeted southerly companion, offers overwhelming reasons for stopping. But Totteridge and Whetstone has always possessed for me a certain creaky charm, albeit a charm sadly insufficient to draw one back more than once every sixty years.

ROY JENKINS

Ah, Venezia! (the Italian word for Venice). It is like no other place on earth, a city blessed with having been the lustrous, historic setting for one of my most memorable novels. Venice! Though it rhymes with tennis, there are few tennis courts there. But it also rhymes with Penice or Penis. Ah, Penezia! To me Venice has always been a young man, his chest rippling with muscles, dragging me to his bedchamber, nimbly unbuttoning my Versace top, pulling out his manhood and slowly yet urgently entering me again and again and again, like the little man in a Swiss weather predictor on a changeable day, full of bright spells and blustery showers.

Let me paint a picture of Venice in words. Plash, plash. Laughter wafts across the canal. Fragments of conversation float under my open window. Plash, plash, plash. Beneath my silk blouson, my nipples sway to the gentle hum and thrust of the *canale*. Only the occasional plash-plash-plash of an oar interrupts the silence. Plash. There it goes again! Plash-plash! And again! The air is aromatic with the scent of coffee. Soon you are transported to a world in which the gentle lapping of your lover's tongue against your breast takes you to a – plash! plash! plash! plash! plash! – hey, is there no end to this infernal plashing?! Quit this plashing NOW! ROOM SERVICE! Oh, someone shut the fucking window, can't you, this fucking plashing's driving me maaad!!

ERICA JONG

May 15th

In dumbing down our culture, it is our culture that has been dumbed down. It was Proust who Searched for Lost Time, but he might have been Searching for Lost *Radio Times* too. A once-proud magazine is now a magazine that was proud, once.

Cultural television has been shown the back door, and that door is marked 'Back'. The jewel is in the crown no more. The crown has drowned, causing the free world to frown. Around town, the crown is a clown, and its colour is brown, proving that rust is no substitute for trust. But as the delightful (and highly intelligent) Britney Spears told me in my seminal *Clive Meets Britney Down Under*, a bust is a must for intellectual thrust.

CLIVE JAMES

May 16th

We've been getting a lot of complaints recently from viewers who have bought themselves trouser-belts from leading high-street retailers. 'I pulled my belt too tight,' writes a typical viewer, Mr P. Randall from Uxbridge, 'and I found that my waist was painful all day.'

The same happened to Mr Trevor Johns from Croydon, who pulled his belt a full two notches too tight. 'I was in no mood to let the matter rest,' Mr Johns told us. 'So I took my complaint direct to the manufacturer. Eventually, I got a letter back saying that the fault was MINE and that I shouldn't have pulled it so tight in the first place!!'

Well, we thought we'd take this scandal further, and we rang a Mr Stephens of the High Wycombe Belt Company in High Wycombe.

'We've been getting a number of complaints about your belts,' we said.

'Oh yes?' he said.

'OH YES!' we said. 'A lot of our viewers have found that if they tie them too tight, they spend the rest of the day in some pain.'

We must admit to being absolutely stunned by the reply Mr Stephens then gave us.

'They've only got themselves to blame,' he said.

'But why have you not fitted SAFETY LOCKS to your belts, to stop people pulling them too tight and hurting themselves?' we asked. Eventually, Mr Stephens said he would 'look into the matter'.

We wonder just how many people will have to walk around with painful waists before LEGISLATION is brought in to guard against belts that can be pulled too tight. Until that day, we have set up a special BELTWATCH number – 0891 6591 3947 – for people to ring, day or night, if you feel that your belt has been pulled too tight. So far, there have been no deaths from overtight belts, but a tragedy can't be too far off, God willing.

ESTHER RANTZEN

May 17th

1878

Thoughtful persons observing me walk those six miles across the hills to market to purchase a carrot for my supper might have regarded me as a singularly fortunate man. But those persons would have known little of the truth, for the truth is always unhappy.

On my arrival at the market, I caught sight of a carrot, cold and long and dusted in dirt, lying all alone on a ramshackle table some twenty yards away. Sacred in its solitude, the carrot spoke to me, and I could not forebear to walk up to the stallholder and offer him a decent price for this sad, pining vegetable.

I had taken but two steps in the direction of the poor carrot when my left foot happened to trip on a loose and callow stone. With nothing in this world to cling onto, I plunged forward, bumping into a gentleman all in green carrying a tray upon which a goldfish swam heartily in a bowl won at a fair in a neighbouring village some five miles away.

A keen-eared fellow passing nearby might then have heard the first harsh mournful grindings of the solemn wheel of fate. The goldfish in question, a second ago so carefree (whistling a ditty popular among goldfish at that time) was jolted a-sudden out of his bowl and span rapidly through the air like a night star plunging into eternal darkness. At the very moment when the fish was hurtling through the indifferent air, a local tradesman, Biggins by name, was removing his cap to a handsome maid of his acquaintance who had the day before found her unfortunate husband crushed to death beneath the weight of a falling oak on a country road. Oh, how the maid, her thick auburn tresses dancing naked in the sunlight, now wished her husband had decided against the prettier route!

The unknown goldfish – its mother had perished by drowning before conferring a name upon it – now ended its flight in the momentarily upturned cap, which Biggins then replaced on his head.

'No!'

Biggins was driven to this profound exclamation as he felt the mysterious dank twitching scales on his hairless scalp.

'No! No! No!'

With that, he flung both arms wide, causing his right hand to hit a passing donkey, recently bereaved, which bolted at the sudden shock, unsaddling its rider, a one-eyed gypsy fiddler whose mother had been found hanged by the neck ten days previously, and the one-eyed gypsy tumbled willy-nilly onto a plank balanced precariously on a boulder, and the bucket of water at the other end of the plank shot skywards, turned over, and landed over the grizzled head of Parson Jennings who, now blinded to his fate, floundered sideways into the blacksmith's kiln and perished in a sea of flames so burning fiery hot that many a raw-faced young lad found himself able to grill a fine-tasting sausage on his embers, though this was no consolation to the poor discomposed donkey who had proceeded to gallop in terror through the market, pitching ladies in fine crinolines headlong into the mud-filled sloughs.

I cast this tragedy from my mind in order to pursue my voyage towards the solitary carrot that had caught my fancy some minutes before. With determination renewed, I bent to pick the carrot up when the recalcitrant donkey, conferring upon it the consolation he sought, snapped it up with his large, gloomy teeth and swallowed it down.

I journeyed back over the hills and arrived home three hours after to behold Mrs Hardy beside a pot.

'Your water is a-boil, Thomas,' she said. 'Now where is that fine carrot you promis'd me?'

'I tripp'd on a stone,' I explained to this woman, who had once been so fair, 'and fate again play'd its hand, as it do.'

THOMAS HARDY

The Beatles were a truly remarkable group of young men. Four lads from Liverpool who conquered the world. Between them, Lennon and McCartney composed to my mind some of the most memorable songs of our time. I had John Lennon on the show once. He could be very outspoken, and was quite a character. I plucked up the courage to ask him the one thing I'd always wanted to know. In this game, timing is everything, so when I felt he was sufficiently relaxed, I slipped in the question. 'Tell me, John, something I've always wanted to know,' I said, '– what makes you tick?' That took him by surprise and no mistake! I forget his reply – probably something about music, knowing John – but it was a truly indefinable moment of classic television, and one that I shall long cherish.

MICHAEL PARKINSON

May 18th

In a curious way, Wayne Rooney has, for me at any rate, all of the grace but little of the marvellous *joie de vivre* of, say, a Wesley Sneijder or a Nobby Stiles. But on the other hand, Rooney has something of the medieval troubadour about him, at once joyous and observant, yet with a strange and unexpected undertow of – what?? Might one call it melancholy?

It was during the match against Russia that I caught a glimpse – swift yet surely undeniable – of the sunshine glinting off the hairs just below the knee on the right leg of Fernando Torres. Instantly, those peculiarly plangent lines from Abba leapt, unbeckoned, into my head:

> There was something in the air that night
> The stars were bright, Fernando
> They were shining there for you and me
> For liberty, Fernando

And I felt at once humbled and curiously elated, almost as though ravaged by gypsy minstrels while eating handmade chocolates from a velveteen clutch-bag.

A.S. BYATT

May 19th

I finish *Tintin in Tibet*. When all is said and done, Tintin is really a very poor reporter. He was a very flawed writer, with nothing to say. The man was a fraud. I do not for one minute believe that he went to the moon and back, and he had no understanding of the Incas. I once met his dog, Snowy. He told me he didn't like him either. A dreadful little man with a quiff. Was he a homosexual?

V.S. NAIPAUL

The only newscaster who isn't common is Peter Sissons, who's an absolute *dreamboat*. Peter and I were very intimate one summer, long ago. He used to look so pretty in his two-piece grey suit. Every night, I'd ask him to read the news to me at a little desk at the foot of the bed, and always with that simply wonderful I'm-being-oh-so-serious face on. And then right at the end, he'd click his pen in that divine way he had, and shuffle those papers with his big strong newswreadery hands of his. I was *agog*.

NICHOLAS HASLAM

May 20th

In the afternoon, reread complete works of Graham Greene. Pretty thin stuff. Deeply unpleasant fellow, and, one feels, highly conceited: he loathed handing out praise to his contemporaries, retaining all his warmest approval for his own works. Later reread various fan letters confirming that I am the leading novelist of my generation. Why is it, one wonders, that my fans are so unusually percipient? Or is it the other way round, and do the unusually percipient tend to be my fans? One of life's deeper questions. Must explore further.

ANTHONY POWELL

May 21st

THE STATING OF THE OBVIOUS

To state the obvious, one is obliged to state the obvious. It is according to how frequently we state the obvious that we determine the frequency with which the obvious is stated.

ALAIN DE BOTTON

May 22nd

Aswan. After a slightly uncomfortable night, I wake up. I pay a trip to the famous Aswan dam, an extraordinary feat of engineering, dealing with a lot of water every day of the year. This is a very colourful country, full of hidden secrets never vouchsafed to the outsider. I ask one of the locals – quite a character – what it is like to live in Aswan. He tells me he enjoys it quite a lot. 'I imagine that the difference between living in Aswan and living in England is literally indescribable,' I say. He mentions that he doesn't know, as he has never lived in England.

'Do you have a funny hat I can wear for the cameras?' I ask him, but he hasn't got one, so my researcher slips out and buys one – a very Pythonesque garment! I put it on beside the Aswan dam, and make a quip – 'It's not unlike wearing a dead parrot!' – and the camera crew creases up! In the afternoon, I bid a fond farewell to an utterly magical country, full of a great many contrasts.

MICHAEL PALIN

May 23rd

Such a striking boy at Binkie's yesterday – perfect skin and teeth, marvellously loose-fitting dark suit, wonderfully flashing eyes, an entrancing (Birmingham?) accent. His name was Enoch, if you please! I asked him how he was, and he became most dreadfully agitated, saying that like the Roman, he seemed to see the River Tiber foaming with blood.

'Frightfully inconvenient,' I agreed, saying that if I were him, I would certainly holiday elsewhere. Had he tried the Caribbean? I insisted that if he visited Jamaica, he should look up Noël. He's just Noël's type, and would look quite wonderful in a crisply laundered pair of Bermuda shorts.

JOHN GIELGUD

Of course I could reveal what Derry told me Gordon said that Margaret had told Jack about what Tony said about Patricia.* But I have no intention of revealing private conversations, so I won't. But it was very personal about Patricia indeed, and something Tony would never forgive Jack, Margaret, Gordon, or Derry for repeating. I used to get on well with Jack, before we fell out.

DAVID BLUNKETT

May 24th

A *soirée* at Campden Hill Square. But make the effort to give over the odd evening to entertaining Neil and Glenys. To set them at their ease, I tend to eschew my normal silks for more down-to-earth 'overalls', and we serve what I believe are known as 'chip butties' with lashings of 'custard', though it suits me to save up and eat something else later.

Neil Kinnock greets me. 'Hello, love,' he says. It's an expression I've never heard before, except in those truly splendid 'gritty' Northern dramas in the 1950s. 'Oh, Neil,' I say, charmingly, 'you simply MUST say that again, so that everyone can hear.' So I call the assembled

---

*Andrew Rawnsley writes: 'Historians are now in broad agreement that what Tony said about Patricia was indeed what Derry told David that Gordon had said Margaret told Jack. It could well have been the straw that detonated the flood of cards if Derry had not told David not to pass it on.'

company to silence and make Neil say it again, exactly as he did the first time, and then again and again and again. Of course by the end of it we are all in absolute fits.

After Neil and Glenys have finished the washing-up, I always insist on pressing some small change into their hands, but they won't hear of it. What a sweet team they are! Harold and I simply can't wait for them to be the next little couple in Number Ten!

LADY ANTONIA FRASER

May 25th

I love film. After a yummy meal for the whole family and some truly great friends we often go out to see something beautiful and unique.

Here's a tip for all you moms. Never ask young children to pay when you go out to the cinema. It is simply unfair to ask a four-year-old to pay for herself.

Why not give her the trip as a very special present? That way, you – and she – can learn so much more about what it is to love and to give. Repayment can come later.

GWYNETH PALTROW

The possibility that Iraq will soon have nuclear weapons could have chilling consequences for the world. It is up to writers who have the power to articulate the unimaginable to stress the urgency of the situation, to pick words of sufficient terror to show that nuclear weapons are the exploding turds of our age, that a nuke-turd is like a liquefied Biro in the top pocket of a beige suit, probably three-piece, that the aftermath of nuclear collar-hoist will be more serious than anything we have so far encountered, like a gob of snot-phlegm – phlot? snegm? – on a shiny kitchen surface, or an ear-glob in a plate of vichyssoise, which is chilling; chilling at the moment in fact: I'm having it for lunch with croutons after tennis with the Hitch.

MARTIN AMIS

May 26th

The liquid runs out of our 'Fairy Liquid' just as we are about to embark on the washing-up. I have noticed the strange fact that this occurs with disarming regularity. Is this a fluke, or is it part of an unspoken policy by Labour? And why should Blair and his busy-body cohorts so hate to see dishes clean? Could it be because they wish to spread MRSA? At the moment it is confined to hospitals, but if they can spread it beyond, to dishwashing, Conservative-voting households, the General Election will be theirs for the asking.

CHARLES MOORE

Samuel Pepys died today, in 1703. A forgotten diarist of little or no distinction.

V.S. NAIPAUL

May 27th

Contemplate suicide.

Look in diary.

Tomorrow, we have Princess Margaret to dinner.

Decide against.

KENNETH TYNAN

I saw JM again on Friday. I was in the area where he lives, and he and his wife offered their home for a rest, which I appreciated. Nice place, not like I'd have done it, very mumsy, but nice all the same, just so long as you're not burdened with a sense of style.

I'd never do anything to hurt him, so I acted very demure, very discreet, keeping all my clothes on while his wife was in the room. But when at long last she popped out to get us a cup of tea, I flung off my coat to reveal the Donald Duck costume I was wearing underneath, ready for my appearance at the Swim To Get Fit launch in Trafalgar Square later in the day.

'If this doesn't get me to Number 10, nothing will,' I said, practising my 'quack-quack' and waddling back and forth. Needless to say, JM was very positive, very supportive, whispering that I was just like Donald Duck, he really couldn't tell the difference, he was sure I'd be a huge success at the launch and that would be a great stepping stone to the Cabinet. But then his wife came back with the tea – she favours the cheaper brands, bless her – so I had to throw my coat back on.

Go home. Ray still in bed with pneumonia. Why me?

EDWINA CURRIE

May 28th

Dinner for Princess Margaret. She is really quite extraordinarily small. Without her shoes, she would be officially reclassified a dwarf. Jill Bennett mistakes her for an occasional table, places an empty glass on her head and drawls for more. Princess Margaret becomes fearfully upset, so I try to draw her back into the conversation.

'Do you not agree, Ma'am,' I say, 'that Chairman Mao's Cultural Revolution is simply the most marvellous thing that has happened in years? How one wishes one were an adorable little Chinesey peasant at this time!' The Princess burps wittily, then follows it up with the most delicious yawn. All perfectly timed, as one would expect of royalty. As Noël once noted, she really is the most exquisite yawner.

Across the table, Mick McGahey is having a fearful row with Debo about workers' ownership of the means of production. McGahey must surely know it is wholly improper to address a Duchess as 'love'. Every time I hear that crude vulgarity, a sword pierces my heart. Really, this is no way for Mick to repay one – and after all the passionate support I have offered the Hard Left over the issue of secondary picketing.

KENNETH TYNAN

I like non-sequiturs, but I wish they'd follow on from what's just been said.

PETRONELLA WYATT

May 29th

Trouser pockets can be an awful hazard around the home. If I've said it once, I've said it a thousand times: do, I beg of you, make sure that your pockets aren't drenched full of petrol before putting your trousers or slacks on in the morning. It only takes one match to light and – whoosh! – the next thing you know you're faced with a desperately sad family bereavement, and the additional financial burden of a new pair of trousers, should the poor love survive.*

CLAIRE RAYNER

'Disobedience'
James James
Morrison Morrison
Weatherby George Dupree
Took great
Care of his Mother,
Though he was only three.
James James said to his Mother
'Mother,' he said, said he,
'You must never go down
To the end of the town,
Or they'll smash your fucking head in.'

HAROLD PINTER

---

*Historical note: this was the entry that sparked the nationwide campaign that led to the passing of the Trouser Pockets Fire Prevention Act, making it compulsory for all trouser manufacturers and vendors to clearly label all trouser pockets with the words 'Unsuitable for Petrol'.

May 30th

These days, people like the Queen are queuing up to see me, but when I was a child we were very very poor. It was like *Steptoe and Son*, we were that poor. Poorer. In fact, now you mention it, I remember actually being brought up by Steptoe and Son, only they never showed me on the scenes they showed on the television, because the old man Steptoe locked me in a cupboard for the six years they were filming. Sometimes you could hear a bump and a yell, but that's the only sign the viewers ever had that I was in there.

Then they put me to work up the chimneys. I was a chimney sweep till the age of eleven, going up the chimneys and coming down all like black and sooty. Luckily, I ran away from my wicked employer and leapt into a river, and luckily I was transformed into a water baby, where I met others in the same situation – and from them I learnt the meaning of love.

From there, aged sort of thirteen, I went to live in Elm Street, where the nightmare took place. I never trusted Freddy Krueger, there was just something about that way he used to kill people at random that I didn't like. So I thought, no, I'm not having any of this, and I managed to save a helluva lot of kids from his clutches. I never told anyone that before, but that's one of the reasons I'm being considered for the Nobel Peace Prize this year, which is great.

HEATHER MILLS McCARTNEY

Joan of Arc died today, in 1431. She called herself the Maid of Orleans. No one else did. She was ruthlessly ambitious. She would do anything for immortality. It was she who built that bonfire, climbed up on it and set light to it. A typical attention-seeker, with nothing to show for it.

V.S. NAIPAUL

May 31st

The President of the United States of America dipped into his desk drawer, awarded me two medals and told me that, truly, I was the wisest Christian he had ever encountered. In turn, I told him he was the seventh President of the United States of America who had honoured me in this manner, and that his Democratic rival for the Presidency, also a decent, God-fearing man, had promised to award me three medals. Out of the goodness of his heart, the President then awarded me a further four medals. Never have I felt so truly humbled in the presence of the Lord.

BILLY GRAHAM

June

June 1st

I am privileged to accompany Her Majesty around the Obesity Unit of the new Farnsworth Hospital. She is in a dress of peacock blue with an elegant straw hat with pink brocade. Her lady-in-waiting informs me she has made it a firm rule never to wear slacks on official visits. I myself am wearing a dark brown Harris tweed suit with sensible check shirt and sober light-green woollen tie. It is what people expect.

The Queen speaks to an obese inmate, a man in his forties. Her Majesty avoids the temptation to call him Fatty, or poke him in the tummy.

'She has enormous tact,' her lady-in-waiting confides.

I approach the patient once the Queen has moved on. He seems delighted at their meeting. 'What a gracious lady,' he says.

I set him at his ease. 'I bet you're relieved she didn't get the giggles or call you unkind names like Fatty Pants or Porky Pig!' I say.

Before each royal arrival, there is a heightened sense of expectation, leading to nervous laughter from those due to be presented. When the Queen arrives in the outpatients ward, I attempt to break the ice.

'Good morning, Ma'am,' I say (pronouncing the 'Ma'am' to rhyme with 'Clapham', as is correct).

'It's nice and warm in here,' she observes. I lead the laughter.

'Boom! Boom!' I say. Within minutes, there are tears literally rolling down my cheeks. Her Majesty is, when all is said and done, a natural comic with a perfect sense of timing.

GYLES BRANDRETH

Message in my hotel pigeonhole from Martin Scorsese.

Martin SCORSESE!

MARTIN Scorsese!

MARTIN SCORSESE!

MARTIN SCOR-FUCKING-SESE!

I feel betwixt myself with joy. He tells me he loved me in *Withnail*. Me?! He loved ME! I stutter something about loving everything he's ever done. 'I just wanna say I thought you were GRRREATTT!' he says. In a mad moment, I think to myself that it's time I showed I don't just KOW-TOW to everything he says, to show that I'm a bit of a fucking REBEL, so I take the plunge. My stomach wrenched with fear and courage, I seek to contradict him.

'NOTHING like as GREAT as the way you directed *TAXI-DRIVER*!' I say. 'You're a FUCKING GENIUS!'

At this point, we establish eye contact. His eyes sear into mine like heat-seeking missiles. Uh-oh. Have I gone TOO FAR? Have I thrown away my BIG BREAK by being TOO HONEST? Scorsese pauses, pulls on his beard. Then he says: 'And you were great in *The Age of Innocence*, too.'

MARTIN Scorsese!

Martin SCORSESE!!

MARTIN SCORSESE!!!

Marty.

RICHARD E. GRANT

June 2nd

SUE LAWLEY: My castaway this week is an artist who is impossible to ignore. She has appeared on *The Frank Skinner Show*, the Brit Awards, *Stop the Week*, *Blankety Blank* and *Room 101*. She regularly adorns the pages of the *Sun* and the *Daily Mail*. She has been drunk to the point of incoherence on live television. As a result of these achievements, she now has her own space at Tate Britain, and we welcome her to *Desert Island Discs*. She is, of course, Tracey Emin. And, if I'm right, Tracey, you're still only fourteen …

TRACEY EMIN: Forty-one …

SUE LAWLEY: Yes, fourteen! So young, and with such a precocious talent! Now, Tracey, you've been raped twice, and –

TRACEY EMIN: Yeah but no but. Like, not really raped as such, well, I s'pose you could call it rape but, like, well not really rape and that. More like heavy pettin'.

SUE LAWLEY: Let's call it rape. So, Tracey Emin, you've been raped three times, you've had two abortions, you've attempted suicide –

TRACEY EMIN: Well, I wouldn't call it suicide exactly.

SUE LAWLEY: Yes, definitely suicide. So that's three abortions, four rapes, and five successful suicides. Marvellous! Your first record, please.

* * *

SUE LAWLEY: Tell me, Tracey, how much has your art, which is so autobiographical, so confessional, if you like, saved you from yourself?

TRACEY EMIN: What I like about my art is that it's like what I like about my art is what I like about my art. No one can take away from me the fact that when I make my art it's the art I make and no one can take that away from me.

SUE LAWLEY: Four abortions, five rapes and six successful suicides! That's an awful lot of pain! Super! But there's enormous professionalism in your work, too. Hard work is very much part of you, isn't it?

TRACEY EMIN: Yeah but no but. With my bed and my tent I've changed the face of art twice. They're inseminal. Most artists don't manage it even once, but I've twice created an absolutely semolina work.

SUE LAWLEY: Your next record, Tracey.

* * *

SUE LAWLEY: Now, alongside your unmade bed –

TRACEY EMIN: You call it unmade, but I made it. Like, I made it unmade. And you can't take that away from me. It's not something you can unmake.

SUE LAWLEY: And alongside your unmade bed there were some lovely little watercolours. They were very beautiful, weren't they? Describe them for us.

TRACEY EMIN: While I was painting them, I was committing suicide. And making toast. But mainly committing suicide.

SUE LAWLEY: Remarkable. And for a long time, you were very, very promiscuous …

TRACEY EMIN: I haven't had any sex for seventeen months, can you believe it!

SUE LAWLEY: But until quite recently you were very, very, VERY promiscuous!

TRACEY EMIN: Yeah but no bu–

SUE LAWLEY: Really EXTREMELY promiscuous for a fourteen-year-old! Marvellous! Your next record, please.

* * *

SUE LAWLEY: All your work is autobiographical. Your bed, your tent. And your remarkable work, *My Chewing Gum* is also intensely personal. Explain *My Chewing Gum* to me.

TRACEY EMIN: Basically, it's my chewing gum. I'd been chewing it for like an hour or more then I decided to turn it into a work of art.

SUE LAWLEY: As I say, an intensely personal work of art. And how did you go about it?

TRACEY EMIN: I scooped it out with my tongue, then I picked it off my tongue, and then, taking care not to alter its shape not one little bit, I placed it on a plinth.

SUE LAWLEY: And it still carries the exact indentations it had when you were chewing it. Remarkable! And since then, you've issued a limited edition of *My Chewing Gum*, Tracey, though some people say you now get other people to chew the gum for you …

TRACEY EMIN: Yeah, other people chew it for me, but I buy the packets of gum, and I decide where it should go on the plinth, and no one does nothing without my say-so.

SUE LAWLEY: Wise words indeed, from one so young. Tracey Emin, thank you very much indeed for letting us hear your Desert Island Discs.

TRANSCRIPT, *DESERT ISLAND DISCS*,
BBC RADIO 4

June 3rd

Before luncheon on the 3rd of June, Picasso changed his shoes from a pair of plimsolls to a pair of light-brown leather walking shoes, purchased six months earlier from the singularly butter-fingered cobbler Monsieur LeBas on the rue Goncourt. He then took approximately eight steps into his dining room, where he joined his uninteresting wife Olga and her dimwitted mother for a bowl of tepid onion soup followed by a nourishing fish stew. After a two-minute break to partake of his ablutions, he returned to his studio, where he completed a further six sculptures, five paintings and a bust of his latest conquest, the under-maid who had served him his fish stew. He was later to portray her as an unfolded napkin, or 'serviette', as the ill-bred Clive Bell, within my pained hearing, used to term it.

JOHN RICHARDSON

Arthur Ransome died today in 1967. Why do none of the Swallows or the Amazons perish in agony? Instead, they all go home to bed. This demonstrates a failure of nerve by the author.

V.S. NAIPAUL

June 4th

CHURCHILL: We shall fight on the beaches, we shall –

HUMPHRYS: What beaches, exactly, Mr Churchill?

CHURCHILL: We shall fight on the landing grounds –

HUMPHRYS: Forget about the landing grounds for one minute. If we could just go back to those beaches. You say you will, and I quote, 'fight on the beaches'. Well, there are strict laws, are there not, about causing a public affray on our beaches, not to mention all the ensuing damage and pollution and so forth. Presumably then, you will be obtaining permission from the relevant authorities for all this fighting you are proposing to carry out?

CHURCHILL: We shall fight in the fields and in the streets –

HUMPHRYS: Ah! In the streets, you now say. Well, this is rather different from your previous statement, is it not, Mr Churchill? Having first told us that you proposed to fight on the beaches and on the landing grounds, you are now telling us that you've just remembered, you also wish to fight in the fields and in the streets. I think what the public have a right to expect from you, Mr Churchill, is a clear statement of your intention, and not the sort of muddled proposal your critics will accuse you of having come up with so far …

CHURCHILL: We shall fight in the hills, we shall –

HUMPHRYS: If I could just stop you there for one second. You say you are going to fight in the hills, but you are aware, are you not, Mr Churchill, that there are very clear government guidelines concerning fighting in the hills, many of which will be in places of natural beauty. Do you intend to stick to these guidelines?

CHURCHILL: We shall never surrender.

HUMPHRYS: Many of our listeners will be left wondering what exactly you mean when you say you will 'never surrender'. I need hardly remind you, Mr Churchill, that many of your critics maintain that, given the right circumstances, you would certainly surrender. In fact, polls today seem to indicate that up to 62 per cent of ordinary men and women find it frankly hard to believe that you would 'never surrender'. Would you really have us believe, then, Mr Churchill, that given the strength of public opinion against you, you would 'never surrender'? Many people would find that frankly hard to believe. I'm going to have to rush you.

CHURCHILL: We shall –

HUMPHRYS: I'm going to have to stop you there, Mr Churchill. And now it's over to Rob for the Sports News.

TRANSCRIPT, WINSTON CHURCHILL
INTERVIEWED BY JOHN HUMPHRYS,
HOME SERVICE, JUNE 4TH, 1940

WEDNESDAY: Breakfast with Henry Kissinger. The guy claims he's a bloody doctor. Oh yeah? When I tell him I've got a bit of a tickle in my throat, he hasn't the foggiest.

He starts to go on about international co-operation to reduce something-or-other, blah, blah, blah, and how the United Nations must resist the temptation to blah, blah, blah, and I'm falling asleep into my fried egg. Lighten up, mate! I think – and I interrupt him.

'"Kissing-'er"? Great name for pulling the birds, mate!' I laugh uproariously. 'Is that the full tongue sandwich, then – or just a bit of a snog?!!!!'

Henry's actually very good fun, and loves my lively and provocative sense of humour, brilliantly managing to keep a straight face throughout. What a guy!

As we say our ta-ras, I get him to sign my autograph book, on the same page as top singer Billie Piper, top *Big Brother* finalist Jade Goody, and top crime icon Reggie Kray. Nice bloke, Henry, but on the way back to the office I wonder if he has much of a moral compass.*

PIERS MORGAN

June 5th

Why's it always me, that's what I want to know?

I've got nothing to say. There's a deadline looming and I've done it all, I've used it all up. My life, I mean. Last week, I had my lovely, lovely, lovely dog dying on me. That'll teach him to sit in a locked car on a hot day with the windows shut.

When I found him there, all sweaty and dead, I shed so many tears on my retro Chanel two-piece that I had to take it to the dry cleaners

---

*Dr Kissinger was later to appear on *Piers Morgan's Life Stories* in March 2009. Twenty-three minutes into the show, he began to cry when Morgan said: 'The bombing of Cambodia – that must have been very upsetting for you, Henry. How did it make you feel?' However, a minute later the sombre mood was lifted when Morgan asked him who he fancied more – Pamela Anderson or Scarlett Johansson.

in Dulverton High Street, and a fat lot of good they were. But in the end it was all worth it – my pooch dying, the dry-cleaning bill, taking the dry cleaners to the small claims court, the lady in the dry cleaners calling me a bloody little rat-faced bitch – because I got six articles out of it, almost as many as I got out of the time I threw myself in front of a train because I had low self-esteem resulting from a spot on my chin and my selfish bastard of a husband telling me that no way was he going to perform a circumcision on himself even though he bloody knew I prefer them less flappy and I was perfectly willing to shell out for the Stanley knife.

LIZ JONES

I hear on the news that Ronald Reagan has died. He never cut a very considerable figure on the world stage. I doubt he is remembered today by anyone who really matters.

SIR EDWARD HEATH

June 6th

The surliness of the London bus driver knows no bounds. This morning, I boarded a Number 14 bus, paid the requested fare, and, with due politeness, asked the driver to turn his vehicle round and transport me to the house of a very dear friend in Somerset in time for Sunday luncheon. I was, I should add, carrying a very heavy case of non-vintage champagne, and my Somerset friend was a lady of advanced years who has since passed on (much to the amusement of her friends, to whom she always boasted she would reach eighty!).

The driver, who was of the black or 'coloured' persuasion, steadfastly refused to accede to my bidding, stating that he was bound for 'King's Cross', somewhere at the far North end of London. The 'rules' would not permit a diversion to Somerset, where most of his passengers would surely wish to go, had they a choice. Even after ten years of

Mrs Thatcher, there are, it would appear, many areas of public life still hamstrung by the rulebook. How very saddening.

PEREGRINE WORSTHORNE

Buses I Have Written Poems to Past Lovers On In the Last Fortnight:

56, 14, 29, 11,
19, 23, 24, 8,
17, 9, 44, 7,
4, 12, 18 (late).

WENDY COPE

June 7th

JM comes round to the flat. I've specially put on my goggles and flippers for him, so he can see what I'll look like on *Good Morning Britain* tomorrow, for my launch of the Diving For More Regular Bowel-Movements campaign. If that doesn't get me a job in Cabinet, nothing will. Today's polls confirm I'm more famous than Denis Nilsen.

JM cups my hand in his, looks deep in my eyes, takes out his clipboard and tells me that the long-term forecast for UK exports of industrial machinery to the Far East has much improved. It turns my heart over, and I weep tears of joy.

EDWINA CURRIE

Lady Blanche lived in Dieppe for the sake of economy. Aunt Natty, as my parents called her, had strong views on French food, and would insist on all her meals being cooked in England, then sent over by ferry.

This caused her dinner parties to be beset by delays. If one were invited to luncheon on Friday, one could not expect the principal dish to arrive before dinner on Sunday at the earliest.

LADY BLANCHE'S FISH PIE

1 tin sardines
Mashed potato

Ask a willing hand to open the tin of sardines for you. Now place the contents in a serving dish. I have noticed over the years that some guests enjoy crunching on the backbone of a tinned sardine, while others do not. One can always remove the backbones from the general mix. Threaded together and painted in lovely deep blues and reds, they make a most attractive table decoration.

Spoon the mashed potato over the top of the sardines and scatter with eggs from the garden. Aunt Natty would always insist on wearing flippers and a snorkel. She said it was the only way to eat fish pie, but sadly in the present day many people have lost the knack of eating in snorkels, and the fashion nowadays is to eat without.

DEBORAH, DUCHESS OF DEVONSHIRE

June 8th

It was probably Italy's foremost poet Eugenio Montale (1896–1981) who taught me all I know about that which is contained within a wet T-shirt. The path to wisdom is seldom less than rocky, but a wet T-shirt prevents even the driest wit becoming shirty: the shirt may be wet, but no tea can be called dry when offered in a teacup by someone in a D-cup.

CLIVE JAMES

June 9th

With fame came sex and encounters with female customers in the ladies' toilets and under the tables while their husbands were finishing off their Introverted Sea Bass Covered with Baby Goose Saliva in a Rhododendron Sauce. The Eighties was that kind of era.

I was briefly married to a Spice Girl, I forget which. On our honeymoon she started to sing 'Tell you what I want what I really really want'. I told her to shut the fuck up and she left me.

As for Delia Smith, I never liked the look of her and I never fell for her goody-two-shoes image. Once she had the nerve to come to my restaurant with a view to eating a meal. I thought I'd give her a taste of her own medicine so I got her in a half-nelson and told my staff to take her outside and give her a good pummelling. I never fancied her anyway.

MARCO PIERRE WHITE

Charles Dickens died today, in 1870. There is so much rubbish in Dickens. He is wordy and repetitive. He uses far too many words, and he repeats himself. And he is wordy and repetitive. There is so much rubbish in Dickens.

V.S. NAIPAUL

June 10th

It was whilst staying at Wombats with Cecil Beaton that I first set eyes on Isaiah Berlin. He was a small dark man, his head packed full of thoughts, many of them interesting.

At dinner that night, I sat between Isaiah and Pablo Picasso. Pablo was also a small dark man, but he was seated to my right, whereas Isaiah was seated to my left, so telling them apart was relatively simple.

Pablo was clever, but very Spanish, some would say unashamedly so. He had nevertheless made quite a name for himself as a painter.

Sadly, his accent was extreme, so I spent most of the dinner simply nodding, but one of his sayings has lodged in my mind to this very day.

Over an overcooked main course of veal with spinach and creamed potatoes, he turned to me abruptly and said: 'Please could you pass the salt?'

Fortuitously, the eighteenth-century salt cellar was within easy reach, so I was able to fulfil the polite request of this remarkable little fellow. I heard much later that he was a ladies' man, but he made no approach to me on that occasion.

CLARISSA EDEN

June 11th

Queen Elizabeth the Queen Mother had an especial talent for friendship. She took everyone on their own terms, and was as happy to be entertained by a duke as by a dustman, in fact much happier.

She introduced an element of fun wherever possible. For her, there was satisfaction in knowing that by her mere presence she could bring intense pleasure to a room. To those she encountered, she gave much. It always greatly amused her to watch as her old friend Ruth, Lady Fermoy, would beg on the floor in front of her, her hands in the air and her tongue out. 'I rather think Fido is in need of a reward!' she would exclaim with an infectious giggle – she was suffering from a bout of catarrh at the time – before popping a Good Boy doggie biscuit into Lady Fermoy's wide-open mouth.

HUGO VICKERS

8.23 A.M.: A woman walks into Tony Blair's Downing Street office with a cup of tea, moving her free outstretched hand like a balance, palm down. It gradually becomes clear that she is the lady who delivers the tea, or, in technical parlance, 'the tea lady'.

8.24 A.M.: Tony Blair reaches out his hand for the cup. The tea lady in turn moves the cup towards him. It is a moment of high tension. If either of them now drops the cup, the carpet will suffer. For a split second, both are holding the cup. Then the Prime Minister holds it alone. He takes a sip. The transfer is complete. A comparatively minor event, maybe. But observers agree it augurs well for a successful resolution to the conflict in Iraq.

8.25 A.M.: It is impossible to know what the Prime Minister is thinking as he sips his tea.

8.26 A.M.: The Prime Minister successfully completes his cup of tea. Now that the war has begun, he is ready to get down to write his speech to the nation. He is keen to address the real issues, tackling real problems facing real people. But as Alastair Campbell, Director of Cosmetics, points out, he must first freshen up his lipstick. Over on the other side of the historic room, a clock ticks. Then it ticks again: a symbol of something undoubtedly momentous but eerily undefined.

'Is this make-up too ... showy?' the Prime Minister asks Campbell. Campbell reaches into his Eve Arden leather clutch-bag for a little concealer. He sets about applying make-up to reduce the effect of the previous make-up. 'Eyes to the ceiling,' he says, and the Prime Minister obeys without a murmur. Campbell reaches into his clutch-bag for the eye-liner stick marked 'Statesmanlike' and begins to apply it with all the seasoned care of a true professional.

SIR PETER STOTHARD*

June 12th

I watch football for purely aesthetic reasons, as though I were viewing a kinetic sculpture or abstract light show. The things I watch for are all contained in quadrilaterals, concern the movement of round balls, and the shifting lines of force and energy made by the players' movements.

Watching Gareth Barry pass to Dean Ashton in the mid-season friendly against Finland, I was reminded inescapably of that wonder-

---

*From *Eyewitless to History: On the Road to Victory in Iraq.*

ful collage of blue and yellow seahorses by Henri Matisse, or, perhaps more tellingly, Vermeer's truly sublime *Young Woman Reading a Letter at an Open Window*. Is she, one wonders, truly pregnant? Or is she in reality hiding a Dutch football beneath her peasant blouse?

A.S. BYATT

I got to go see an execution, it was so great. Roy Cohn phoned to say he'd got the tickets from J. Edgar Hoover, who didn't want to go himself because then he'd have to miss the party for Martha Graham that Margaret Trudeau was giving in the Village, but I'm kind of bored by Martha now so I said I'd take the tickets and I asked Candy along, she was so thrilled, said she'd never been to an execution before, not even a minor one.

So the cab ($32) took us to New Jersey State Penitentiary and we got there in good time with great seats right at the front and just a little to the left. After a bit of waiting, this guy was led in, no one I knew, he had a terrible haircut, and they sat him in the chair and someone must have pulled a lever backstage because then he went all jerky and died, it only took a few minutes at most, so I said 'Is that it? We've come all this way just for that?' It was kind of a disappointment, I guess. In the cab on the way back ($32) we ate peanuts, dry-roasted, which was great.*

ANDY WARHOL

---

*Andy Warhol's *Man Undergoing Electrocution No. 53* sold for $21 million at auction in September 2009. This is the highest price yet recorded for a Warhol Execution Portrait. It is now hanging in the VIP area of the Hard Rock Café in Cleveland, Ohio, alongside the Fender guitar played by Jeff Beck on his classic hit 'Hi Ho Silver Lining'.

June 13th

On, or should I say 'aboard', a train the other day, I was gently wondering why on earth a motorcar is called a motorcar (what, perchance, is, or are, a 'moto', and what in heaven's name can a 'rcar' be?: the mind quite literally boggles!) when a ticket-collector came lurching into view.

'Ticket please,' he enunciated, holding out a machine which looked for all the world like one of those contraptions great aunts were once in the habit of employing for retrieving stones from the hooves of gee-gees.

'Might I be forgiven for thinking that your over-riding purpose at the present time is to cast a beady eye over my railway ticket, or absence thereof?' I inquired with due geniality.

'Ticket please, sir!' he replied, a mite testily I thought, holding out an ungloved hand for my inspection.

'Come, come, my dear fellow,' I said. 'A little more specificity – if such word exists! – might help matters immeasurably. A ticket to the Proms? A ticket by rickshaw to Timbuktu? Please define your terms before venturing into such a veritable menagerie of possibilities.'

As his clenched fist landed on what I suppose I must learn to call my 'hooter', I reflected that all might not be quite right in the baffling world of transport. Alas and alack, my subsequent observation to the incensed collector that he might consider punching my ticket rather than my nasal protuberance resulted in another swift jab, this time to my jaw. Thinking it best to reveal myself to be in full possession of the travel documentation in question, I was driven to wonder whether the art of conversation is a skill much prized by the modern world.

ROBERT ROBINSON

June 14th

What are my plans for the future? I don't think about the future but when I think about the future I'm like, the future's not here and now, and the future's not in the past, the future's like, in the future. And that's like really, really weird.

If I have a baby then I'll definitely be a working mum, but then again being a mum is a full-time job, so I'll have like two full-time jobs, so maybe I'll have to choose between being a mum and working, so the best like compromise is probably to be a working mum. But then again being a mum is a full-time job.

And that's like really really weird.

STELLA McCARTNEY

I've come here to hoity-toity Royal Ascot, don't hog the sausage rolls, love, to see how the other half live. I'm with one of their horses in the snooty paddock, very nice if you can afford it, and at these prices there's not many who can, and what I want to ask this horse is what class it thinks it belongs to – upper, middle or working?

At the moment, it's refusivating to speak to me. Typical. These over-privileged horses won't speak to a bloke they consider's below them. And now it's just standing there on four legs while the rest of us have to make do with just the two, and it's chewing on a raw carrot. That's what they all eat – raw carrot, ooh, very posh, very fashionable – while the rest of us have to make do with pie and chips. Did someone mention meat pie? Ooh, I could murder a meat pie, I love me meat pie, don't stint on the chips.

These snooty upper-class horses, you can just feel them looking down their noses at you, thinking to themselves, what's HE doing here, he didn't go to a private school like what we did where they play polo and sing opera and hang around all day in their tail-coats and their powdered wigs, oh, no, he's definitely working-class, and I'll tell you another thing, I've seen these horses glancing from one to the other, I know their sort, and they're muttervating to each other under their breaths, they're saying, all snobby, 'I say, Algernon, old fellow, who on EARTH let HIM into our naice upper-class horse-box?' and it makes me sick.

JOHN PRESCOTT

June 15th

To tea with Chairman Mao. Do I detect something Chinese about him? Curiously his wardrobe seems not to run to a shirt and tie. I set him at his ease. 'My dear – those are workmen's overalls! But how witty!'

Not so much as a smile in return. I try again. 'Diana tells me Debo ordered no fewer than twenty magnolia cushions for the Blue Room – but they arrived in a simply ghastly shade of cerise!'

It barely registers. One sometimes wonders why one bothers.

JAMES LEES-MILNE

June 16th

JOHN: What do we mean when we say we feel 'happy'?

ROBIN: It's probably best described as feeling the opposite of 'sad'. Most people are 'happy' some of the time and 'sad' some of the time. But most of the time they feel somewhere 'in-between'.

JOHN: Neither very happy nor very sad?

ROBIN: Quite so.

JOHN: And what comes after the letter 'D' in the ABC?

ROBIN: For most people, 'E'.

JOHN: And then 'F'?

ROBIN: Usually.

JOHN: And is 'E' a happy letter? Or a sad one?

ROBIN: Probably somewhere in between.

JOHN: I suppose that in many ways it's infantile and regressive to talk about letters being 'happy' or 'sad'.

ROBIN: Certainly.

JOHN: After all, they're only letters. They have their off-days like everybody else.

JOHN CLEESE AND ROBIN SKINNER

June 17th

Others may have found him tiresome, but Captain Hook was always frightfully sweet to me.

It was a moonlit night. A piano was gently tinkling somewhere far away.

'You are so very lovely, my dear,' he said, 'and I do so want to place my arm around you.'

With that, he placed his right arm around my shoulder. Alas, his prominent hook, never his strong point, caught the strap of my brassiere and then with a resounding snap unloosed my ballgown.

I stood naked on the dance floor.

Among the assembled onlookers were the Governor of the Bank of England, Lord Beaverbrook, the Duke of Devonshire and the Admiral of the Fleet, all of them interesting people.

Before the tune had drawn to an end, all four of them had requested my hand in marriage.

I never saw Hook again, but I will always remember him as someone rather special.

BARBARA CARTLAND

Today I get to do a bit of your actual straight-up-and-down honest-to-goodness steady-as-she-goes your-place-or-mine motoring. It's the new Bluebeard HRT that's waiting for Clarkson today, and from the look of her she's positively raring to go, like a Dutch airhostess, brunette, hair done up in plaits, full lips, pert as hell, who's been stuck on trolley duty since Bangkok.

You ain't seen nothin' yet. Oh boy. You can say that again, mate. In my twenty-year career in motoring, I've never seen nothin' like this babe. Let me tell you this, if this car was a woman, she'd be on her back and gagging for it before you could say Peugeot CDM.

I lollop hard down on the shaft-neck, strike the fuchsia into suction, drag on the marrowbone and before I know it I'm clocking up fifty aspidistras on the zimmer. Slam on the footstool, into third and then it's easy on the old scrofula. The underwench is looking good, the V-neck is great, and one glance at the thrombosis tells me the entire Preston Candover is pure state-of-the-art.

Into fourth, and it's basting the turkey all the way. The grasshopper's pulling on my left leg, the scavenger is coming along nicely, and all that's between me and the road is the well-cooked sprout. Boy, is this one hell of a sexy hedgehog!

I'm up into fifth now, giving it the full aspirin, and the baby's mewling like a woodlouse. Heavy on the camiknickers, and she's taking the corner like a bantam. You can forget all that stuff about the antelopes, because this lemon-squeezer could shuffle a six-pack and still have change for a scarecrow. Phew – and to think I might have left my duck-warbler in the snuffle-shank.

JEREMY CLARKSON

June 18th

To the far-flung reaches of Kent to record an edition of *Any Questions?*. The audience seems to appreciate my languid humour and my rather droll delivery, coupled with my pleasantly 'anti-establishment' opinions, delivered in mercifully aristocratic tones.

'I think that Colonel Gaddafi is perfectly beastly,' I say, 'and Saddam Hussein of Iraq seems to me like an awful prig. But, on a more serious note, Jonathan, might I add that I deplore the killing of innocent people?'

This goes down well with the studio audience, who clap and cheer, so I add: 'And may I also say how passionately I care for this great country of ours?'

Another enthusiastic round of applause. 'And one final point: I don't mind admitting that I simply adore freedom of speech. Goodnight and God bless.'

At the end of the show, the good people in the audience clamour for signed copies of my most recent book, *Rumpole Pops Over to Tuscany*. An immensely civilised occasion, a far cry from the rooftop protest at Strangeways that has come to symbolise so much of what is wrong with Thatcher's Britain. Prisons are perfectly ghastly places, much like I imagine Marbella to be(!). I would have been on that rooftop myself, had not my attendance at a Foyle's Literary Luncheon been arranged some months ago.

JOHN MORTIMER

All things come from within us; except that which comes from without.

SHIRLEY MACLAINE

June 19th

I'm composing my next project, a screen version of *The Life of James Last*, the brilliant – controversial! – and hopelessly misunderstood Scandinavian orchestral leader who lived for his music as no other man had ever done and sweated blood to conjure up his own mad and incredible vision of things. I've called it – controversially! – *Lastomania!* and it opens on the Golden Gate Bridge, transposed to the Swiss fjords, where James Last (played by Oliver Reed) is practising frantically with his baton as the rain thunders down in loud guitar-bursts:

MRS LAST: Oh James, James, James! Have you not suffered enough? Must you always live for music! Music! Music! and nothing else? Let us to bed! (Mrs Last removes her leather one-piece costume decked out in swastikas. Beneath it is another leather one-piece costume decked out in swastikas) Take me, maestro!

JAMES LAST (pulling out a thirty-foot-high phallic symbol, dousing it with petrol and setting fire to it): Not now, dear! Before the dawn cometh, I must, must, must finish my new work, *Non-Stop-Party-Hits-A-Go-Go Volume 10*, or my very creative juices will fail me and I will shrivel to nothing! Art is torture!

MRS LAST: Your music is a hymn to nature, sure enough, James Last. But what about me? Do I not have my own needs and desires, husband? You may have conquered the world of easy listening, James – but still you cannot conquer your own wife! (Mrs Last erupts in a mad cackle. She strips off and dives naked into the fjord, which becomes awash with the bodies of dead nuns. Choking on her own vomit, she struggles desperately and drowns. The stirring soundtrack is – poignantly – Last's own version of 'Build Me Up, Buttercup'.)

JAMES LAST: Did you say something, dear? You see, like many mad and crazy artists, I sometimes become so involved in the act of creation that I am prone to neglect those around me. But at least the new album will be arranged by tomorrow, and that's the main thing, eh dear? Dear? Dear? (Suddenly he realises that his wife is floating face-down beneath the bodies of dead nuns) Oh my God! What have I done for my art?

Not a bad scene-setter, eh? By a series of subtle hints and juxtapositions, here a clever metaphor, there a suggestive symbol, I introduce the viewer to the massive torments and contradictions in the paradoxical character of James Last – his passionate love of music coupled with his inability to reach out beyond fantasy into a darker reality. By the end of the first scene, he has composed his next album, his wife has drowned and his penis has been set on fire. And then things really start happening.

KEN RUSSELL

One takes care to watch *Neighbours* on the television. I've always had a special place in my heart for the poor people in the East End of London, and that's where it's set. They all have the most delicious cockney accents, reminding me of the time I visited the brave little

East End during the war. It seems much sunnier now, I must say, so perhaps I will visit it again soon. They absolutely adore the Royal Family there, you know, bless them: we lend colour to their lives.

**HM QUEEN ELIZABETH
THE QUEEN MOTHER**

June 20th

As I grow older, I find myself taking up interests that, in my youth, I might well have eschewed as immature. Until last week, for instance, I had never felt the need to tie my own shoelaces, finding it more convivial to employ someone else for the purpose. The Moggs, true to their Somerset blood, have never set much store by the base technicalities of existence. Consequently the art of tying a shoelace was one I never learned. As a child for a short while, and then as Editor of *The Times*, Vice Chairman of the BBC, Chairman of the Arts Council and later Deputy Chairman of the Milk Marketing Board, I found that employing someone else for the chore saved me time I could usefully spend on rereading and improving the great works of Peruvian literature.

But in Wessex we have a particular love of walking, and this, last Sunday, was to prove my – and my shoelaces' – undoing. As I was perambulating in a meadow, reflecting that Edward Heath might still be Prime Minister to this day if only he had followed my advice on the Gold Standard, I noticed to my horror that my right shoelace was utterly undone.

What was I to do? My Latin education – even my Presidency of the Oxford Union and later Vice-Presidency of the Mothers' Union, followed by a holiday job as Chairman of the World Bank – had not prepared me in any way for this fearful eventuality. It seems to me that Plato, for all his admirable efforts in other fields, teaches us little about shoelaces. At first, I attempted to stumble on, but in so doing fell face downwards into a circular pool of mud, marking the spot where a cow had been recently standing. I then fiddled with the laces, but found that my mind existed on too high a plane to be able to deal with such hapless threads.

At last, the solution came to me: I removed my trousers, tore them neatly in two, and then knotted each trouser leg around each shoe. Though slightly bumpy, my walk back was hugely enjoyable and enlivened by a fine breeze circulating around my legs and lower regions. Henceforth, I will be urging the present Cabinet when next they come to see me to do away with shoelaces. This will have the effect of taking our minds off the recession, and so sterling will recover in no time at all. In many ways, life is like a great shoelace, useful only when done up, standing for what it stands for, a solid yet impermanent knot.

WILLIAM REES-MOGG

June 21st

There was a constant parade of visitors to the house in Chester Square so we bought another in Cheyne Walk, and when that began to fill up we moved to Eaton Square. So we now have three houses, all full of heads and freaks, but Mick hates untidiness, so he says we have to move anyone who isn't still breathing out of the upstairs bathroom and into the basement. I'm secretly involved with Spanish Tony who doesn't realise I am also intimately attached to Japanese Frank, who has no idea I'm having a scene with Nicol Williamson, from whom I'm keeping my on-off relationship with Hurricane Higgins a firm secret, as I'm worried that if he finds out he'll tell Moroccan Herbert, who's intensely jealous of Freddie and the Dreamers, with whom I'm beginning to grow heavily involved, and I'm at all costs determined to preserve my dignity.

MARIANNE FAITHFULL

A game I used to enjoy playing with Aunt Phyl was one of our own invention. We called it 'Numbers'. I would think of a number between one and a hundred. Aunt Phyl would then have to guess what it was. On one memorable occasion, it took her eighty-four guesses before she came up with the correct number, which was thirty-nine! On another memorable occasion, it took her seventy-two guesses before she came up with the correct number, which was fifty-one! After precisely an hour and a half, timed on a kitchen clock bought by my great-grandmother in Sheffield in 1876, we would switch roles, and it would be Aunt Phyl's turn to think of the number, and my turn to guess what it was. We always made a point of playing this game around a little low oblong table in the front room, even though the game did not require a table. I forget why.

MARGARET DRABBLE

I am a serious.

It is novels that I usually write: what I usually write is novels. And you know why I write? I write to fill the chiliastic lacuna of the aberrant psychotheatre in my headipops.

And it all adds up to one thing.

I am a serious.

MARTIN AMIS

June 22nd

Say what you like about King Ethelred, he was always ready.

SIR EDWARD HEATH

June 23rd

Khartoum. Another place with an 'h' in an odd place in its name! I suppose that's just my somewhat Pythonesque, surreal way of looking at things! After a very comfortable night, I meet some marvellous old characters in the main square of the town. 'Do you enjoy it here?' I ask them. 'Yes,' they reply. I come away with the firm impression that they enjoy it here!

Africa is a vast country, with great distances between one spot and another – far greater than the distance between, say, Nuneaton and East Croydon! Still, you've got to laugh. It's only by taking this humorous approach to things that one can see the world for what it is – a vast sort of globe, full of all sorts of places which might be fun to visit.

After some highly concentrated investigation by your intrepid traveller, I discover that 'Khartoum' is not in fact the place where the 'cartoon' was invented. My fellow-Python Terry Gilliam will be much distressed by this news, methinks!

In the evening, after filming me wearing a totally barmy hat a researcher picked up somewhere, we watch the sun setting over the horizon: a literally indescribable sight.

MICHAEL PALIN

June 24th

They tell me they have now developed railway trains jam-packed with hundreds of seats. This means that ordinary travellers are obliged to travel hugger-mugger with hundreds of complete strangers, regardless of whether they are family. Nor is there a drawing room where one might relax by oneself with a good book. It sometimes seems to me that the people in charge of these things haven't the foggiest idea of what ordinary people want. Railways always represented the most perfectly civilised way to travel around the country in silence whilst enjoying one's own company. Alas, I fear those days may be gone forever.

HRH THE PRINCE OF WALES

June 25th

Tragic Michael Jackson has died tragically. Mike was a lovely, lovely bloke. I first met him when he was a complete unknown. He came to me as a tot, a lovely little tot, and he said to me, 'Max, I want to become the world's biggest star pursued by demons before dying tragically aged fifty.'

I said to him, 'Michael,' I said, 'Michael, leave it to your Uncle Max.'

The rest is the proverbial history. Back then, he didn't have the foggiest how to sing and dance. Not the foggiest. He had two left feet and a squeaky little voice. But I taught him those fantastic steps, and gave him a lesson or two in singing. Result? The whole world adored him before going off him and then he tragically perished.

Yes, I made the man what he is today.

Now all we are left with is cherished memories of Michael and, between ourselves, fantastic video footage of his autopsy.

MAX CLIFFORD

Jackson could dance like there was no tomorrow, and, like no tomorrow, he could dance. His moonwalk was the walk that made you moan. And then it made you walk. When he walked on the moon, it was as if the moon itself could walk. He sang 'Got to be There', and there is where he had got to be. And even when he was not all there, he was certainly here. Now he is no longer here, but hear him we still can. He longed to heal the world, and it was on his heels that he whirled for so long.

CLIVE JAMES

It is fair, in my opinion, to say that Michael Jackson – one of the Indiana Jacksons – will soon get over this latest setback to his career. He has never allowed himself to be the victim of trauma or neurosis. He is, by all accounts, a robust and healthy young man, with a pleasingly straight-forward outlook on life. It seems clear to me that, despite his reported death, he has rarely been in better shape. All the signs suggest that he will bring renewed vigour and panache to the fifty-or-so concerts he has planned for the O_2 arena. Some commentators have predicted the cancellation of some or all of these concerts. My own view is that his premature death, such as it is, will interfere very little, if at all, with his innovative and undeniably popular song-and-dance routines.

WILLIAM REES-MOGG

He touched a lot of young people in a lot of different ways.

The sudden death of this Dionysus, this Orpheus, this Midas, this Canute, this Colossus, is a strange kind of victory. Instead of entering middle age and letting himself be chained to earth, Michael has floated away like a wisp, annihilated on the brink of a fifty-date concert tour that I for one was dreading.

I wasn't there for Michael when he died, and that's something I'll always regret. I would have held him to my chest and kissed him, not so as to revive him – his young heart did not want to grow old – but so as to let him know that he was cherished, just as Persephone was cherished, and Ulysses too. And we might have taken one final dance together, Michael and I, with Michael clutched to my bosom like Clytemnestra.

But it was not to be. Michael is no more. Yet in another way, he is with us for all time. When I sing, it will be Michael singing. When I dance, it will be Michael dancing. When I touch people, it will be Michael touching people.

GERMAINE GREER

June 26th

Many good friends beg me for any tips I may have on how to get leggings on quicker. My in-house leggings guru advises rubbing five spoonfuls of extra virgin olive oil with turbinado sugar and coarsely ground coffee onto your legs in advance.

GWYNETH PALTROW

Polly put the kettle on,
Polly put the kettle on
Polly put the kettle on
Polly put the kettle on
Polly put the kettle on
Look here, Polly, chum,
How many more fucking times
Do I have to tell you
To put that fucking kettle on?

HAROLD PINTER

Word reaches one that President Amin has been forced into retirement. Idi had a remarkably sensitive eye for Tang Dynasty chinaware. Of course, his country never stopped giving him trouble. But he was a man of great character, and he never allowed his tiresome people to distract him from amassing a most impressive private collection of exquisite vases.

Some say now Amin was a cannibal, that he enjoyed consuming his enemies. That may be so, but he was also a great gourmet, and would have made sure that they were cooked to the highest possible standard. Nor should we allow these minor details to distract us from his very real charm. Do not let's carp. Historians may argue, with the benefit of hindsight, that I should have taken a leaf from his book and consumed Margaret Thatcher during her disastrous spell as my Secretary of State for Education. But I did not have the necessary implements. Besides, I can't abide gristle.

SIR EDWARD HEATH

June 27th

Catch up on the latest Philip Roth while in the taxi to a meeting with Gilbert and George, to catch up on their latest mammoth artwork, the truly magnificent *SodArse*, made entirely out of used faeces and tulips.

While catching up on the Roth – and, take it from me, it's truly irresistible, what a great writer he is, enjoying a brilliant Indian summer – I catch up on the latest Arctic Monkeys on my iPod, and am once again amazed by those guys' versatility and sheer youthful energy. Catching up on the Arctics, I manage to catch up on my latest Armani suit at the same time: a fine new ultra-contemporary cut, retro-modernism at its best.

ALAN YENTOB

There is no great writer or painter who is not at heart an African. 'To be or not to be' – the rich reggae rhythm is undeniable.

MAYA ANGELOU

June 28th

Sandringham. Up at 7 o'clock. Not much sun. Luncheon with Mama and then to my stamp collection.

Bacon puts his head round the door to inform me that the Archduke Franz Ferdinand and his wife have been assassinated. No further interruptions until tea-time.

My new stamps from our dominion New Zealand look splendid on the page.

Bed at 10.45.

HM KING GEORGE V

Every time I get a letter, I say to myself that she never asked to be put on those stamps, she's a very private lady, but everyone jumps on the bandwagon and they gag her and they say, 'You're bloody well going on those stamps or else,' and so they push her to the edge and they make money out of her misery. She's been waving at us for help for so long but we've ignored her but now I intend to take a stand. I'm going in there and saying to her, 'Look, you've been Queen for long enough. You must be going out of your mind. It's time someone else took over. Pass me that crown, love, and we'll say no more about it.'

HEATHER MILLS McCARTNEY

June 29th

London Weekend sends me the tape of my *Audience with Rod Stewart*. Bloody brill! They love me!

(Rod enters. Applause. More applause. Rod turns round and wiggles his bottom at the audience. Standing ovation)

ROD: Woooh! (Pause) Nah, bollocks!
AUDIENCE: Hahahahahahahahaha!
ROD: Woooh! Any ques-tee-o-nez, nah? Make it all above board, will ya? Nah. Bollocks!
AUDIENCE: Hahahahahahahahaha!
ROD: Me old mate, the late, great Ronnie Wood! The legendary Woody! Rock 'n' roll! Nah! Yeah, mate?
WOODY: Burp! Gorra bidda wind, Rod! Hahahahaha!
AUDIENCE: Hahahahahahahahaha! (Wolf whistles)
WOODY: Burp! Nah, Rod, wodda wonnid to arse wuz – air ye doin', mate?
ROD: Couldn't arf do wiv a right good shaggin', mate! Nah! Bollocks!

(Raucous laughter. Standing ovation)

ROD: Here's a song written by me old mate wossisname – the crafty old shagger!!! Nah!

Ah m say-lin
Ah m say-lin
Harm gen crass d seey
Ah m say-lin
Starmy wart tuz

T be wiv yer
T be freey
Ah m flar-yin
Ah m flar-yin
Harm gen crass d seey

(Applause. More applause. Cheers. Catcalls)

ROD: Wooh! Yeah! Anyone gorra quessie for me? Yeah – the bird in the third row with the nice tits! Ha! Ha! You smooth-talkin' ladykiller, Rod, you! Nah!

(Laughter. Applause)

ULRIKA JONSSON: Rod …
ROD: Hi, darlin'!
AUDIENCE: Hahahahahahahahaha!
ULRIKA JONSSON: Rod, what's the most fun you've ever had ever in the whole of your life in the entire history of the world bar none?
ROD: Can't beat a good shaggin', love! Nah, seerzly, lez think, I dunno, I carn answer that, nah –
WOODY: You old goat, Rod, mate!

(Laughter. Applause)

ROD: Down boy! Hahahaha! Nah! Great mate – lays an gennelmen – the legendary Woody!

(Applause)

ROD: Please wowcum – Baby Spice!

(Applause)

ROD (singing): Cumarn angel ma harse on far
BABY SPICE (singing): En doan denar yermar desaar
ROD: Spread y wins and lemme carm insaard

BOTH:

> Tonaarght's the naarght!
> Tonaarght's the naarght!
> Sgonnabe yallraaaght!
> Tonaarght's the naarght!
> Tonaarght's the naarght!

ROD: Wooh!

(Standing ovation. Catcalls)

ROD (sings):

> Way kup Mageh ar thing
> Ar gos umfin ter say chew
> Slay Setember an ah
> Really shoobe backa skoo

(Applause. Yells. Catcalls)

DESMOND LYNAM: Rod, despite all your success, you've managed to remain an ordinary bloke with both feet firmly on the ground. How d'you manage it?

ROD: I shag the wife somethin' rotten! Hahahaha! Wicked! Nah, seerzly, I'm a normal bloke, like my birds, like a glass or six of the old boozey-woozey …

WOODY: Make mine a pint, Rod! Hahahaha!

(Audience cheers and laughter)

ROD: The legenry Mister Ronnie Wood, lays an gennelmen! Nah, but we live a normal life, go darn the pub. Well, we don't actually go darn the pub, nah, we get the landlord to dismantle the pub, bring it to our place in a container lorry and reassemble it at our place, just for the sake of convenience, know what I mean? Nah. Here's one yer might recognise. Cheers.

ROD (sings):

Dooyer thin Karm sek see
Just ree chout an tarch me
Carmon baby lair me know

(Wiggles bottom. Applause. More applause)

ROD: Bollocks! Hahahahahaha! Ta-ra! See you darn the boozer! Hahahahaha! Classic!

(Audience rise to their feet, cheering and clapping. Camera pans around celebrity audience of Rod's contemporaries, all swaying in rough time to the beat, including Alan Freeman, Jimmy Savile, Angela Rippon, Douglas Hurd, Janet Street-Porter, Quintin Hailsham, Kenneth Kendall and Penelope Keith.)

ROD STEWART

June 30th

Hong Kong. To dinner with Governor Patten. He has been my Governor here for a good many years now, following his outstanding success in introducing our Community Charge to a grateful British people.

'If you'll just let me finish,' I say to his wife, Mrs Patten, when she offers me a canapé before the meal. 'It's never advisable to wear your hair like that. Your type of hair is much better short. Otherwise it gets in the eyes, and one can't have that.'

After another glass of Scotch, I set about solving the poor woman's curtain problem. 'You don't want them overflowing at the bottom, dear,' I am good enough to advise her. 'That way, they gather dust. You want them cut off an inch to an inch-and-a-half above the floor. That way, the dust drops to the ground – and your dust problem is solved!!'

I dip into my handbag for my trusty pair of kitchen scissors. I never go anywhere without them, not since 1983, when I asked Francis Pym to leave my Cabinet and the poor man proved difficult.

MARGARET THATCHER

News comes through of John Aspinall's death. Aspers, as he was affectionately known, was my lifelong inspiration and guide to the wonderment and beauty of animals. His private zoo was quite marvellous, and he was lucky enough to employ a range of devoted keepers who would think nothing of having the odd arm or leg bitten off now and then. Inevitably, there was the odd cry-baby. When one of them came running up to Aspers whining that his friend's head had just been ripped off by a playful lion, Aspers simply said 'Just a scratch!' – and placed the errant head back on the keeper's neck! Needless to say, it fell off soon afterwards – that's keepers for you! – but at least the incident gave us all the most tremendous hoot!

ANNABEL GOLDSMITH

July

July 1st, 1923

My dear Lady Cholmondley,

I cannot thank you enough for that simply splendid picnic you gave us yesterday. We both thoroughly enjoyed ourselves. The food was delicious and the situation idyllic. We are tremendously grateful to you for the abundance of your generosity. My only regret is that you and your guests refused to follow my entreaties and enter into the spirit of things by throwing off your clothes and dancing naked under the blazing sun before throwing yourselves headlong into intercourse. I was left to go behind a bush to put my clothes back on. And the god Priapus howled in pain.

Is masturbation your only real interest, woman? That is the message you signalled to me – you were lurking in your clothes as a skeleton lurks in its coffin! Do you suffer like your fellow-countrymen from the grey disease of sex-hatred? Why do you refuse to surrender to the sacred sex-flame of life? Instead, you insist on you and your fellow picnickers 'engaging in nice conversation' – as though this miserable globe was not already sinking in the steamy excrement of 'nice conversation'!

My God, this country of ours! Propriety will see that we starve to death regardless of how many grey, morose dishes are laid before us. Away with your death-desiring picnics, you slattern! Have you no impulse to love?

Oh, and might I add how very clever you were to pick such a perfect location. The meadows at this time of year are particularly lovely, don't you find?

Thank you again for the most thoroughly enjoyable day.

Yours ever,

David

D.H. LAWRENCE,
LETTER TO LADY CHOLMONDLEY

July 2nd

Reread *Hamlet* by Shakespeare, a competent but unreliable author, though now rather dated and always prone to wordiness. Never to my knowledge managed a novel. *Hamlet* is a not uninteresting play, but the plot is flawed. The Danes are really extremely minor royalty, even by Scandinavian standards; scarcely worth a lengthy play. Tremendous hoo-ha in final scenes, characteristic of a particular sort of empty-kettle Dane. Prince Hamlet wouldn't have lasted long in Pratt's, where Danish royalty is taken with a fairly hefty pinch of salt. 'Hamlet', a peculiar name – any relation, one wonders, to the Fotherington-Hamlets of Much Hadham? Much to-ing and fro-ing with ghosts, incest, madness and so forth – always the sign of a writer grasping at straws. I would guess that Shakespeare stole many of his more notable lines from the immortal titles in my own 'Dance to the Music of Time' sequence. But I should hate to pass judgement.

ANTHONY POWELL

'More tea, Prime Minister?'

The Queen sat on one chair, the Prime Minister on the other. Buckingham Palace has 775 rooms, including nineteen state rooms and seventy-eight bathrooms, but today the hand of fate had brought them – the ashen-faced Queen and her white-knuckled Prime Minister – together in the same room.

Both of them knew, deep down, that it would be at best unseemly and at worst politically catastrophic to be found sitting on a single chair. The ravenous press would have a field day if they found the two of them on the same chair, Gordon Brown perched on the Monarch's lap. So, in a mammoth PR operation, two chairs – one each – had been put in place. Any disappointment either person felt at this enforced physical separation – and insiders, including at least one former Home Secretary, are at pains to stress that there was 'none at all', as they 'barely knew each other' – would be at least partially assuaged by the knowledge that the country was on the brink of a seismic earthquake of titanic proportions.

And, their panic-stricken advisers warned them, this was one earthquake that would not vanish in a puff of smoke. No: it was an iceberg, and an iceberg that was waiting for the music to stop – to make way for the gathering storm.

'I don't mind if I do, Ma'am,' seethed Gordon Brown. He glared down at his shoes. Black lace-ups, they had been bought by his wife Sarah at the New Bond Street branch of Russell and Bromley for £89.50 at a sale the previous January. Also in the sale were brown leather zip-up boots with Cuban heels, offered at £169 a pair, but, offering no explanation, even to her closest friends, Sarah Brown had decided against them.

He held out his cup for more tea. If he dropped the cup now, the delicate china would be sure to smash into a million pieces, possibly sending lethal shards into Brown's sole remaining eye. He had already lost one eye. He knew – as everyone close to him knew – that he could ill-afford to lose another. This realisation turned that teacup into a ticking time bomb. If he dropped it now, he could be plunged into eternal darkness. There was no doubt about it: this was the single most important tea-refill of his political career.

The scalding tea gushed out of the expensive Palace teapot with all the hellish fury of a woman scorned. With deft handling born of years of experience, Gordon Brown caught it in his cup. Now he could breathe again. He wanted to put an issue on the clear blue ground between them. Then, and only then, could they dance around it.

'Milk, Prime Minister?' the Queen stonewalled. From the other side of the fully-carpeted room, an unnamed corgi glowered manically. The tail of this short dog – insiders insist the breed was introduced to Wales by Flemish weavers in the Middle Ages – beat uncontrollably against the side of its basket, a bleak reminder of catastrophic times ahead.

Gordon Brown's in-built radar spiralled into overdrive. He realised instinctively that the woman opposite expected an answer – and fast. Behind that demure sovereign-like exterior simmered a boiling cauldron of know-how. The world-famous Queen of the United Kingdom and the British Isles had not held onto her power-base at the uppermost storey of the British political ladder for over half a century without knowing how to out-manoeuvre her opponents into checkmate. Should Brown demand milk – or not? One wrong move and he could find himself trumped into the double-whammy of a lethal own-goal. It was a power struggle he could not afford to lose.

'Yes, please, Ma'am,' he thundered. The unnamed corgi suppressed a terrified whinny. He knew, as well as anyone, the dangers that lay in making his feelings clear. Only a few short centuries ago a previous monarch had offered his kingdom for a horse. What price a corgi?

The die was cast. The Queen seized the milk jug by the neck. In a split second, the milk was flowing mercilessly into the tea. Never had a cup felt more isolated or more poured-upon. Now there was no going back. This was to prove the most important top-up of Brown's political life.

A dark pall descended over the Palace like a hammer blow on a learning curve. The Prime Minister grabbed a teaspoon. In Downing Street, he had become notorious for his ruthless way with teaspoons. 'He would use them. You'd see him just stirring and stirring. And then he'd just put them to the side of the saucer and forget about them,' recalls one top aide with a shudder.

And then it happened. Brown's rabid stirring – the most singularly ruthless stir one observer had ever witnessed – whipped the stricken tea into an unstoppable whirlpool of mayhem and discontent. Some witnesses recall seeing at least two tiny ships – a passenger liner and a luxury yacht – frantically sending out anguished distress signals from somewhere close to the middle of the hurricane. Others looked on helplessly as a miniature rescue helicopter was engulfed by the unforgiving waves. This was nothing short of a typhoon in the Ty-phoo.

'I've literally never seen anything like it,' recalls one terrified observer, reeling from the blows. 'There's only one way to describe it: a storm in a teacup.'

ANDREW RAWNSLEY

July 3rd

You know why they calling it Henley Regatta? No? I tell you. Name after multi-murdering English King Henley VIII. That no way to treat wives, rest your head here my dear, whoops my axe it slip, what shame, you lost your head in bucket, weep weep, now I marry my girlfriend, OK? That no way behave. How English letting him get away I want to know – and then they naming Regatta after this crook like he some kind of VIP.

Henley Regatta very crowding, so many people, women, homos, the lot, all chatter-chatter, so everyone want getting away as fast as poss but I tell you my friend no one can getting away because so many traffic is all jam. So what they do? Only escape is on water – so clever ones, they give two fingers to Establishment, yes, they hire skinny boats and make getaway fast possible by river, so they no having chatter-chitter and eat bloody strawberries no more.

MOHAMED AL FAYED

A mild case of the squitters. Write it in my diary. The public has a right to know. And I'm putting it in the diary for all women, everywhere. For too long, these things have been brushed to one side. It's the most hard-pressed people in the community, those with fully-fledged diarrhoea, that I feel most sorry for. I am determined to make their voice heard.

EDWINA CURRIE

July 4th

To Cuba. I am immediately struck by how very Cuban it all is.

Fidel Castro honours us with a truly splendid dinner. I sit next to the great man himself. He has a truly splendid beard. 'There's something I really must know,' I say to him over the first course. 'Do tell – have you read the new Joanna Trollope yet?' Fidel tells me – through an interpreter – that he hasn't. I tell him he simply must, she really is truly splendid at the turmoils besetting the middle-to-upper-middle classes in the Cotswolds. He tells me he has never been to the Cotswolds, which I must say I find quite astonishing. I tell him he'd adore it, and when he does go he simply must stay in a truly splendid hotel there ('one of our absolute favourites') called Château Talbot. 'It's where Harold wrote his poem "Crap",' I tell him, and he's obviously fascinated.

Harold, sitting across from us, hears his name mentioned. Like me, he is simply astonished that Fidel hasn't read 'Crap', so he calls for silence by smashing a glass and reads it out, quite brilliantly, lending wonderful emphasis to those magical last three lines –

> And it's not just my crap
> It's your crap and their crap
> That bungs us all up good and proper, chum

– by banging his head on the table.

Needless to say, everyone is terribly appreciative. Harold tells Fidel that 'Crap' still hasn't been published in a major American newspaper. 'I'm afraid – deeply afraid – that that's the kind of regime we're dealing with,' he says. 'If there's one thing they can't abide, it's free speech.'

I join in. 'I adore free speech, don't you?' I say. 'So much better than expensive speech, especially at a time when things are getting so pricy! My new Jean Muir culottes cost me £600 – and that was in the sale!'

Everybody around the table nods in agreement, greeting my little *aperçu* with respectful silence.

All in all, an evening of great jollity.

LADY ANTONIA FRASER

July 5th

Acting's a dreamerooni, so I always try to get my feet back on the ground after a hard day's sweat on set. I meet close friends for a drink and talk about ordinary down-to-earth things like acting and films and future roles and so on. Tonight, I relax over a drinky-fucking-poos with Uma Thurman and Gary Oldman. We exchange views on Sean Connery and Julia Roberts with Tim Robbins and Val Kilmer, who are staying with Lauren Bacall, who told them she just loved *Withnail* – very humbling. Later, I need a bit of exercise and meditation, so I walk down Sunset Boulevard with Steve Martin, and we quietly share our euphoria about, among other things, Marty S. And Dan Day-Lewis and John Malkovich. Just then, a young boy comes up, looks at Steve and says, 'JEEEZ! You're STEVE MARTIN!' and asks for his autograph. It hits me with a jolt that these people – ordinary guys, personal friends of mine – are seen as so SPECIAL by members of the public, who love to DROP their NAMES! How odd people are, and what a bizarre, upside down, crazy, wobble-inducing world this Hollywood stuff really is. I determine to tell this to Barbra Streisand if ever the day comes – JUST THINKING ABOUT IT MAKES ME GASP FOR BREATH – when I am privileged to meet that SCREEN-BLOODY-GODDESS.

RICHARD E. GRANT

July 6th

There seemed little doubt that the tour had been an outstanding success. Queen Elizabeth had embarked on it a joyous, vivacious and delightful wife and mother. She emerged from it a delightful, vivacious and joyous mother and wife, but expert observers noticed an added enchantment, natural dignity and radiant beauty.

But there was to be no let-up in her hectic schedule. All were agreed that there was not a worker in the nation who toiled as hard as she. Just five days after her return, she was booked to attend a luncheon in her honour with a few close friends at the Savoy Hotel. 'The poor woman must have been exhausted,' remembers one of those in attendance, 'but she refused to show it.'

She arrived at the Savoy dressed informally in a white satin dress with square *décolletage* and puff sleeves flounced with old lace, embroidered over the previous three years by elderly members of the Royal School of Needlework with diamanté emblems of the British Isles and Empire. Three rows of gold galloon lace ran around the edge of the train. She was greeted by her old friend Ruth, Lady Fermoy, who showed her to her place at the top of the table, where she sat with a consummate ease born of long tradition.

'I frankly don't know how she did it,' recalled a delighted guest, 'but somehow, in this single perfect gesture, Her Majesty bent her knees and sat down straight onto the chair. I truly can't remember when I last saw someone sitting down so perfectly, and with such ineffable grace.'

The table was presented with a vast meat pie. With her wonderful manners – widely regarded as the most wonderful manners in the world – Queen Elizabeth set her guests at their ease by lifting both hands, as though in a wave, and then plunging her fingers straight into the pie.

'It was a magnificent spontaneous gesture,' one of them recalls. 'Without the slightest bit of fuss or bother, and with an intuitive empathy for the pie, she put both hands straight into that pie. Queen Elizabeth confided in me later that it was a trick she had picked up from her morale-boosting visits to the East End during the war. Lovable Cockneys who had been bombed out of house and home loved to watch this beautifully dressed lady stepping out of her Bentley to share their plight for a few minutes. In return, one of them must have taught her how to stick all one's fingers in a pie. Absolutely delicious and utterly delightful!'

As Ruth, Lady Fermoy struck up a delicious selection of wartime favourites on the Savoy piano, a delighted Queen Elizabeth wriggled her delightful fingers in the delicious pie.

Her simple pleasure was evident to all present. 'Her Majesty's ability to wriggle her fingers about in that pie was both infectious and inspiring,' recorded Lord St John of Fawsley in his diary. 'It was a habit, much enjoyed by her friends, that she had perfected over so many long years of stalwart and dutiful service to the people, both human and native, of the Commonwealth.'

What was it that allowed Queen Elizabeth to stick her fingers in so many pies? Many saw it as her intuitive sense, derived from years of experience, that socialism sought to drag everything down into uniform and unimaginative drabness. To the end, she remained firm in her belief that the pie was best served by her fingers, and hers alone.

Her perspicacious wit remained very much to the fore. 'Oh yummy, yummy!' she remarked, with her trademark spontaneity. With that, she pulled her fingers out of the pie and waved them around and around, to the delight of guests and staff alike. In the corner, Ruth, Lady Fermoy struck up 'Any Old Iron' on the pianoforte, and the delight of the world was unconfined.

WILLIAM SHAWCROSS*

July 7th

Woozy-on-down the street – STRIDESTRIDESTRIDE – just walking along, like an everyday person in this city of drea-fucking-ms, yakyakyaking with Steve (Martin!!!) about the other, that and this. It's one of those magical, hope-filled, fine and gorgeous, yet not really so fine and gorgeous, with an undertow of banality and pessimism, LA-ish sort of LA days, very LA yet with its own kind of particular feel to it that's not really LA at all but yet which also is LA: there's an indefinable SOMETHING to it that's definitely not LA, but not LA in a very LA-ish sort of way. In many ways, it's one of these EASYPEASYLEMONSQUEEZY kind of days when you want to drag someone into your heart and tell them what's REALLY ON YOUR MIND.

---

*From *Most Beloved Ma'am: The Authorised Biography of Queen Elizabeth the Queen Mother.*

'Did I tell you I just loved *The Man with Two Brains*? We've got it on video,' I say to Steve.

'Did I tell you Victoria and I saw *Withnail* twice, no, nearly three times?' says Steve.

We walk on in silence, the raw emotions of two human beings reverberating into the winds like leaves on quite a windy day.

RICHARD E. GRANT

July 8th

Dinner at Mo Mowlam's. The sexual tension is highly charged.

'Piers,' she says. Like everyone in government – Tony, too – she loves rolling my Christian name around her mouth. 'Piers,' she says, 'this is strictly between ourselves, but I hate Peter and Peter hates Gordon and Gordon hates Robin and Robin hates Geoff and Geoff hates David and David hates Jack and Jack hates Peter and Peter hates Gordon – or did I already say that?'

I reassure Mo that her secret's safe with me. When I get home, I jot it down in my diary and send it to my publishers, for safekeeping.

PIERS MORGAN

Dear Diary, It's now summer 1975. My boyfriend Martin Amis has become as famous as his father, and his feelings of profound unattractiveness and physical inadequacy (he sometimes takes a stepladder to parties, just in case he bumps into someone taller, like Dr Jonathan Miller) have given way to a Byronic magnetism. When he leaves a room, metal filings stick to him.

Suddenly, the whole of literary London yearns to go to bed with him. I've spotted tell-tale signs all over the place: Germaine Greer's headband on the hatstand, Andrea Dworkin's thong beside the fur rug, William Golding's beret on the bedside table. I suppose I really only twigged that things were getting out of hand when I walked into our bedroom and found Martin naked in bed with a young woman who didn't seem to have had a book recently published. This was going too far, even for Martin. When I questioned her, she insisted she had written one, but I could find no evidence for it.

JULIE KAVANAGH

July 9th

What happens when galaxies collide? When galaxies collide what happens? What happens when galaxies collide? This is the mega-question, you know: galaxies having collided, happens what? That's the gammily effluent inquisitorial presupposition – the question – that rocks and tosses – never flosses, not now – the veined and corpuscled American football in my skull the neurosurgeons know as my brain, intricate as a spider's web of phlegm, though disappointingly less tasty.

The speed of light is 186,000 mps and one light hour is 670,616,629 miles. This means that when 'Martin Amis' – not me, but 'Martin Amis' – is yearningly staring at the mug-reflector on the ceiling at night (when men cry) and he sees two blackheads – headblacks – protruding from his cheeks like hooded negroes on the prowl and he loftily squeezes them and pounds them and knocks them about and they squirt their tears of pus skywards, and there's a hollow-caustic mess on the mug-reflector, he takes a few seconds to see it. And that's what happens when galaxies collide. When galaxies collide, that's what happens.

MARTIN AMIS

Visiting Cardiff with Her Majesty, I decide after close consideration to wear my dark made-to-measure pinstripe suit with a pink-and-white-spotted tie. It is what people expect. The Queen is wearing her customary coat, dress and hat. I feel desperately embarrassed that my own perfectly judged Savile Row splendour will divert attention from her, but decide on a policy of least said, soonest mended.

'Wales is very important,' she tells me as we sweep into the St Swithin Day Care Centre for the Elderly. I roar with good-natured laughter, and repeat her little joke to the assembled line of nurses so as to 'set them at their ease'.

We are greeted in the day room by a massed band and male voice choir, all performing a fanfare of 'Vivat Regina' while fifty schoolchildren dressed as druids and leeks enact some sort of Welsh pageant. I study the Queen's face throughout: she doesn't yawn or raise her eyes to the ceiling once.

'Very Welsh, Ma'am!' I whisper as the whole effort appears to be drawing to an end. I attempt (unsuccessfully, I may add!) to stifle a giggle at my own jest. I then make my famous comical hand-pinching-the-nose chain-pulling gesture that has set many a dinner table a-roar. Greatly to her credit, Her Majesty manages to maintain a straight face. She then looks at me with what on anyone else would appear to be a furious expression, but which I know to be a face full of natural empathy and good humour.

The Lord Lieutenant tells me Her Majesty's tour of the day care centre for the elderly has been planned meticulously over the past six months. Yet still they couldn't somehow devise a route avoiding all those old people! I decide to 'help her out' by briefing her before each encounter and steering her away from obvious danger zones.

'Ca-veee! Definitely one to avoid, Ma'am!' I hiss in her ear as she approaches an old bird who looks, to my practised eye, a little over-keen on meeting her. But Her Majesty is, sad to say, obviously a mite hard of hearing.

GYLES BRANDRETH

July 10th

And so we move on, as move on we must. No man, no woman, no child, no nation, ever reached his destination by standing still.

The man or woman who stands still stays in the same place. And that place may be a far distance from the place to which they had once intended to travel.

Time and again, men and women have moved on, I tell Malia Ann.

Time and again, these noble men and women have toiled to construct their sandcastles, employing no material but the sand beneath their feet.

'Let us go build that sandcastle,' I tell Malia Ann. 'And in building this, our sandcastle, let us reaffirm once again the greatness of this nation.'

'But Daddy,' she says, 'I'm bored with all this talk! Let's just get on and dig our sandcastle!'

'You do well to remind me, little Malia Ann, that action is the natural accompaniment to words. Faced with words, our Founding Fathers sought action. Yes, action was what they sought. And their ideals still hold. The success of our nation has always depended not on words alone, but on action. From sand alone, they have built their castles. Today, Malia Ann, we are called to build another. Ours will be a castle that shall withstand all the elements. The sea shall not flatten it, nor shall the fierce winds prevail against it.'

'Daddy,' says Malia Ann, 'are you kidding?'

BARACK OBAMA

July 11th

Today JM said he liked talking to me.

'Underneath, you are as soft as butter,' he said.

'Why, thank you, kind sir,' I said.

'I'm not talking about when it's frozen, because then I find it really quite considerably hard to spread,' he added, 'but after it's been out of the fridge for a minute or two, three at the most, and you can cut it into thin strips and thus apply it to your toast neatly in an appropriate manner.'

EDWINA CURRIE

People say that my failing is that I cannot concentrate – interesting word, spelt backwards emerging as 'etartnecnoc', a meaningless jumble of letters – but this is intolerable and untrue. They also say that I am a master of the *non sequitur*, leaping from one subject to another when they do not follow. For the past year I have not been following the patchy progress of my neighbour Graham Greene, a very undistinguished writer and a grumpy old bat, with whom my argument escalates, though the escalator, in French, *escalateur*, goes down as well as up, echoing, in a quasi-mysto-mechanical way, the descent and subsequent ascension of Lord Jesus Christ, who was, of course, not a Lord at all, as the Anglo-Saxons, being riddled with snobbery, like to think, but a carpenter, in fact I believe in this country there is a sporting commentator called Harry or Harold Carpenter, though whether he has ridden on a moving staircase or not we have no way of knowing. Where was I? Ah, yes: concentration. There is a concentrated orange juice – Kia-Ora, now there's a funny word, bivouac, there's another – but when we talk of concentration we mean something more than orange juice, moving staircases, sporting commentators, Graham Greene, or even Jesus Christ, but now I've lost my thread, which few people realise is an anagram of 'dearth'.

ANTHONY BURGESS

So now I'm staring at myself naked in the full-length mirror wondering what the hell to write about.

I'd do the postman and that dreadful way he has of grinning and putting his sweaty hands on my post and how he could do with losing a good three stones and even then he'd be as fat as a double-decker. But I did him the week before last, and then I did a follow-up piece about the way he had a hissy-fit about it. I mean, some people in my village really can't take the tiniest piece of constructive criticism, can they? He must be gay, the way he reacted. His wife, who cleans for me, if you can call it cleaning, looks as if she's not had sex for a year, so I must be on to something. And when I wrote about her total but total failure to clean my toilet (nickname Sally) properly (I'd just had diarrhoea, owing to low self-esteem, and Sally was crying out for a really good going-over with the Domestos) she threatened to walk out on me, talk about thin-skinned. So I wrote about her threatening to walk out, and then she got in a right old strop, so I wrote about that, too.

LIZ JONES

July 12th

I am persuaded by an albeit rare outbreak of sun to honour the beach with a visit. But I first proceed to a shop, the proprietor of which maintains a meagre display of sun-hats.

'Pray, sir, are you in possession of any headwear relevant to my needs, albeit of a type that does not bear either this or a slogan similar?' I ask, pointing to a hat bearing the elitist legend, 'Kiss Me Quick'.

'Sorry, mate,' he replies.

'Please neither interrupt nor hector me, my dear sir,' I riposte, in my usual measured tones. 'If I have no wish to be kissed, quickly or otherwise, neither can I be persuaded to be heckled. Please assist informed democratic debate by answering my simple question – yes or no?'

'No.'

'Yes or no?'

'No.'

'Ah! Did you say yes?'

'No. I said no.'

Touché! Through a combination of fastidious cross-examination and razor-sharp instinct, I have cornered the aforesaid gentleman into admitting that he has no appropriate sun-hats for the purchase thereof.

'In the circumstances, I am not prepared to continue our discussion,' I say, turning on my heels in a manner reminiscent of Gene Kelly in his evergreen if overrated *Singin' in the Rain*. The gentleman is flabbergasted, little realising he has just taken on an opponent who, as the linchpin of every major post-war Labour government, has established himself as something of an expert at the art of debate.

GERALD KAUFMAN

July 13th

Day 18,450 in the *Big Brother* house. 11.36 a.m.: Nikki and Satnav are in the kitchen.

NIKKI: Remember wosisface?

SATNAV: Who?

NIKKI: You know. Wosisfuckinface. Thassit. Frank. What fuckin' happened to Frank, then? He was fuckin' voted out, was he?

SATNAV: No fuckin' way. He only fuckin' went and fuckin' DIED, didn't he?

NIKKI: When was that, then?

SATNAV: Eight, nine years ago. Maybe ten. Old fuckin' age.

NIKKI: Oh. Right. Yeah. See if I care. Used to so get on my fuckin' tits, he did. I really liked him and I got a lot of respect for him, but he got on my fuckin' tits he did. So what did we do with the fuckin' corpse, then?

SATNAV: Big Brother made us bury it in the garden. It was startin' to piss me right off anyway, rotting and smelling and that. Least Big Brother gave us a luxury fuckin' hamper in return.

NIKKI: I hate corpses. They're so two-fuckin-faced.

July 14th

I still haven't found what I'm looking for. I love money, but don't get me wrong – I don't love money just for what it is: I love it for what it can buy. To wholly involve yourself with this world – this so-beautiful world – I believe you have a moral duty to the universe to ensure your income off capital remains as tax-efficient as possible by retaining your disposable assets in earner-friendly offshore holdings.

I was very humbled when my accountant, Skunk, explained the inner wisdom of transferring the heart of my fiscal operation to the

Netherlands. Tax avoidance has a strong spiritual dimension, a dimension of such joy that it could bring a tear to the eye of an orphan child. As usual, my good mate the Dalai Lama put it in a nutshell. But mine wouldn't fit in a nutshell, so instead I've put it in a portfolio of global investments.

BONO

July 15th

Incidentally, how many writers possess surnames at loggerheads with their personalities! Housman, as well all know, loved the great outdoors, Robert Graves is still not dead, and Donne died with his life's work incomplete …

Do you enjoy eating with a knife and fork? I count it as one of the last truly civilised pleasures of life.

GEORGE LYTTELTON,
LETTER TO RUPERT HART-DAVIS

July 16th

With French wine soaring beyond the prohibitive £2.50 mark, I boast to friends of having found a very reasonable substitute for red wine. Water and tomato ketchup, in roughly equal proportions, with a squeeze of purple paint for colouring, makes for a more-than-acceptable alternative. Likewise champagne. Mix your own urine with a splash of soda and your house-guests honestly can't tell the difference.

MAX HASTINGS

July 17th

I started the day in a foul mood and it got worse. For crying out fucking loud, TB was getting on my tits, he just wasn't doing what I was fucking telling him to do. 'Look, mate,' I said, 'if you want to carry on being Prime Minister, you'd better shape the fuck up you miserable wanker or I'll see you're shafted good and fucking proper.'

It seemed to clear the air. After he'd wiped his tears away, we got on with the job. He was worried by yesterday's poll: people thought he was insincere and couldn't think for himself. 'Tell me it isn't true, Alastair,' he said. He begged me to draft a speech to show he was sincere.

That moment, the sun caught that slight hint of auburn in his hair. Fuck it, I love him when he needs me.

'You know what I really want, Alastair?' he said. 'I want to be known as the People's Princess.'

'That title's fucking taken,' I told him. He's always been crap at market positioning. 'But I could arrange to have them say you were the People's Prime Minister.'

'Were? What do you mean – were?' he said.

He just didn't get it. 'You'd obviously have to agree to die first,' I explained. 'That way, you'll have them eating out of the palm of your fucking hand.'

He said he wasn't sure about that, not if it meant GB taking over. I said, 'No way, GB's not going to be PM in a million years, the guy's a fucking arsehole.' I tell him I've heard it was GB who balanced that bucket of water on the lintel back in April, making it fall on himself, just to make himself look like he was being persecuted. 'Believe me, I know these things,' I said. 'A loser like that's never going to be Prime Fucking Minister.'

ALASTAIR CAMPBELL

The White House in Washington is nothing to write home about, and much smaller than one might have expected, in fact very Haslemere. President Eisenhower is said to be the most powerful man in the world, but I do not find him so. Quite the opposite. He has little taste in home decoration. He looks utterly blank when I suggest it might look more distinguished and 'in keeping' as the Beige House or the Off-White House. He may be clever, I suppose; but he is also very American.

CLARISSA EDEN

July 18th

Having traced a sun-hat, I venture down to the seashore. I am frankly appalled by the conditions that greet me. I make haste to summon a duty officer.

'This standard of flooring is wholly, but wholly, unacceptable,' I complain.

'But it's sand,' he whines. 'People expect it on a beach.'

'That is not the issue,' I remonstrate. 'The issue is whether they have a right to expect something of an altogether higher standard. You'll hear more of this.'

'But the kiddies like to build castles with it,' he bleats.

'If you wish me to point a Building Standards Officer in your direction, so be it,' I rejoin. 'But I would have you know that you are talking to someone who served upon the Royal Commission into the Construction Industry, 1969–1973, so I am something of an expert in the field. And what, may I ask, is all that water doing there?'

'It's the sea!' he says.

'Please don't it's-the-sea me – this is a very serious matter,' I correct him. 'And it may well lead to a number of alarming consequences. That "sea" could make a number of elderly or underprivileged persons intolerably damp. The issue at stake is the public's right to wear dry clothes, free from the fear of drowning. If it is cleared away by tomorrow at the latest, I will say no more about it.'

GERALD KAUFMAN

Jane Austen died today, in 1817. What small success she had didn't last. She never married, whereas I have been married twice. She is little read today, except by sodomites.

V.S. NAIPAUL

Janey Austen became one of the greatest novelists of all time – after I'd helped her with the spelling, mind – but even then the media wouldn't stop persecuting her, asking her like, 'So when are you going to get married, then?' or making snide and wicked comments that she wasn't the marrying type. It beggars belief. Even after all the books we wrote together had been filmed, they were still on at her with their made-up lies, calling her stuck-up and saying 'Why d'you wear those prim, stuck-up, old-fashioned dresses, Jane, when you could be wearing hotpants and that?' I feel for that lady, I really do.

HEATHER MILLS McCARTNEY

July 19th

How right you are, my dear George, on the *sujet* of writers' names being out of sorts with their personalities. One only has to think of Trollope – now there was an upright man! – to have one's confidence in God's (is there one, I wonder?) choice of names for his scribblers hopelessly undermined. On the one occasion I met Edith Sitwell I found her to be an extraordinarily fidgety woman – up and down, up and down, all the time. I am reliably informed that Muriel Spark cannot so much as change a plug. H.E. Bates is one of the gentlest of souls.

... Indeed, I am never without a knife and fork when I eat, unless soup is served, in which case I use a spoon. Indispensable instruments, all, and, it must be said perfectly suited to the job.

RUPERT HART-DAVIS,
LETTER TO GEORGE LYTTELTON

And now I've died and gone to heaven and everybody told me it would be just grand up here but I tell the Archangel Gabriel it's not it's as mighty a disappointment as ever there was. And with that the tears start flowin' down my cheeks like the Niagara and I'm weepin' and weepin' and weepin' and I'm weepin' so hard that St Peter himself comes over and offers me his linen hankie.

This is Heaven, says he. You've got everythin' you could possibly be wantin' – beautiful white suits, lush music, stupendous clouds, gorgeous angels, great craic and God Himself in attendance and there's a name to drop. So tell me this, Frank – what more could a fella need after he's died? What's the problem?

So I wipe away the tears, and I wipe away the tears that follow the tears, and the tears that follow the tears that follow the tears, and finally I look St Peter in the eyes and I tell him fair and square where those problems lie, just like Dad would have lain, all flat on the floor, if only he'd been able to afford a floor.

In Paradise, I tell him, there's misery for the finding, if only you'll turn your Irish eyes towards it and catch a peek. Just take a look at that harp, I say.

Sure, 'tis a splendid harp, says he. What can possibly be wrong with that harp?

But, I say, those skinny little strings all in a row remind me of the frets and the furrows on me dear Granmammy's brow, frets and furrows as deeply dug as the deepest dug ditch owing to her life being one of abject poverty and misery and degradation and abuse at the hands of men for whom alcohol was the very devil. And take a look at that angelic choir! I continue.

Sure, says he, 'tis a splendid angelic choir: what is there to fault about that angelic choir?

'Tis their wings, I explain. Their poor darling wings remind me of that sad little bird, a little red robin, that died in me mam's own fair but wizened arms on the very first day of May one dark December morn deep in the howling cold of March. The poor little thing it didn't stand a chance no it didn't after me Granpappy hit it over the head with his shovel because he swore it was starin' at him and twitterin' too much. With terrible twisted tormented tangled torturent turbulent memories like that, it breaks my heart to set my eyes on that angelic choir.

I tell him I'm Frank McCourt and I'm sorry to say I've just passed away and now isn't that a terrible shame, all things considered. And Mam is dead I tell him and Dad is dead and me Granmammy is dead and me Granpappy is dead and –

I'll have to stop you there if I may, Frank, says St Peter. I'm a little pressed for time, though to hear the full details at a later date would be a rare treat indeed.

Not to worry, I tell St Peter, you can read all about them in me bestsellin' book *Angela's Ashes*, and ain't that a blessing? I say.

To be sure, Frank, says St Peter, that's one thing I cannot do up here in Paradise, as we don't have your book in stock.

You don't have me bestsellin' book in stock? I say.

'Tis the case, explains St Peter. There's no misery memoirs here in Paradise. Why else would we call it Paradise, would you answer me that?

FRANK McCOURT

July 20th

I'm an artist, I'm obsessed, I put all of myself into my work. Like, my new song, 'Whoo! Touch My Sex!', is basically about my struggle to come to terms with my childhood, and the Roman Catholic Church and my obsessions with guilt and with insecurity, and it represents one of my most complex statements of self-revelation so far. So the lyric goes:

I wanna screw you, screw you
All thru the nite, nite
Wanna get thru to you
Let's do it right, right
CHORUS: Whoo! Touch my sex!

That's outasight
Whoo! Touch my sex! Touch my sex!
Turn on my life!

Well, I'm delving very deep into myself there, I'm exploring my unconscious paranoias in a way I've never allowed myself before, and I think it represents like a very clear and positive statement about the way I am now, you know, and I think that should help a lot of people who are still searching, I guess we're all searching for something.

MADONNA

July 21st

I'd never tell anyone this but I was abducted by aliens aged fifteen and a half and it wasn't at all pleasant really. It was when I was fourteen. I was just walking down the street one day, wondering how I was going to earn enough money to pay for a great holiday at Disneyland for all the other poor kids in the world when this spaceship came down and abducted me. And I was only thirteen at the time. I'll never forgive my alien abductors the way they treated me – clean this, clean that, do this, do that, the lot.

But when you suffer in life, you go one of two ways. You're either like, 'I've been mentally and physically abused by aliens, I'm going to get really angry and abusive and get eaten up with it.' Or you're like, 'No, I'm going to make a difference, I'm going to put all the love I feel inside me into helping others less fortunate than myself and if that means becoming the world most famous international charity worker in the process then that's something I'll just have to come to terms with in my own way and if some people don't like that well they'll just have to lump it.'

So now when people say to me, 'Even with your unlimited capacity for caring, Heather, will you ever be able to forgive those aliens who abducted you when you were only eleven?' I say, 'They made me who I am today, and though I'll never voluntarily return to their flying saucer, and though I disapprove of many of their methods, I hope they'll come some day to understand what I wrote in that song all those years ago: "All you need is love – love is all you need".

HEATHER MILLS McCARTNEY

Hardy often complained of the cold, Pater had no children and Jane Austen couldn't drive. How thankful we should be that authors write books, for if they did not it would afford biographers a hopeless task in assessing their lives …

I blow my nose with a handkerchief. Et vous?

GEORGE LYTTELTON,
LETTER TO RUPERT HART-DAVIS

July 22nd

Since time immemorial, the Cavendishes have spread their marmalade on the bottom of their toast. I adhere to this family tradition, but I regret to say the marmalade does not always adhere to the toast. More often than not, it prefers to fall on one's chin or one's bib, and when replaced on one's plate it tends to stick to it. For this reason, we mix our Oxford marmalade with a little glue – Gripfix or Uhu – and that seems to do the trick, though it ruins the taste, of course.

ANDREW, DUKE OF DEVONSHIRE

July 23rd, 1966

TO NOBBY STILES, ESQ.

Dearest Norbert,

I can't begin to tell you how very deeply impressed and moved I was by your performance in the World Cup.

I daresay you may be tempted to feel a smidgen of resentment against 'Bobby' Moore and those frankly unprepossessing Charlton brothers (couldn't some brutal angel tell them to do something about that hair of theirs?).

But it struck me that you went after that soccer ball like a veritable will o' the wisp, injecting a note of the very purest humanity into your performance as you 'took a tumble', and rolled over on that grubby turf, clutching manfully at your shin.

And what beautifully curvaceous knees you have, Nobby! Do you mind me calling you Nobby?

Yours ever, Johnny

JOHN GIELGUD

July 24th

I, too, swear by the humble handkerchief when it comes to the blowing of the nose: heaven forfend that I ever contemplate the usage of another. How eminently civilised we both are!

As for Gibbon, he never even set foot up a tree and Elizabeth Smart is, I fear, generally under-dressed.

Tell me, my dear George, what do you think of death, if anything?

RUPERT HART-DAVIS,
LETTER TO GEORGE LYTTELTON

To New York, New York – otherwise known as the Big Apple – to catch up on the latest exhibitions in the famous Chelsea district and to chair a few more cutting-edge committees. It's true to say that BritArt is taking the BA (Big Apple) by storm, and Keith Tyson's brilliant, epic installation at the Pace Wildenstein Gallery is as brilliant and epic as ever.

Hop over to the space where the famous WTC (World Trade Center) used to be – it's an epic space, a timely reminder of that great tragic day – the day on which, for me, television finally came of age, and for that we should be thankful. Alas, I'm one of those people whose mind never stops whirring – for my sins! – and looking at the seriously tragic site made me suddenly realise that a late-night current-affairs TV celebrity quiz show on serious, tragic issues – everything from tsunamis to beheadings – is long overdue. Memo to self: text Graham Norton about it soonest, how about a George Steiner (new book out) or a Dawn French as team leaders.

Hook up with Charles (Saatchi) and Mick (Jagger) in a gaff to eat a brilliant, epic soft-shell crab and to chew over a number of relevant issues concerning the arts, global warming and Britney with Bobby (De Niro) and Al (Gore), among others. Suddenly, everything seems possible in New (York). That's the magic of the place. I once heard someone say it's so great they named it twice.

ALAN YENTOB

What is a wall with no writing upon it? I would not know, as I have yet to see one. Yet there is little of any purposeful use and/or useful purpose in the world in the last decade of the second millennium. The sloppy armies of Barbaria are on their ill-shodden march, dragging civilisation headlongly to its doom. In the United States of America, the President's daughter is pictured dancing at a 'night-club discotheque'. In South-East Asia, the Spice Girls appear on daytime television, yet Gustav Mahler continues to be denied his own show. In Switzerland, Heinz baked beans make inroads into the supermarket shelves. In England, few schoolchildren are fluent in twelve languages before the age of nine. Instead, they watch television programmes like *Oasis* and gyrate to the primitive sexual rhythms, at once tribal and solipsistic, of the Teletubbies, none of whom, save perhaps La-La, could hold down a post at any major European university.

GEORGE STEINER

July 25th

The sparrow sits on the fence. The fence does not sit on the sparrow. When the fence sits on the sparrow, the sparrow finds it hard to fly.

SHIRLEY MACLAINE

July 26th

Off to watch *Punch and Judy* on the beach. It is, for all its undeniable ups and downs, a profoundly Christian marriage. From my own dealings with Mr Punch, I have long found him to be a most impressive individual, very different from his media image – outgoing, direct and with real authority.

Much has been made by the media of the sufferings of his wife Judy.* It cannot be denied that she is a very popular figure who has managed to gain the sympathy of the crowds. But from my many private conversations with Mr Punch, over excellent dinners, superbly served on the finest silver by liveried staff, I have learnt that there are two sides to every story.

If circumstances have driven Mr Punch to hit his wife on the head over and over again with a big black stick, it is not for the rest of us to sit in judgement. Instead, we must sympathise. Might his undeniable sense of fun have been stifled by his marriage to a woman who has – for all her undoubted qualities of persistent nagging – never really tried to understand him?

As I watch them together on the beach, I am struck by how very different they both are from the image projected by the media. Mr Punch is a warm and friendly fellow, his concerns deeply grounded in issues relevant to today. Far too much is made of him whacking Judy over the head with a stick. It is high time we looked beyond these playful thumps to the devoted husband beneath.

RT REV GEORGE CAREY

---

*Judy's bestselling misery memoir, *Ouch! Stop Hitting Me with that Stick!: My Dreadful Ordeal at the Hands of Mr Punch* (Century), was Oprah's Book of the Month in September 2008.

July 27th

My mother never forgave me for helping myself to an extra biscuit without asking her. It was on March 3rd 1949. 'You really should have asked,' she said to me, and then – typically – she changed the subject. I was only nine or ten years of age but those awful words wound me to this day. They were not only sexist – I was a little girl at the time – but they were also anti-biscuit. Sixty years on, whenever anyone offers me a biscuit, or if I am driving along a motorway and a car passes me in which someone happens to be eating a biscuit, I emit an involuntary shudder. I used this involuntary shudder in my novel *The Meaningful Silence*, but I changed it into a nervous twitch, for reasons I no longer recall.

MARGARET DRABBLE

July 28th

Wonderful to visit West Kensington again. It is the site of one of the most rewarding, if under-appreciated, tube stations on the entire District Line (with the notable exception of Turnham Green, which rivals it in sophistication and, to my mind, surpasses it in comfort cossu.

I first visited West Kensington in the spring of 1980. I was, by that time, both General Secretary of the World Trade Federation and Chairman of the World Bank, as well as President of the European Commission, three posts which, I am happy to relate, left one ample time to get on with more useful and more pleasurable, if not necessarily more remunerative, pastimes.

It was not my wish to embarrass the far from disagreeable staff of the District Line by landing on them 'out of the blue', as it were. They would not, I surmised, be used to dealing with a man not unblessed with my undoubted lack of indistinction, so with due forethought I had a message posted in advance that the President of the European Commission, etcetera, etcetera, would be arriving at such-and-such an hour on such-and-such a day, giving them plenty of time to lay out the red carpet and so forth.

As I remember it, I had just stepped onto the 'down' escalator when the red carpet they had earlier laid upon it began to 'ruck up' at the bottom, causing myself and my honoured guests – who included the Lord Provost of Glasgow, Sir Isaiah Berlin, the Duke of Westminster and Dame Anna Neagle – to hurtle head-over-heels down forty-odd steps or more. An unfortunate occurrence, perhaps, but what it lacked in dignity it more than made up for in exhilaration, so we immediately climbed the stairs and did it all over again.

ROY JENKINS

Sandringham. After luncheon, marked my new stamp catalogue. Bacon interrupted to inform me that my government had declared war against Germany. Most regrettable.

Ham with carrots and boiled potatoes for dinner. Excellent.

Bed at 11.15.

HM KING GEORGE V

July 29th

Today would have been Benito Mussolini's birthday. I don't know about his war record, and it frankly doesn't particularly interest me, but Benito had the most wonderful sense of fun.

DIANA MOSLEY

They had called it the Wedding of the Century. But – hey! – that was five years ago, and a helluva lot had changed since that fateful day. To Princess Diane, sitting sultry on a settee in super-swanky Kensington Palace, it now all seemed more like a pile of doggy-do. Wooh, she couldn't get that crappy nightmare day out of her head, covered by hair recently shampooed by world-class mega-hairdresser and dynamo-former-husband-of-pop-star-Lulu John Frieda.

That longago morning, the Royal couple had power-marched up the aisle of top marital location Winchester Abbey, just a mile from world-famous Harrods department store. Unknown to the rest of the world, and revealed here for the very first time in human history, Princess Diane had secretly employed the veil of the billowing hyper-expensive designer-label wedding dress as a cover for a last-minute call on her mobile to glamorous soon-to-be-divorced multi-millionaire hotdog heir Hiram Vernon Hiram Jr.

'Hey, babe – it's still not too late to change your mind!' Hiram had blurted as Diane arrived at the altar.

'Got to go now, huggy-bear! Byee!' whispered Diane, forgetting to switch off her mobile. 2,863 miles away, on the other side of the Atlantic Sea, in his penthouse valued at $120 million, and with a deluxe bottle of vintage Cristal champagne chilling in his state-of-the-art Frigidaire, the next words to echo in Hiram's ears were: 'I do.'

Hell, he thought – Diane's gone and done it. Hiram let out the crazed money-soaked sigh of a jilted multi-billionaire.

'Beepity-beep! Beepity-beep!' Just as he was power-kissing his new bride on the specially-fortified exclusive power-balcony of Buckingham Palace that sultry Autumn afternoon, Prince Charles of Wales heard his mobile go off like a crack of mega-thunder.

Those underlings near the front of the billion-strong crowd gathered outside the Palace that day recall him power-barking, 'Not now, Camilla, I'm shamming it for the cameras!' into his mobile, before carrying on with his super-snog of wretchedly tearful bulimic Princess Diane, her wedding dress spattered with thousands of melted chocolate-stains from the family-size Yorkie bar she had smuggled into the classy, cash-rich cathedral.

Behind them Helen Mirren-lookalike Elizabeth 2, pumped-up mega-rich silver-spoon sovereign, burned like a meteor with the bright, flashy glow of real power. Those regal, rancorous, rough-hewn eyes seared through her son and his unsuitable new wife like a $5,000 kitchen knife from top store Macy's on New York's fashionable

Madison Avenue through butter served in the in-crowd, book-six-months-in-advance brasserie of super-sassy boutique hotel McDitzys, Park Avenue.

TINA BROWN*

July 30th

North Pole: This really is an extremely cold place, with ice absolutely everywhere! It's at the very top of the world – or bottom, depending on which way you're looking at it! As I say, my main impression of it is of its great chilliness: literally indescribable!

MICHAEL PALIN

July 31st

You were kind enough to ask me for my w.'s of w. on that old bugbear, Death, my thoughts on the aforementioned. One of its most overlooked aspects is that, but for the missing 'r', it anagrams neatly into 'thread', a by no means unacute observation, since doctors and poets are as one in their belief that this is all that divides the living from the dead. What will happen to me when I die? I dread a heaven without barley sugar, and, on a deeper level, I'm not sure I could cope with the crowds.

By the by, what is your favourite method of walking? I myself place on foot in front of the other (which necessarily involves the leg, or legs) and, repeating this process *quid pro quo*, find myself ambulating with no little efficiency. And you?

GEORGE LYTTELTON,
LETTER TO RUPERT HART-DAVIS

---

*From *Diane, Princess of Wales.*

Dear Diary, We are in the middle of a heatwave and it brings with it an oppressive air of foreboding. I suppose Martin and I both know that this is the end. For some time, I now realise, his notes to me have all been alibis. 'Popped out for pack of fags. Back late tomorrow,' reads one of them, and another reads, 'Off to complete new novel. Probably finish it early Mon. Taken toothbrush and clean pr of pants and two bots. of Lambrusco and pk of cndms for literary reasons you wdn't undrstnd bcs you didn't go to Oxford.' Reading between the lines, I suspect he is playing on my feelings of inadequacy for never having gone to Oxford.

JULIE KAVANAGH

August

August 1st

Which came first: the egg or the chicken, the chicken or the egg? You may believe one thing, and I may believe another.

I think about my Mom, who would never eat an egg without cooking it first. And I think about my Grandmom, who always liked hers fried, sunny side up.

Yes, we should rejoice in those differences. It is our differences that make us so alike.

But I promise you this. That egg and that chicken: these are two very different things.

It avails us nothing to dip our toast in our chicken, nor to spit-roast our egg on our barbecue.

On those points we find agreement. And it is our agreements that make us what we are today, what we have been in the past and what we will continue to be in the future.

So let us not put our past behind us, nor let us fail to learn our lessons from the future that is here with us now. Instead, may we continue to heed what the present was once, is now, and will be forever.

BARACK OBAMA

August 2nd

I was the first person in Britain to develop a passion for good design. But what enormous opportunities were missed by the generations who preceded me! The River Thames, for instance, has many major design faults, and is long overdue for a corporate makeover in order to radically alter public perception of it as something 'outdated' and 'worn out'. This week we have accordingly developed a three-point Thames Re-Imaging Plan:

DESIGN PROBLEM: The Thames curves randomly, without due regard for the sadly outdated buildings alongside it. This is bad design: fussy, obtrusive, and lacking the 'human dimension'.

DESIGN SOLUTION: Radically redesign the Thames, banishing all fussy curves to form a marvellous bold and simple straight line, in a stroke making it user-friendly, democratic, gutsy, passionate and ready for the new demands of the twenty-first century.

DESIGN PROBLEM: The Thames is far too moist and splashy. It is made up entirely of water, creating an almost insuperable access barrier between the North and South of London, making it wholly unfit for pedestrians.

DESIGN SOLUTION: Tile the Thames in richly checkered Italian tiling, terracotta and a marvellous deep lush green, blocking out the water and allowing full pedestrian access, affording it a marvellously 'Continental' street-market feel, full of marvellously evocative bustle and hub-bub.

DESIGN PROBLEM: 'The River Thames' is a tired, yesterdayish logo, too strongly associated in the public perception with a lack of vibrancy and drive. It is crying out for a radical rethink in its corporate identity to reflect its new, all-dry, user-friendly, updated competitive edge.

DESIGN SOLUTION: A new corporate identity for an old river, radically altering perceptions with a dramatic new logo, incorporating a go-ahead new one-million-pound designer typeface that is impacting for change:

thaMes: the river

SIR TERENCE CONRAN

August 3rd

We do some mad shit together, the Dalai Lama and I. Listening to the bald guy rap on, I begin to understand something very special about the meaning of life. DL taught me an important lesson and it is this: 'What, me worry?'

Yes, that's a beautiful, beautiful sentiment, and one that I have attempted to convey in the lyrics of my new song, 'Get Your Ass Off and Rock this Joint, Baby (Homage to Rwanda)'.

You learn a lot about life from all sorts of different human beings. Put it this way, the other day, when I was last talking to DL, there was a knock on my door and who should it be but the lovely Benedict, an early U2 fan who's currently doing a truly great job as Pope. Loved the new album, he says, couldn't get enough of it, reminded him in a funny way of Buffalo Springfield in their mid-period, with a touch of Jefferson Airplane thrown in.

So we were rapping on – I told him I just loved that last Easter address of his – when there was another knock at the door. 'Kofi!' I said. 'Come in, me old mate! And would you be knowing Ben here, who's the Pope? And have you met our new rhythm guitarist, Gusset?'

Two minutes later, who should walk in but this beautiful guy with a truly great sense of humour called George W., says he has a bit of time to spare, thought he'd just hang loose and generally chill for a while. You know, it's easy to underestimate George, but the guy rocks. At heart, he's just one cool laidback dude.

BONO

On the beach, I come across a tiny outdoor theatre showing a truly terrifying drama called *Punch and Judy*. Hugely talented dwarf actors highly versed in the Noh drama of India somehow manage to convey, with a beautifully circumscribed range of expressions and gestures, all the grotesque hatred and suffering and shabbiness that informs our twenty-first-century world. For me, it is a literally shattering experience, with performances of an unbelievable intensity that put what is laughingly called our National Theatre to shame.

I insist on going backstage afterwards and find all the main actors – Punch, Judy, the Policeman, the Baby – in a state of nervous collapse. And who can blame them? It's as though the four of them have been made visibly thinner by what they have just been through, unable to move or even to speak after undergoing such a momentous journey into the heart of darkness.

GERMAINE GREER

August 4th

It had grown uncommonly dark and sultry, the clouds painfully laden as though ready to sear the earth once more with their translucent acid, when I set out on my Summer holidays. Holidays! The word itself, a stifled and tortuous amalgam of 'holly', that fiercest and most spiteful of all trees, with its sharp, shiny, pox-green edges ready to strike out and pierce human skin, causing blood, a dark reddish-grey, greyish-red, to drop out, willy-nilly, onto the earth below, staining the soil in perpetuity, and 'days', with its dull echo of daze, in which I so often find myself after finishing these sentences, some of them as long and distracted as those sentences handed out with unnerving efficiency by the Guatemalan Lord Chief Justice to the Netherlandish invaders of the Indonesian island of Iwu-Miju in 1473, after the Brecon uprising commemorated in the poem by Swinburne after he had taken a cup of tea – a cup fatally calamitous for two pure-white sugar lumps, which can have known little of their destruction but for those few dreadful seconds when they experienced the unsettling feeling, common to all human civilisation, of being dropped into hot, brown liquid with an abrupt flick of the wrist, there to disintegrate into nothingness, never to return – the entire and dreadful word, 'holidays', forcing one to attempt to suppress a mounting sense of dizziness in the face of looming catastrophe.

W.G. SEBALD

August 5th

It has been a tough, tough decision. But, as it's August, I now feel that the time has come to break my silence.

I haven t spoken on the subject of Diana, Princess of Wales for these past five minutes. It's been a lonely, harrowing time. Believe me, it has been quite a struggle to stay silent. Five long, long minutes ago, I made a vow to the memory of the lady never to tell all her secrets. But, as the minutes ticked by, I came to understand that my first duty is to history. The serialisation of my second volume of royal revelations in the *Daily Mail* is, I now realise, just what the Princess would have wanted.

For as long as I live, I shall never forget that conversation I had with the woman I always called The Boss. We were together in Kensington Palace, just the two of us, enjoying a quiet game of Scrabble.

Suddenly, she held me by the hand, looked imploringly into my eyes, and said, 'Paul, if ever I am killed in a tragic car-crash in Paris, I want you to promise me to spill all my right royal beans – and not just once, but twice. Yes, Paul – if ever I die, you must be sure to cash in.'

Those prophetic words haunt me to this very day. I owe it to the memory of that wonderful lady to share her secrets with the world.

PAUL BURRELL

August 6th

Dear Diary, I'm so sad. Martin Amis has dumped me for my best friend, Emma Soames, just because her grandfather was Winston Churchill. He's had her on the beaches, he's had her on the landing grounds, he's had her on the fields and in the streets, he's had her on the hills. It's the heady pull of an aristocratic world that drew Charles Ryder to Brideshead, and I cannot compete.

JULIE KAVANAGH

Day 18,474 in the *Big Brother* house. 11.41 a.m.: Lea is in the diary room. Lea's bosoms are in the garden.

BB: Lea, you have been nominated for eviction by your fellow housemates 3,726 times over the past half-century but you are still here. How are you feeling?

LEA: I've been bored fuckin' shitless these past fifty fuckin' years.

BB: Lea, during your time in the *Big Brother* house, you've performed your own breast enlargement seventeen times. They are now a housemate in their own right, and come into the diary room by themselves. Unfortunately, Lea, they can't stop slagging you off behind your back. Why do you think that is?

LEA: I'm just too fuckin' real for them.

August 7th

You have to pinch yourself, you really do. You lay on a generous, must-have picnic for ordinary people and they show no gratitude whatsoever. Dismay and despair are the only natural emotions for today's picnic-provider – roughly 56 per cent dismay and 44 per cent despair.

It was left to me to unpack the two hampers. The men, being men, sat around doing nothing. Needless to say, the women had their hands full trying to prevent their irresponsible underage offspring running into the busy traffic (congestion on the roundabout up a staggering 29 per cent in just three years, according to my sources).

'Bread and butter, anyone?' I said, showing them the main course.

'What's the choice?' asked an ungrateful child.

'Let's hear no more about choice!' I rebutted. 'You can have bread and butter, or just bread, or just butter. In a civilised society, that's far too much choice as it is!'

'Anything to drink?' asked a parent, who, like 89 per cent of today's bloated citizens, should have known better.

'There's as much water as you could possibly want!' I said. Looking around at the picnickers, I was continually disappointed by the ill-suppressed expressions of dissatisfaction on their ignorant, selfish faces. Did they not know that in some parts of Africa, 51 per cent of the population would be 93 per cent grateful to be invited for a glass of water and a nice piece of bread and butter on a highly-regarded roundabout on the northern outskirts of Hatfield? Hosting a picnic in this pampered day and age is indeed a thankless task.

Instead, we have created for ourselves a have-it-all, me-me-me, grumble-grumble-grumble society in which picnickers who would once have been delighted to eat a decent bit of grass and perhaps the odd dandelion now turn up their pampered toffee-noses at a delicious bit of bread-and-butter. Sitting here on the roundabout in Hatfield, it suddenly strikes you what Labour is up against: a nation of sour and selfish consumers, pumped full of things they would be better off without.

POLLY TOYNBEE

Pork tenderloin is common, and so is any pasta, though, paradoxically, not spaghetti. Francis Bacon is common. Everyone has to have one of those screaming Popes – such a bore. The only Pope who wasn't common was Pope Paul VI. I never saw him screaming, not even when I pinched his BTM. He always looked quite wonderful in emerald green, which set off that lovely neck of his. He was so petite, but marvellously well-proportioned. With the incense billowing everywhere, he reminded me of the young Rudolf Valentino.

NICHOLAS HASLAM

August 8th

He who wishes to come back must first go away.

SHIRLEY MACLAINE

August 9th

I went toad-hunting this morning. The most obviously useful of all forms of hunting – no one likes a toad – it also has a strange beauty about it. Is there a sound closer to the deep, mystic spirit of the English countryside than the sudden squelch of toad beneath Wellington boot?

We gathered at dawn, each of us wearing boots several sizes too big, for maximum impact. Never has the English countryside looked more peculiarly beautiful. In the distance, the early sun bounced off the warty, dappled backs of a squadron of basking toads. It was as if, in some mysterious way, these toads were beckoning us over, yearning for the firm squash of reinforced boot upon their enticingly rubbery bodies.

My host, the Earl of Crowborough, represents the fifteenth generation of his family to have squashed toads in their corner of East Sussex. Toad-squashing is close to the heart of an aristocratic approach to life because it is communal, ceremonial, democratic (in the true meaning of the word – '*demo*' meaning 'toad' and '*cratic*' meaning 'let's stamp on a') and makes a beautiful sound – like an explosion from a Whoopee cushion, though less vulgar.

In the evening, Johnny Crowborough led us into his delightful neo-classical barn for the Toad Dinner. A piper gave us a fine rendering of 'Nearer, My God, to Thee' on the natterjacks, a more plangent version of the bagpipes, sewn from the matured bellies of twenty natterjack toads.

The main course consisted of a magnificent toad stew, cooked from the morning's bag. When we had finished our feasting, we were led by Vince, the friendly lower-class Head Toadier, down a long corridor to a centuries-old marble basin. At a given signal from Vince, we proceeded to 'vomit up' the entire feast in the traditional manner.

As the evening sun shone through the fine neo-Gothic tracery, spreading its warm dappled rays o'er the lively yellows, greens and browns of the gloriously regurgitated toads, I couldn't help but feel that this was one part of England that Blair must wish to see abolished forever, along with fresh air, the Royal Family, and white people.

CHARLES MOORE

It was a dark, overcast day when I arrived on the beach with my bucket and spade, or it would have been if the sun had not been blazing down on me, as though spurred on in its hatred by some half-remembered vendetta, unforgiving in its burning, hell-like cruelty. My feet seemed to blister in despair and to scream out in silent agony as the sand slithered and slimed its way, viper-like, into their misshapen crevices, holes between limbs, all worn away by the ravages of time. What could I build with my spade and my bucket, the two of them working in unison, that might hope to endure longer than a single tide? I strode despairingly along the beach, taking note of what others had constructed. Sandcastles! But to me the idea of erecting a castle of sand was out of the question if there was no cement-mixer to hand. I hesitated no more, immediately walking, all alone with my bucket and spade, to a distant builders' merchant in the outer reaches, terrifyingly isolated, of the locality. 'I will be immediately needing a cement-mixer for the construction of a beach-castle,' I told the merchant. 'You may be assured I shall be providing my own sand and water.' He looked at me with the bemused expression I have observed before on those startled to find a stranger among them, however proficient he may be in the language of English. There was no time to lose: I soon found myself back at the same stretch of beach, pulling my cement-mixer behind me, the grains of sand, like so many tiny eyeballs, staring in mute hatred at me as I prepared to turn them to stone.

W.G. SEBALD

August 10th

Until now, I have said little about my relationship with Her Majesty the Queen, but the truth must now outweigh the need for me to protect her little secrets.

Her Majesty was a lovely lady. She thought the world of me.

She would often call by on her nights off. I got used to that tell-tale knock on the door. She would drum out the opening bars of the National Anthem with her clenched fist. That way, I knew it was her.

I'd open the door, and there she'd be, dressed in casual clothes – a pair of designer denims and a favourite kaftan. Often, she'd let her hair hang down, so it flowed over her creamy shoulders. It gave her the more relaxed and carefree look she had always craved.

'You know, you should keep it like that, Ma'am – you look truly fabulous!' I once ventured, but she looked downcast. 'My public would never accept me like that, Paul!' she said. 'They like me with it up.'

At that point, she got out her guitar and sang me one of my all-time favourite songs – Ralph McTell's 'Streets of London'. It was a very private moment, which I have decided to write about only after a great struggle. But one thing I know. I will continue to cherish my memory of a special evening of rest and relaxation spent in the company of a very lovely lady.

PAUL BURRELL

August 11th

It was in the warm glow of a delicious August afternoon that I first set eyes on Warren Street underground station. It is not, perhaps, a first-rate station, still less a second-rate station, but as the lower-third-rate stations go, I have always considered it ranks really rather high; if not at the very top, then quite near the upper-middle.

It was during my time, not entirely wasted, as Minister for Transport that I found myself passing through Warren Street. The train itself was less luxurious than utilitarian. In terms of comfort it could never, I think, compare with the Orient Express or, for scenery, with the Trans-Siberian Express, both of them very considerable trains. But it possessed features rarely found in some of the more ostentatiously fêted vehicles, as I pointed out to Valéry Giscard d'Estaing and Pierre Trudeau, who were journeying with me at the time.

'That's a really rather charming cushion over there,' I remarked to Pierre, pointing to a soft yellow item on the banquette opposite. 'If not exactly a first-rate cushion, then certainly high among the lower seconds.' At this point, Pierre, a man with an adventurous, if not perhaps always sagacious, turn of mind, stood up and walked over to the cushion in question.

'This is, I fear, no cushion,' he said, sniffing it with the instinctive delicacy of a French-born Canadian. 'It is a pool of vomit.'

Up to that point, I had never, I confess, come across quite such a pool of vomit on the banquette of a major underground railway train. For this reason, I was drawn to study it more closely. Rather to my regret, I found it altogether less impressive, both in hue and texture, than a pool of vomit most memorably produced by George Brown outside the Savoy Hotel in the cold winter of '66.

ROY JENKINS

The sky appeared blue, but I knew that, somewhere else in the world, yet more clouds, black and bruised, were gathering. Immediately above me, a seagull swooped, its wings stretched fully out, as though an unseen torturer were pulling them to breaking point until it disclosed its secret. But what secret does the seagull hold? This one conducted its incessant squawking with an earnest intensity, yet its almost bird-like language meant nothing at all. Whenever one cuts in half a seagull that has been killed with ethyl alcohol one is struck by how utterly useless it now looks, each half unable to flap in even the most basic manner. Anton Chekhov must have known this distinctive, bewildering feature about seagulls when he wrote his play *The Cherry Orchard*, for almost exactly three years and two months earlier and only six hundred and forty-seven miles away, a Prussian fisherman with pale brown hair had finally assembled the largest collection of ostrich eggs under a single roof. Ten years on, due to faulty sand-based cement in the fixtures, the roof was to crumble, and the entire collection was to lie in smithereens. High above me in the air, the gull continued upon its vacuous and erratic journey through a sky still glowering in fury at the ceaseless intrusion of the crazed sun.

W.G. SEBALD

August 12th

Some bloody holiday this is turning out to be! Along the beach I find, to my absolute horror, rides being offered on donkeys. Could someone please tell me just how ignorant people can be? Don't these guys realise that a donkey is not some kind of mule but closer to a fish or an amphibian, which should be permitted to go back into the sea to its home underwater for at least half the day?

GERMAINE GREER

August 13th

Another beach, another holiday. The day begins with me dressing my darling cats – Monsieur Wenceslas Muff, Canon Simpering Screamer, The Right Honourable Peter Pussykins, Bishop Blubbering Bumboy and The Rt Reverend Pompous Twat – up in their Victorian beachwear and telling them to mind their manners and not to go too near the water.

'You must remember, my little pussies,' I tell them, 'that at the tender age of twenty-six, your master became the youngest-ever Director of the National Portrait Gallery, no less; by the age of twenty-seven he was being invited to dine by Her Royal Highness Princess Margaret-Rose, the sister of Her Majesty the Queen; and before he turned thirty he was setting tables of Duchesses a-roar with laughter at his finely-honed anecdotes concerning the dullness of unimpressive dons!'

The cats are noticeably impressed, purring with simple pleasure at my fond reminiscences.

'To some extent,' I continue, excitedly, 'one foxes everyone by simultaneously being scholar and academic, populariser and communicator, and sticking to the belief that these are not incompatible!'

Could it be just my imagination, or do these cats stand up on their hind legs and applaud as my little speech draws to its powerful close?

Together, the cats and myself parade along the sands, me in my stripy one-piece swimming togs, looking perhaps almost too like the divine Tadzio in Mr Mann's mournful masterpiece, *Death in Venice*. Close to the sea, the common folk are deliberately flying tawdry-coloured kites, making a hideous mess of the seascape. Thank heavens for a sharp pair of scissors, I say to myself, as I dip deep inside my Edwardian clutch-bag.

SIR ROY STRONG

August 14th

An amusing story which may well raise a chuckle among the more humorously inclined. Mrs Margaret Thatcher recently fell over and hurt her knee badly while at the seaside, putting her out of action for several days. Like all the best stories, it's perfectly true, and somehow appropriate. Anyway, it made me chuckle.

SIR EDWARD HEATH

August 15th

The sky loomed over me like a bright blue package containing heavy objects about to fall on the world from a great height.

'Strawberry or Orange, mate?' said the man. I had asked for an ice-lolly and now the salesman in the van was cross-questioning me as to my exact meaning.

'A Mivvi,' I replied.

'I know that, mate,' he responded, curtly, 'but Strawberry or Orange?'

It was then that I remembered that Orange is the colour of the robes that adorn the corpses of women in Delhi who have died hideous deaths, a haunting and melancholy detail I have never been able to shed from my memory when ordering a lolly. 'Orange, please,' I said, mournfully.

The Mivvi, I was later to discover, is named after Dr Hans Mivvi of Zürich, the eighteenth-century apothecary whose *Almanac de Mivvi*, first published in Rome in 1781 – the very same year that a ninety-two-year-old woman was burnt as a witch in Bury St Edmunds – pioneered the notion of an iced comestible wrapped around another iced comestible, the two of them placed on a stick and priced accordingly. Yet the Mivvi ice-lolly has always seemed to me godforsaken in its bewildered iciness, an iciness brought into savage relief by the plaintive flavouring of its outer lollyhood, so that the insertion of the Mivvi into the mouth induces a terrifying sense of *déjà-vu* in the hapless consumer, as though mankind itself were frozen for those few minutes on a stick, to be placed into the mouth of nothingness until it melts, the sole memento of our existence a few fast-fading orange drips on the chin of oblivion. With the sun setting behind me, reminding me of a bad egg thrown haphazardly into a darkening bin, I end my first day on the sodden beach. On this very day three hundred and ninety-seven years ago, something unspeakably dreadful happened. But what? I spot a congealed chip on the worn beach, pick it up, suck on it, and struggle to remember.

W.G. SEBALD

KARL'S TOP 5 TIPS FOR SURVIVING THE CREDIT CRUNCH

1. Don't eat. Eating is so Seventies and this is Today. I eat only celery and even that I am not enjoying. Pale green is so uninteresting.
2. Dismiss your assistant chauffeur. No one has an assistant chauffeur any more. Assistant chauffeurs are so Yesterday.
3. You do not need more than two hundred white shirts at any one time. Anything more is excessive. I threw the rest of them away when I heard of the arrival of the credit crunch and I tell you I felt so good about myself!
4. Forget charity. Charity this, charity that. Tcha! I try to avoid charity. It is so boring, like tomato ketchup. I avoid charity. It doesn't happen for me. I'm rich enough not to have to do that. Thank God I don't have to do that. There are so many poor people who dress deplorably with no sense of style and they look so ugly and stupid and are always out begging. Do

you want to encourage them, hm? Of course you do not! It would be different if they possessed any sense of bravura, if they styled themselves on the Ballets Russes, or they came out onto the streets with the Audrey Hepburn look. But they do not. The only charity that is acceptable is Save the Tiger, because at all costs we must not lose the real tiger fur, I just adore it, it is so chic.

The whale? Tcha! I would never save the whale. It is so fat, and who is to blame for that? The whale has let itself go, so it is not even size 18, it is something so much more, like size 35. And why should I save the whale, when it has let itself go so ugly and morbidly obese? And all the spouting it does is so horrible. Imagine your reaction if I were to come in here spouting water out of my backside and into the air? I tell you this, you would not be offering me your chic charity money, and that is for sure.

5. Never travel first-class. It is so common. No one should travel first-class, with all those strangers with their coughs and their germs. No: a private jet, or nothing at all.

KARL LAGERFELD

August 16th

Elvis Presley dies tragically on the toilet. But not before he got in touch.

'Max,' he said, 'I'm the undisputed King of Rock 'n' Roll. But I've eaten far more than is good for me, I've taken many too many pills and now I'm sitting on the toilet and I'm frankly not feeling my best. As my oldest friend in the business, Max, I'm hoping you'll be able to get me out of this pickle.'

Sadly, I was stuck on the other phone at the time. I was talking to a senior member of the Royal Family who shall remain nameless. So by the time I got to hear Elvis's message, he had already passed away.

But the story has a happy ending. Luckily, I've been able to tip off the gentlemen of the press – the *Sun* was able to give his tragic toilet-based death a front-page exclusive. Thanks to my quick reactions, his *Greatest Hits* now looks to go straight to Number One in the charts!

Memo to self: give a bell soonest to Lysol, of toilet-cleaning products fame. Go halves on rights to Elvis's tragic toilet.

MAX CLIFFORD

Peel an apricot. Place it between your toes. Put on a sock and walk to work. When you arrive, your foot will be very messy, but the sky will still be blue. Yoko loves you.

YOKO ONO

August 17th

Tea with Martin McGuinness. Lovely man. Really super warm smile. Wouldn't hurt a fly. 'I frankly deplore the way this Government allows its media to describe you as a terrorist, Martin,' I say, pouring him another cuppa. I can't help but notice he's fiddling with something. 'What's that you've got there, Martin?!' I ask, with a chuckle.

'It's a fly, Tony,' he replies with that lovely Irish lilt of his. 'I'm just pulling its wings off. For its own good, of course'.

'Quite,' I say. 'It's probably sick to death of all that flying nonsense. They work them far too hard. Needs a well-earned rest, eh?'

Having finished pulling the wings off, Martin kindly squashes the fly flat as a pancake, 'to put it out of its misery'. What a really super, kindly chap he is. A tear comes into my eye when I think of this great act of kindness he has performed on a little fly.

'No life for a fly, without wings,' I say reassuringly, and we hug one another.

Early Christmas card from Augusto Pinochet, 'To the best Leader the Labour Party never had'! I'm tickled pink, obviously. Very sweet of him. What a nice old man he really is. In the past, we had our differences, but I now feel a very real affection for the guy. So much more genuine than that dreadful little phoney Tony Blair.

TONY BENN

Sir V.S. Naipaul was born today, in 1932. He is undoubtedly our greatest living writer. His fiction and non-fiction are characterised by a commitment to truth that gives them a unique brilliance. The winner of the Nobel Prize, he has produced a formidable body of work, full of gentleness, humanity and feeling. He remains consistently undervalued by spineless nitwits.

V.S. NAIPAUL

August 18th

I received a telephone call from a Professor Wildenstein at Princeton University. He wanted to give me a large amount of money. This is the sort of thing the Americans do very well.

ANTHONY POWELL

Last night, I woke to the sound of handfuls of gravel being hurled against my bedroom window. Putting my head out from my second-floor room, I recognised the tell-tale sparkle of the Queen's tiara glistening in the moonlight.

'Hang on, Ma'am!' I whispered. 'I'll be down in a jiffy!'

The lady was clearly distraught, with her tiara thrown on any-old-how, her evening dress trailing in the mud, and her lank hair dripping all over the place.

My heart went out to her. 'Come in and warm yourself!' I said, leading her into the kitchen.

Previously, I have always maintained that Her Majesty and I were never on terms of great intimacy. In my last diary, I even went so far as to suggest that our conversations were few and far between, and that we did not speak to one another as equals.

That, I can now reveal, was a white lie aimed at stopping speculation that the Queen and I had ever become engaged.

But the truth is very different.

Last night, with the two of us huddled up all alone in my kitchen, that gracious lady revealed a side of herself that few ordinary mortals had ever seen.

'Let's face it, Paul,' she said, and I detected in her tone a very slight Northern accent which she had long kept hidden from the world at large, 'my husband is getting on. He has served me well, a stalwart companion in times both good and bad. But one is only too aware that he won't go on forever. Before very long, one shall have to face the world on one's own – and, frankly, it is not a prospect to which one is greatly looking forward.'

I felt instinctively that HM was leading up to something. And, once again, I was proved right.

For all her public image of self-assurance, this intensely private lady was finding it hard to get the words out.

'I was wondering, Paul … if by any chance … after a decent period of mourning … that goes without saying, of course … you might be prepared to … how shall one put this … slip into his shoes?'

It came as a bolt from the blue. Never in my life had I received an offer of marriage from my sovereign. I felt truly humbled.

For a moment, I found her plan attractive. After all, I already knew the ropes. For my part, I would be able to serve my country as the Queen's husband, greeting people with a smile and a friendly handshake, whilst enjoying an intoxicating jet-set lifestyle. And from the Queen's point of view, I would be able to give her the normal life she had always craved, away from the trappings of Royalty which had both defined and stifled her. As my wife, she would be able to be an ordinary woman, vacuuming, dusting, doing the dishes, ironing, making the bed.

But HM's plan had a fatal flaw. I was already a married man. Not for the first time, I found myself torn between my duty to my sovereign and my duty to the Burrell family.

Alas, I knew then that our marriage was not to be. But my years in service had also taught me a very important lesson: a refusal may offend.

'Get this down you, love!' I said, handing Her Majesty a silver schooner of warm whisky, mixed with honey and lemon. I had to pick my words carefully.

'I thank you for your kind offer, Ma'am,' I said, 'but, alas, it is not to be.'

She moaned inwardly, before collecting herself. 'Only promise me this, Paul,' she said, choking back the tears. 'You will never breathe a word of what has passed between us.'

My heart went out to her. 'I promise,' I said. And I have kept my promise from that day to this.

PAUL BURRELL*

August 19th

My portrait is coming on apace. Lucian Freud has been making a magnificent effort, truly magnificent. But sadly it isn't going quite as one would have planned.

'You don't want to do it like that!' I said, rising up from the couch. I pointed to the cactus he was painting onto the canvas, due east of my buttocks. 'No one likes a cactus in a painting. There's nothing cheerful in a cactus. The cactus is not a BRITISH plant. It does not bat for Britain!'

So out went the cactus. I took another long, hard look at that canvas. One does so hate mess. It was a sorry sight. Mr Freud had pictured me looking unkempt and bedraggled upon an unmade bed, my legs jutting out at peculiar angles. As any woman will tell you, if one wants a job doing well, one simply has to do it oneself. So I prised the paintbrush out of poor Mr Freud's hands and set about making some improvements.

'That whippet's got to go! No one likes a whippet!' I said, painting a lovely sunset in prosperous reds and yellows all over the scraggy, mean-spirited little hound. I then set to with my brushes, painting an open window onto the bare grey wall. 'Fresh air – we British love a bit of fresh air, Mr F!' I explained. The poor man didn't reply, he

---

*From *Love Forbidden: The Diaries of Paul Burrell.*

simply looked daggers. 'Chin up!' I said. How one hates a moaning minnie!

In the corner of the painting, where a very smudgy half-full waste-paper bin had once been, with a few good, strong strokes I added a doughty British Tommy with a tremendous smile on his face proudly running the Union Jack up a flagpole. Magnificent!

'B-b-but ...' moaned Mr Freud.

'If you'll just let me finish!' I said.

MARGARET THATCHER

Reread *Huckleberry Finn*. Very American.

ANTHONY POWELL

August 20th

Mousse is, to one's mind, the perfect summer dish. My sister Diana was a great judge of mousse. Diana and her husband Oswald, who was a huge success in politics, would always serve a liver mousse to start a meal, and often a fruit or cheese mousse to close it. Diana always said that the secret of the perfect mousse was to find the very best mousse chef and leave him be. Incidentally, she always insisted that the second 's' in mousse remain silent, growing simply livid if any of her guests lingered a moment too long on their 's's.

This particular mousse receipt is named after a dear old friend of Diana's from the pre-war years. How very long ago it all seems now!

MOUSSE DE ADOLF

7 hard-boiled eggs
7 fl. oz double cream
¾ pint mayonnaise
2 tablespoons dry vermouth

Stir the mixture with a spoon for a minute or two, then pass it over to chef, who will know what to do.

Diana always used to say that for all his faults, Adolf always left his plate spotless, particularly when his favourite mousse was being served. It is all too easy to criticise him, and in many ways he was far from pleasant, but this is the sort of thing chefs really appreciate.

DEBORAH, DUCHESS OF DEVONSHIRE

August 21st

Back in Londra, I catch up with the 100th edition of *Granta*, which lets me catch up with the latest brilliant, epic love poem by Harold to Antonia:

I shall miss you so much when I'm dead,
The loveliest of smiles,
The softness of your body in our bed.
And if ever anyone should say otherwise
You should tell them to fuck the fuck off, chum
Or you'll come round and splash their brains
Over the fucking pavement, just like Bush.

Once again, a work of undoubted genius.

Catch up with the latest from Salman – the guy's a magician with words, a master storyteller at the peak of his powers, the Amy Winehouse of the printed word.

ALAN YENTOB

Our lovely director Ang Lee takes us through our meditation and exercises. We sit on cushions and breathe deeply, imagining ourselves to be fallen leaves, slowly disintegrating into the deep brown rich English ground beneath us. Sadly, someone neglects to inform Fred, our lovely assistant studio manager. He arrives with a broom and attempts to sweep us up. I observe to myself that, on occasion, humans can be dreadfully prone to muddle. I fancy the lovely Jane Austen might have rather approved of this observation!

EMMA THOMPSON

August 22nd

I've had a good week. My name was mentioned by the deputy political editor of the *Derbyshire Examiner* as a possible future vice-chair of the party.

I sometimes wonder how the party can afford to do without someone of my obvious talents. All this morning I sat in my office, dressed up in my wetsuit, snorkel at the ready, just waiting for a call from Smith Square asking me to publicise whatever new water-based government initiative was going. But call came there none. I worry they don't understand that I am a highly serious politician whose undoubted gifts must, for the sake of this country, be put to good use. And if I have to strip stark naked, cover myself in chocolate and streak through Central Lobby to prove it, then so be it.

EDWINA CURRIE

Wake up in middle of night. Teensy bit weepy. Try to picture myself as Bosnian refugee, starving from lack of food. Imagine the hunger. Tearful. Suddenly feel peckish, wolf down a Mars Bar. Feel dreadfully guilty – much guiltier than the philistine cohorts of this discredited Tory government have ever managed to feel.

EMMA THOMPSON

August 23rd

Around this time of year, ancient Provençal tradition dictates that one or more chaps from the local community get together to visit the foreigner's beautiful old home. Then, with hand outstretched, they request cash, folklore suggesting that this will ensure the survival of the beautiful old home throughout the coming four seasons. Happily entering into the spirit of this delicious old tradition, I hand over my wallet. In return, I receive the customary trophy of a marvellous piece of *le gob* jettisoned from the mouth of Monsieur Bogusse with native accuracy straight onto the toe of my Clark's Leisurewear Sunsoak Sandal.

Looking down, I note with excitement that the shape, colour and texture of *le gob* are just like the truffle soaked in oil and green pepper I enjoyed yesterday at Le Petit Bistro Solange run by the estimable Madame Valerie. It is then that I remember that Monsieur Bogusse was her Head Chef. *Ah, le cuisine de la campagne! Toujours, Provence dans août*, I think to myself.

PETER MAYLE

Spot on chin. Fuckity fuck. Hate Mars Bars to buggery. Stressed. Bit weepy. Light anti-stress candle in bathroom. Have a pee. Misfire and put out candle. Fuck. Sob.

EMMA THOMPSON

August 24th

Every time I ride in a motor automobile, the familiar twirl of the wheels transports me back to the singularly ill-favored city of Dallas in the November of 1963. I had known Jack and his lamentably less masculine wife Jackie for years, though our intimacy had always, at my insistence, stopped short of the carnal.

At some point in the late 1950s, Jack and I had met to discuss which of us should run for the office of President. Jack had insisted that I was by far the better candidate, and who could blame him, but I had informed him, in the requisite tone of mild regret, that the *arriviste* interior decoration of the White House was not to my taste, and thus I was prevented from accepting his kind invitation. Jack took little persuasion; he was never backward, as my old friend Princess Grace used to say to Eleanor Roosevelt when the two of them were *in flagrante*, in coming forward. So he had become President instead, in public at least: he tended to leave the day-to-day running of the country, and the major decisions, to my own good self.

GORE VIDAL

August 25th

It is by now recognised that ice-lollies are responsible for the tragic breakdown of our society.

Just look at the statistics.

Twice as many ice-lollies are sold today as were sold thirty years ago. And over the same period of time there has been a five-fold increase in teenage pregnancy and a three-fold increase in vicious murder involving illicit firearms.

Yet ice-lollies continue to be sold openly on our streets.

These days, it is considered perfectly acceptable for hooligans to urinate and vomit in the street, over the flower stall and from the upper tier in the opera house.

Old ladies are whistling the latest rap tunes as they knife each other to death in broad daylight.

Primary-school children are trafficking hard-core porn videos to one-eyed asylum seekers in exchange for opium, killer bees, faulty condoms and casual sex.

Hard-bitten foreign terrorists high on Bacardi Breezers are leaping out from behind garden hedges and throttling much-loved family pets before committing suicide by hurling themselves any-old-how off public buildings.

Is this an Orwellian nightmare? No.
This is the British summer.
Frankly, it makes you want to weep.

MELANIE PHILLIPS

I moved into Mart's sock – where you lived was your sock; your rug was your hair. Your knee was still your knee: we couldn't think of another word for it. We called our penises our willie winkies and our shared lavatory the bog. There were a lot of brilliantly inventive word games of that kind. What if you changed the word 'heart' to 'dick' in any well-known song or phrase? Bury my dick at Wounded Knee. Dickbreak Hotel. Don't go breaking my dick … They may, in retrospect, seem infantile, but they built intellectual muscle and taught us all we knew about philosophy, psychology and other ologies too numerous (and humorous!) to mention. It was at the time of the wholly reprehensible bombing of Cambodia. These dazzling jests were part of the reason why, when Mart and I got together, nobody felt able to leave the room, or sock-toe. A glimpse, if you will, of another era, a time when Mr Wilde had sparred so felicitously with Mr Whistler across their effortlessly groaning table at the imperious Café Royal.

CHRISTOPHER HITCHENS

August 26th

In the evening, Edward and his wife arrive. We all shake hands.

She has fair hair.

'Hello, Mummy,' he says. 'We were just passing so we thought we'd just drop by to say hello.'

I say hello.

'Hello,' says his wife.

'You remember Sophie, of course,' says Edward.

'Of course,' I say, making her feel at home. 'Have you come far?'

She says she hasn't come all that far: they live quite near Windsor.

She starts stroking a corgi. 'That's Patch,' I say. 'He's a lovely lovely boy, aren't you, Patch? Yes, you are – you're a lovely, lovely, lovely boy! Who's a lovely boy, then?' Patch loves a little chat.* I suppose we all do, really, when you think about it.

I turn to Edward. 'Have you had a busy day?' I ask him. 'Do you live nearby?'

HM QUEEN ELIZABETH II

On lavvy with bowel problems. Start to hate myself. Omigod. Grow a little weepy. Thank fuck I have a fully developed sense of humour or I don't know how I'd survive! Thank you, *Monty Python*, Jane Austen and a hundred other influences. At least I have learned to laugh at myself. But now is neither the time nor the place for jokes – frankly, I just don't see what's so funny, that's all. Why the fuck SHOULD I laugh at myself? Instead, I light a joss stick, massage my pressure points and try to lose myself in the mirror. Spot back on chin. Fuckity fuck.

EMMA THOMPSON

August 27th

I venture down to the Pier. We must always allow room for 'fun' in our lives. Sitting next to an impressive youth on the 'Big Wheel', I reflect that life is like a Big Wheel.

'One moment, you may be up. And the next moment, you may equally be down,' I observe. 'But you must always sit well back in your seat for safety and comfort.'

He replies with an impressive Biblical allusion, delivered with a force and directness I greatly admire.

'Ark of,' he says.

'Ah, yes!' I say. 'The Covenant!'

---

*Patch was later to publish his bestselling misery memoir, *A Prisoner in the Palace* (Blake Books, 2009).

We have begun a meaningful dialogue.
'Oh, peace of!!' he says.
'… the Lord be always with you,' I continue.
'God help us,' he mumbles.
'Amen,' I concur.

THE RT REV GEORGE CAREY

August 28th

Went to the beach at daybreak, pulled my hat low, found some driftwood, and sketched out a plan for a semi-aquatic solar house right there on the sand. Jogged home and Blanca made me a protein smoothie. Good times.

But the thing about great art is that it will not leave you alone, it rips off its shirt, tugs you to its breast, then demands you make urgent love to it. So back I will be drawn once more, into the arms of art. Like Shakespeare, I have played many parts in my time. One movie, I'll play Death with maybe an English accent, a James Dean quiff and a tight shirt, the next I will do a whole different trip and play a troubled cop with a Chicago accent, an Afro beard and a tight shirt. My next movie? I want to be Diane Arbus,* but with a goatee and a Spanish accent. It's time we began to appreciate that great artist's sense of humor, her *joie de vivre*, her positivity.

BRAD PITT

Without anything being said, there were no women at our lunches. Not that we were talking pussy. Or not much. But it was a chaps thing. Seasoned observers all, we set the world, such as it was, to rights, offsetting our intellectual know-how with truly wondrous flights of

---

*Arbus's iconic photograph *Spotty Siamese Twins in Drag Sit in Cardboard Box in Subway Squinting*, New York, 1961 recently sold for $630,000. It is now hanging in the Sushi Bar at the Radisson Plaza Hotel, Tampa, Florida.

fancy. It was at the time of the ruinous yet avoidable civil war in Angola, in which far too many people died, or, in our immortal parlance, became deadified. It might have been anyone – actually I am sure it was our poet friend Craig Raine – who came up with the appalling yet unforgettable idea that there is a design flaw in the female form, and that the breasts and the buttocks really out to be on the same side. For myself, I have oft been perplexed as to why our heads are where, in a truly just world, our penises really ought to be, and one's arse is not located between one's chin and our nose, allowing one mellifluously to talk out of it.

CHRISTOPHER HITCHENS

August 29th

There's not enough compassion in our society and I intend to drag our politicians through the mud until we get it. Tug-of-love tots, to-hell-and-back teenage mums, kiss-n-tell reality stars, there's an awful lot of lovely, lovely folk hurting out there, and a bit of extra cash in their pockets is always welcome.

Today proves a good for-instance. I was alongside a level-crossing in my limo this morning when I saw a young lady trapped in the way of an oncoming train, screaming.

'Tell me what you want to achieve, sweetheart,' I said, 'and I'll tell you what I can do to help.' She told me there was a train hurtling towards her, and she desperately wanted to be rescued from the jaws of death. Fair's fair. My heart went out to her. But I had to tell her that, short-term, she was looking at certain death. But long-term, we could probably earn the train driver anything up to £100,000, and if he was looking for a career on the variety circuit I could introduce him to Des O'Connor, two members of Showaddywaddy and the showbiz editor of the *Daily Star*.

Very sadly the young lady died, but every cloud has a silver lining. The train driver's on *Richard and Judy* tomorrow and Piers Morgan the day after and we've already secured him a season in Weston-Super-

Mare come the winter. You've got to put something back, you really have. For me, compassion's never been a dirty word.

MAX CLIFFORD

August 30th

To Paris. It's always so dependably French, I say. 'True. Very true,' replies Harold. Harold always insists on a chauffeur-driven car. It's an obsession of his. Geniuses often have these great obsessions. Another of his great obsessions is superior suites at five-star hotels. He says they are much better for writing in.

We spend the morning writing. I am writing one of my Jemima Shore mysteries. This one is all about a murder in a country house. A dead body is found. One of the guests must have done it, but which one??!! Thankfully, I don't have to decide before I start writing the last chapter!! I love it when these wholly original ideas come to one out of nowhere.

Harold finally finishes a short play he has been writing for the past six months. Triumphantly, he reads it to me and I time it on my new watch from Cartier. 'It's exactly two minutes thirty-one seconds!' I tell him. 'That should be about right, with an interval,' says Harold.

We decide to indulge ourselves with a celebratory luncheon at the Ritz. I wear my truly splendid new green suede dress from Chanel and I carry a nosegay of beautifully sweet-smelling freesias. I am Maid Marian, as painted by Burne-Jones, with Harold my Robin Hood. Like that illustrious couple of legend, Harold and I would always elect to rob from the rich and give to the poor, but sadly the pound is weak at the moment so we simply can't afford to, particularly as we've just spent a small fortune on a truly splendid set of Waterford glass. Waterford glass is one of Harold's great obsessions, and, in a cut-glass sort of way, proof of his genius.

LADY ANTONIA FRASER

August 31st

I love old land. And new buildings. I combine these two passions by placing new buildings on old land. It gives me a great buzz. It all feels so real. Which must be why they call it real estate.

I've been truly humbled to discover that the begetting of real estate is not only a creative act but one of the most natural forms of communication known to all mankind. So as I create my thirty-one-floor residential development by the side of the Liffey river in my beloved Dublin, I know, deep within my heart, that I am somehow communicating with my fellow citizens of Ireland, and of the world.

Next year sees the commencement of our multi-million-dollar Let's Put an End to World Greed Tour* which we'll be undertaking with our lovely new roadie, Zit. Across forty-three dates, we will be seen by over one million beautiful people in nineteen different countries, whilst retaining global film, TV and publication rights for our own portfolio. How much will we gross? That's a tough question. But you know one thing that life has taught me? Sometimes the hardest questions are the ones worth asking.

BONO

I end my horrific summer beach experience by being forced to queue – goddammit! – at a lorry for an ice-cream. When I finally manage to reach the front – and why, could someone please tell me, should middle-aged women be obliged to use their elbows and toe-caps just to gain their rightful place at the front? – the inconsiderate vendor presents me with what he calls – of all things! – a '99'. It turns out to be an erect chocolate penis violently and despotically embedded in a vanilla vagina. And that says all you need to know about the British seaside in summer: unbearable, nightmarish sexual agony and torment parcelled up in a wafer cone and sold to the highest bidder for £1.25.

GERMAINE GREER

---

*Sponsored by Lehman Brothers.

September

September 1st

To be or not to be. That was the question posed by one great man. It's a tough one. My choice? To be.

I love being. There's so much wisdom in it. You wake up in the morning and you think, hey, isn't it great just BEING?

But not to be would be just as great too, I guess.

Next week, I'm learning to make yummy Blueberry and Broccoli Ice Cream served with Arugula and Coconut Water.

GWYNETH PALTROW

'Tell me,' I say, wiping the last dribs and drabs of a perfectly acceptable leg of lamb from my chin before reaching for the pud menu, 'do you believe in God?'

I'm interviewing the Deputy Leader of the Labour Party, Roy Hattersley, for the *Sunday Times*. I'm fascinated to hear what his answer is going to be.

'One crème brûlée for me. No, better make that two – one always leaves you wanting more, don't you find?' The waitress has arrived. Having placed his order, Roy returns his attention to the problem in hand. 'Sorry, John,' he says. 'I forgot the question. Do I believe in …?'

'Steam pud, with extra treacle and perhaps just a spot of double cream, terribly kind.' It is now my turn to place my order. I toy with a fudge sundae, but eventually plump for the steam pud, that fine old pre-Thatcher dish. Once again, I resume our conversation. 'Sorry, Roy, you were saying?'

'You asked if I believed in something or other, but I didn't quite catch what,' says Roy, dislodging a stray smidgen of smoked salmon from his hind teeth with the deft movement of a toothpick.

'Do you think we might manage a Beaumes de Venise? Could be just the ticket,' I reply.

'A most agreeable suggestion, which I am unafraid to endorse wholeheartedly,' chuckles Roy.

'Now, where were we?' I ask, resuming our interview.

'Which of you's the steam pudding?' says the waitress.

'That looks jolly good,' enthuses Roy.

After Beaumes de Venise, a good cup of strong coffee and a plate or two of petit fours, I ask Roy a question that always fascinates me. 'Do you believe in God?' I say.

'Your car has arrived, sir.' It is Lorenzo, to tell me that my car has arrived. Bidding farewell to Roy Hattersley, I depart for home, where I will get my excellent secretary to write up my profile of this most intriguing of politicians – a man who, from what one gathers, has not yet quite made up his mind about God, one way or the other.

SIR JOHN MORTIMER

September 2nd

This writer's wind has settled now, belligerent in its bluster, sad, happy, soft, hard, loud, quiet, calm, blowy, pungent, perfumed, but above all adjectival. But the memory of it will never settle. For centuries on, young writers will sniff the air and ask how they, too, can blow off with such muscle, with such force, with such style. To them, this I declare: write as you fart, with precision. To exaggerate is to be fatally wounded. To generalise is always a tragedy. Chase subtlety in all her nakedness, and when you have caught her, promise this old guy you'll make her moan. Turn in sentences that don't sound like ones that with a bit of extra time could be rewritten with a betterment that seizes profundity. But above all else, respect the spooky fart.

NORMAN MAILER, 'THE SPOOKY FART'

September 3rd

The moment war broke out, the King and Queen threw themselves into hard work on behalf of a grateful nation. The King learnt how to break into his own boiled egg with a spoon; for the duration of the war he insisted upon doing the job himself, brushing aside all offers of assistance. Seeing him hard at work at the breakfast table, the Queen would clap her hands together in an expression of delight. 'So clever!' she would presently exclaim.

Her own war work was regarded by many as a crucial factor in the Allied victory. 'Herr Hitler will not defeat this great country of ours,' she could often be heard saying, 'as long as the Royal Family eats up its cream buns.' And with a defiant laugh she would stuff another cream bun graciously into her mouth.

HUGO VICKERS

Attended luncheon at Buckingham Palace. Unexciting guests, mainly philosophers, writers, artists, with a smattering of politicians and showbusiness types. Infinitely dreary. Valiantly trying to inject a little life into the gathering, I raised the interesting question of the knee in literature. 'Tolstoy is sparing with his knees, Dickens mentions them only rarely, and Jane Austen not at all,' I began. 'Can anyone think of any great knee passage in English literature?' This question was met by a fascinated silence, so I enlarged upon the point. 'It is an aberration of modern times that so often the "k" in knee is kept silent. It is a perfect example of contemporary vulgarity that so many younger people – "television newscasters" and so forth – choose to go for the awful pronunciation "nee", with a soft "k". But I am delighted to say that the upper classes continue to pronounce it with its "k" intact.

Incidentally, has anyone read the latest *Eton College Chronicle*? Any good?'

ANTHONY POWELL

September 4th

I go golfing. I join my companions in the changing room. How to describe them? Let my powers of observation take over, for I must note down all their characteristics, if any, for future use. So here goes: there are three of them, they are human beings on the brink and they are here to take their stab-stabbing stabs at golf, the bastard cruel Nazi sport that stalks the innocent like a centipede in bandages.

I put on my tartan trousers, blood-red and bile-green. I signal for a caddy. There is no caddy my caddy has gone I have no caddy. And he has taken my clubs.

Caddy, I have had to kill you
You took my irons away
Coffin heavy, a bag full of golf
Clubs with a five iron
Missing
And a single tee, red as a virgin's
Period.
Caddy, caddy, you bastard.

SYLVIA PLATH

September 5th

My second day of golf. We walk to the first tee, my legs moving apart then coming together then moving apart again like a surgeon's blood-soaked pliers. I push a tee into the ground, like a hypodermic syringe pushing into a corpse, and take a golf ball from the compartment. It is round, pitted with dimpled craters, dimpled craters like a leper's buttocks, and, like a leper's buttocks, meant for hitting. Why do we keep hitting lepers' buttocks? Through the rain, I imagine myself a leper, my golf-ball buttocks slammed and swiped by a million satanic golfers.

I am that leper.

And I feel rage.

I splutter and gasp, now certain of my doom. Golf grips me by the throat and chokes me 'til I scream and scream and scream for mercy. I have done it again, one year in every two I do it. On the second tee, I use my driver. The ball soars high, high, high into the air before plummeting into the bunker, stubbornly circular and untwitching, like a dead hamster someone has chewed on.

'Bad luck!' shouts one of my companions. I shiver beneath her scorn. I want to wrap my driver round her female neck and strangle strangle strangle her to death, as she would club to death a baby seal, if only she could.

I stand knee-deep in the bunker, swinging, swinging. Sand grains scatter everywhere like another Hiroshima formed of so many bloodthirsty flying rabbits, the long white floppy ears of the sand waggling to and fro like torturing-irons. Sinking deeper as I swing, I curse my caddy.

> Why? What does it mean?
> Why does this golf ball hate me so?
> When I try to smash it, it stares back
> Undaunted, accusing, like Pilate in Dachau!
> Devilish golf-ball! Now you
> Crucify me
> With your global intransigence.
> You would poke me with a sharpened stick
> If you only had the hands for it.

SYLVIA PLATH

She was a lovely lady with a very curvaceous body and fabulous hair but Mother Teresa was forced to hide it all under this wimple and long grey gown because otherwise the paparazzi would be sure and try to snatch a picture of her cellulite, I mean it makes me so angry.

HEATHER MILLS McCARTNEY

September 6th

Day three. I am still here, still in the bunker. Above me, the sky looms, glowering blacky blackest black like an electric eel in dark glasses spreadeagled on a blackboard against a black night sky. It is raining mercilessly hard, or would be if it weren't dry and sunny. Scattered showers are expected, if not today, tomorrow. And if not tomorrow, the day after. Or the day after that. I will be drenched like a goldfish. But I will not leave until I have extricated my ball. We shall make our home here, here in the bunker. My golf ball is Adolf Hitler, and I his Eva Braun. Oh, caddy!

On the one hundred and eighty-ninth swing, the golf ball rises, slashing the air. Now it is in the rough, the roughest rough of roughs. The ball is back, back, back in the air. I have described the golf ball, but how to describe the air? It is virtually invisible, almost see-through, yes – and sparsely furnished. There is not much going on in it: no men, no panthers, no lizards, no nothing. In short, it is airy.

The ball teeters on the edge, looking over into the dark centre of the gaping hole. I knock it and it falls, falls, falls. Main fear: I am well over par. I am the prisoner in a cell of my own golfing. But was it like this for Virginia Woolf? When Virginia paraded around her local links did she cry out in pain after bunker trouble on the 2nd hole – or did she take a long, straight drive, ready for a straight birdie on the 3rd? A green seethe of jealousy bursts through the veins. But I bet she was wretched useless rotten with her number five iron the cow.

> The earthen womb
> Cries out for her baby ball back

With my putter, I knock the white round baby
Back into the womb.
The golf ball, shrieking, shrieking,
Hisses into the hole. Then –
Plop.

SYLVIA PLATH

September 7th

Bill and I are in the midst of our troubles. Stevie Wonder calls to say he wants to sing us a song of reconciliation.

Stevie is escorted into a room where there's a grand piano, and he begins to sing a haunting, lilting melody with beautifully moving lyrics, something along the lines of 'Nah nah nah, forgiveness in your heart, nah nah nah, feels so right, nah nah nah.'

Tears fill my eyes as I tiptoe away and close the door. By the time I get back from my duties, Stevie is almost done. He's kicked his seat backwards and is saying, 'C'mon, ever'body – clap yo' hands!' I don't like to tell him we're alone in that room. Instead, I treasure it as a beautiful gesture from a truly international celebrity.

HILLARY RODHAM CLINTON

September 8th

Word of Stevie Wonder's visit has got out. Today, our good friend Barbra Streisand calls and asks if she can come and see me at the White House, to ease my sadness with a medley of her greatest hits. Her gesture touches my heart. But I have to tell her that Gene Pitney, Gloria Gaynor, Kris Kristofferson, Shania Twain and Huey Lewis and the News are first in line, with top magician David Copperfield booked for a week next Thursday.

HILLARY RODHAM CLINTON

Why do our womenfolk insist upon handbags? I've managed to get through well over half a century without the need for one, so why on earth couldn't they?

One of the many joys of leading our boys to victory in the Falklands was that none of them carried a handbag onto the battlefield. Just imagine the kerfuffle if they'd all wanted to rootle around in the handbags and powder their noses at the same time.

Don't get me wrong. I have the heartiest respect for the skills and talents of women. Colourful characters, they brighten our lives with their incessant chatter. And some of them are hugely capable. The best secretary I ever had was a woman, and the best cleaner too. I recently taught my wife to skin a rabbit and she took to it like a duck to water.

Nevertheless, it would be quite wrong to let them loose on the battlefield. When the order to charge was given, they'd never be ready, wanting at least another fifteen minutes to complete their gossip and continue to make arrangements for coffee mornings, whist drives and suchlike.

MAX HASTINGS

September 9th

So what am I going to write about now? I've done my battle with anorexia and my battle with bulimia and my battle with fat thighs and my battle with thin thighs and my battle with my Brazilian waxer and my battle with my colonic irrigator and my battle with my neighbours and my battle with my neighbours' grandparents and not only that but I've done my beloved pony dying (it all got a bit nasty when it refused to canter when I asked it) and my lovely cuddly goldfish dying (for Chrissakes why don't those lazy good-for-nothing pet shops make it clear that fish have to live in water?) and my former boyfriend not being able to get it up (even though I was paying for the luxury five-star hotel suite and had bought the fruit-flavoured condoms too) and my battle with the villagers for being so greedy and pug-ugly and my battle with the puny lily-livered dimwits in all the surrounding villages for not having the guts to join me in my battle with the villagers. Don't these people know what it's like to be a sensitive young woman living all by yourself with nothing to write about? Or are they just too thoughtless and bloody-minded to care?

LIZ JONES

I hear Mao Tse-Tung has passed away. A hugely efficient chairman of an often uncooperative country. It took a great deal of effort and selfless determination on his part to silence his political opponents. But he had the sheer guts and energy to see it through. On a personal level he was immensely thoughtful. He was always pleased to see me. In pride of place on my dinner table is a delightful sculpture of a peasant worker, constructed with extraordinary skill entirely out of human skin. A most treasured gift. Predictably, the right-wing fringe claim he was a 'mass murderer'. Utter nonsense. Mao did not murder people. He had them put to death, which is quite different. And if you don't appreciate that, you're dafter than I thought!!

SIR EDWARD HEATH

September 10th

I've been designing my own costume for my next video to accompany my new single, 'Pump Your Stuff, Big Boy'. I've gone for a complete change of image to reflect a whole new outlook in my emotional and spiritual development.

When I recorded my massive worldwide hit, 'Let My Fingers Feel Your Body (Krishna Krishna)', I was really into Zen Buddhism, and my stage costume – a leather G-string with spiked brassiere and fishnet tights – seemed to draw on this very Eastern approach to my religious fears and obsessions.

Then I was seriously into feminist studies and the role of oppressed woman in the twentieth century when my next big hit, 'Find Me a Guy (Who Wants Me Bad)', came out, so I changed my costume to present a positive image for women everywhere – a rubber bondage-style body-stocking with high heels.

Finally, I was reading up a helluva lot on vegetarianism in the 1990s, and I wanted to make a strong pro-vegetarian statement, so I recorded my biggest hit yet, 'Suck! Suck! Suck! (You're Mine Tonite)', wearing a specially designed costume of lurex brassiere and suede thong.

'Pump Your Stuff, Big Boy' is basically about the insanity of celebrity and the urban nightmare of twenty-first-century society. To express this in costume I have had Gaultier make me something totally different, like a real break with the past. It's an all-black PVC cling-shirt with leather straps, and it exposes a sexual side of my art and my personality which I have previously been too insecure to portray before. It's an entirely new me – obsessive, reclusive, concerned.

And very, very private.

MADONNA

To dinner with Her Majesty and Prince Philip. Buckingham Palace v. bourgeois. No furniture worth noticing. Paintings very second-rate, some third- or even fourth-rate. With all their money, I would have made it a real treasure house. But they simply can't be bothered. I sit at the over-polished table with mounting impatience.

It is one of the great unfairnesses of my life that I was not born into a senior position in the Royal Family. Queen Victoria remains a vastly overrated figure. I would undoubtedly have brought much more zest to the role, and I would have made infinitely more of myself than that little dumpling of a woman ever managed. Yet she continues to get rapturous reviews and worldwide fame, whilst all my work is dismissed with a supercilious sneer by jealous rivals.

I toy with a proposal of marriage to Princess Anne, and plot my advancement from there. I tentatively suggest such a plan to HM. She curtly informs me that her daughter is already spoken for. I curse this feeble, peremptory age!

A.L. ROWSE

Day 2 of my mega-novel – and, hey, it's going so great it's almost writing itself!

Jake Bronze had the longest tongue in the whole goddamn business. Sitting at the table in the exclusive Hollywood restaurant, he released it from his oversize mouth.

It snaked feverishly down his chest, turning outwards past the expensively-laundered crisp white tablecloth, straight along the length of the bottom of the solid teak table, and up Andrina's perfectly-chiselled inner thighs before coming to rest on her red-hot diamond-studded $25,000 black lace thong.

'Jeez!' she gasped. Her phenomenal nipples sprang to attention like the magnificent guards in their busby hats she had seen only last summer outside Buckingham Palace, London, England, the priceless piece of highly desirable real estate owned by world-famous ruthless property tycoon Queen Elizabeth Two.

Over the other corner of the restaurant sat gorgeous, natural, body-to-die-for Maribella Slinke. Ever since her Mom died in the act of saving her from the path of an oncoming train when Maribella was only three years of age she was through with being hurt.

Since that day, Maribella hated violence, just hated it. Hated it. She was through with being hurt. These days, she couldn't see a head being snapped off another human being by an oncoming train without flinching somewhere deep inside.

'Huh!' grunted John Travolta-lookalike top Hollywood director triple-Oscar winning Salvatore Franco. He had no need of words.

'Huh?' replied Maribella, quizzically. She was through with being hurt.

'Huh!' confirmed Franco, firmly.

'Huh,' agreed Maribella, good-naturedly.

'Huh!' exclaimed Franco, defiantly.

'Huh,' thought Maribella, thoughtfully. 'I'm through with being hurt.'

Yup. One thing was for sure.

She was through with being hurt.

JACKIE COLLINS

September 11th

What just happened – what happened? Picture this: two upended matchboxes, knocked over by the sheer force of paper darts. Only it was much, much worse than that. In fact, words alone cannot adduce how much worse it was than that. September 11 was an attack on words: we felt a general deficit. And with words destroyed, we had to make do, we had to bolster truth with colons and repetition: not only repetition: but repetition and: colons. This is what we adduce.

Osama bin Laden is an identifiable human type but on an unidentifiable scale. It's as simple: as that. He is an enormous stirrer – a titanic mixer. Basically, the guy's truly massive spoon is 500 ft long. And we, the citizens of the world (CWs), are his fruit cocktail. Look how he's shaken us up, both in the heart and in the head. Truly, never before in world history has a fruit cocktail received such a great big world-historical stir from an oversized spoon, causing a stir which will reverberate in the world-tumbler for centuries.

Countervailingly, the suspicion remains that a suspicion remains. We may notice, in this *embarras* of the inapposite, this interlockingness of the mutually exclusive, this forcible handcuffing of the opposites, that any attempt at an exact meaning is lost among the word-need – needy-word – of filling space, the final frontier.

MARTIN AMIS

Well how about that, I thought as I flicked on the television in order to observe the airplanes making their way with such unAmerican precision into the World Trade Center. Or, as my grandmother in Oklahoma might have said, 'Jist watch dat cookie crumble.'

How about that, indeed. Needless to say, the world's media in what we are still pleased to call, in our sweetly innocent way, the Land of the Free, were anxious for my thoughts on the matter. So for the rest of this nondescript mid-September day I have been sitting in a geranium-filled garden *en Italie*, the blustery breeze playing havoc with my hair, attempting to explain by satellite the true meaning of what has just occurred to an American population now largely subliterate.

'It should ne'er be forgotten,' I informed the ostentatiously feminine presenter when I appeared on the top-rated *60 Minutes*, 'that the whiskery Mr Osama bin Laden is, of course, a senior backstage figure in the Disney Corporation.'

This was, it seemed, news to the white-toothed Miss Sawyer, who was also, it emerged, blissfully unaware that the far-from-dead Elvis Aaron Presley, has now donned a beard and head-dress and is living in a luxury cave somewhere near Kabul under the direct command of the Taliban and their flat-footed apparatchiks in the CIA.

A brief lesson in history, if I may be so bold. The so-called Twin Towers was, of course, in fact the Triple Towers, the existence of the third tower being kept from the Great American Public by its government for what are euphemistically known in those high-falutin' circles as 'security reasons'.

It was the virtually unknown Third Tower – where, back in 1966, the infamous moon landings were secretly staged and filmed under the direction of our old friend Mr Walt Disney – that was, of course, the true target of the 'terrorist' assault, for here it was that your own Prince Edward, fifth son of Queen Elizabeth II and a full colonel in the SAS, was training the heavily-disguised Yeti, who had entered America under a false name, clean-shaven and wearing a Fedora, to mount an all-out attack on the city of Beirut.

GORE VIDAL

When I heard the news, I was so mega-shocked I abandoned my great new novel and sat just staring into space in sheer disbelief for what must have been minutes. But then I told myself I owe it to the world to carry on. As a novelist, I have to take this thing on board. Yes, I have to reference it in my new novel.

And – hey! – it went great!

Over the other corner of the restaurant, fading thirty-nine-year-old mega-star Pasta Vermicelli fingered her vastly expensive, expertly-prepared sashimi with her long, aquiline toes.

Ever since top Hollywood surgeon bespectacled Jack Lemmon lookalike Dr Mike Decent had so expertly fixed those wrinkles around her fingers, she now had the beautiful smooth hands of a ten-month-old baby girl, even if it did mean she had to eat with her feet.

'You're SURE I now look as good as it gets?' she had begged Dr Decent as he stripped off the plasters from her head, hands and chest.

She stared down at her naked body with mounting excitement.

She now had the gorgeous bosoms of Marilyn Monroe. One on either side of her own.

'How can I thank him enough?' thought Pasta, her eyes riveted to his huge crotch. It was like the guy had two of them, swaying gently in the breeze beneath the thin covering of his expensive Harrods of London pure cotton trousers. No wonder they called him The Twin Towers, she thought. Only difference was, his never looked like coming down.

JACKIE COLLINS

September 12th

Super visit to the aquarium. My charismatic husband Jimmy used to dote on our adorable shark, Jaws. Jaws went on to make quite a name for himself in the famous series of movies that bore his name, but I'll always remember him as a very dear pet. He once ate the Duchess of Abercrombie when she went for a dip in our pool without asking, but luckily the Duke didn't make a fuss about it, and married very happily again soon after.

LADY ANNABEL GOLDSMITH

September 13th

10.23 a.m. Tony Blair is working with Alastair Campbell on the first line of a speech to the press. Observers consider it the most important of his political career so far today.

'So I'll start by saying: "Good morning, ladies and gentlemen,"' says the Prime Minister.

'No!' interjects Campbell. 'It'll be night in America.'

'Good point, Alastair!' How about, "Good, ladies and gentlemen"?'

'Good has too many religious overtones. Let's keep good out of it.'

'Fair enough! How about "ladies and gentlemen"?'

'"Ladies" is sexist. You can't be divisive.'

'Of course. Why didn't I think of that? So I'll start with: "And gentlemen."'

'Drop the "and". You don't need it.'

'Right. So I'll just say "Gentlemen." Yes, that carries real punch.'

'Too lah-di-dah. No one says "gentlemen" any more. You've already lost your audience.'

The Prime Minister crosses out his opening sentence with a decisiveness born of experience. He reaches for a HobNob. Some say it is the second most important HobNob of his political career.

SIR PETER STOTHARD

September 14th

Nelson Mandela is top of the A List. Lovely, lovely man, but where would he be without the proverbial leg-up from yours truly? Right first time: tragically locked up behind bars. When Nelson got in touch with me, ooh, forty-odd years ago, I said, okay, Nelson, you're at a career low point, give it to me straight, tell me what you want to achieve and I'll tell you if it's feasible. He said he was looking to be out of prison and behind the President's desk in a decade or two, so I said, right, first task, build up public awareness, I'm looking to introduce you to people in TV, friends in the press, movers and shakers in local radio, you name it, my friend. And of course, they absolutely loved him, they said, we've just got to have this guy for President, colourful shirts, lovely smile, high-pitched voice, the lot. I'd like to tell you the full story but I can't. Fast forward to the 1990s, and I was able to give a welcome boost to the careers of Kerry Katona and Michelle McManus, to name but two, by arranging a photo-shoot with the guy, who was then at the height of his popularity. It's a win–win situation. Fingers crossed we'll have Nelson attend Jade's funeral, maybe Bono too, the guy owes me one, plus Simon Cowell, baby-faced dad Alfie Patten and *Celebrity Big Brother* winner Ulrika Jonsson.

MAX CLIFFORD

My good friend Nelson Mandela phones to say, 'Heather, you're so loving, so compassionate, so caring. Everyone says it. How can I learn to be even half so compassionate as you?'

I tell him it's not easy. Like Nelson, I was put in prison for years and years, just for the simple so-called 'crime' of being nice.

But I made the best of a bad situation. I gave my rations – just two crumbs of stale bread a day, plus a thimble-full of water – to those that needed them more, and what remained I fed to a sweet little song-bird which popped its head through the iron bars of the window. And you know what? By the end of my incarceration, I had taught that little bird to sing 'Yellow Submarine', a song I composed all by myself.

HEATHER MILLS McCARTNEY

September 15th

A brisk coastal walk in the midst of the historic English countryside on a sunlit day does much to expose the repellent inanities of the Creator. Hills and hillocks, predictable beyond endurance, regurgitate their irksome bumpiness as far as the eye can see; grass, bladish, modishly vertiginous and tiresomely damp, seemingly unabashed to be coloured such a preposterously vivid and idiotic green, spreads itself far and wide over mountain and valley, like the venereal disease of a poxy tart. And what, may one be excused for asking, lies beneath this conceited assortment of rural rubbish? The answer is dirt, dirt and more dirt, grubby beyond endurance, ready to soil one's fingernails if ever one were to exhibit the generosity to allow them, unvarnished, within its vicinity. The sense of symmetry and balance in the countryside is execrable too. Trees, 'shrubs' and wild flowers popping up any-old-how, and the hopelessly overrated sea, much beloved of the pusillanimous panjandrums of the Arts Council and such weary old deadbeats as the dauber Turner, is merely noisy, brash, tediously repetitive, incoherent in its splutterings and vulgarly moist. Overall, there is no evidence whatsoever to suggest that anything higher than a fifth-rate mind has been at work, slipshod and vapid, entertaining itself with flimsy doodles more expertly executed by a blind lesbian black spinster pupil at a fortnight's summer school in Little Piddlehinton. Few contemporary critics possess the moral probity to voice such honest opinions about these wretchedly scruffy shibboleths of our lacklustre age. I daresay I tell an uncomfortable truth, but mine is a voice that shall not be stifled, even by the Stalins and Hitlers who now wield their monstrous power in the boardrooms of the Royal Academy and the Tate, and who desire abject subservience from all scribblers. Bah!

BRIAN SEWELL

On two legs, a man may walk a mile; but on one leg, he must hop.

SHIRLEY MACLAINE

September 16th

Reread complete works of Dostoevsky. No light touch. His characters lack *bounce.*

ANTHONY POWELL

Walking down Madison Avenue with Nina Ryan, the daughter of Otto Kahn, to whom my uncle Cecil Ponsonby had been sports tutor, I ran into the neat little figure of Franco Zeffirelli, whom I had talked to at one of Biddy Baxter's dinners on Capri. I told him that the films of Ingmar Bergman were common, and he reluctantly agreed. 'The figure of Death is unforgivably common,' I explained. 'And the only game more common than chess is Scrabble.' The most common square in Scrabble is the Double Letter Score. I might have added that by far the most common of all the properties on the Monopoly board is Water Works, but by that time he had run off to have dinner with Gee Marvel, the former wife of Sonny Whitney, whose black velvet drawing room I perked up with cyclamen pink banquettes a couple of years ago.

NICHOLAS HASLAM

September 17th, 1927

My dear Lady Cynthia,

What an awfully jolly weekend that was! I liked it ever so much. A simply splendid time was had by all. Frieda and I will remain forever in your debt.

And do please commend us to your husband, whose carving of the roast chicken at luncheon on Sunday was as delicate and sensuous as a spring rose, by which I suppose I mean that it would have been better if he had attacked that roast chicken like a man, not like a scared mouse. Did he have to be so damnably prissy about it? But it is this sitting tight, this inability to let go, which is killing modern England. The blasted prigs with their libraries and their tweeds and their silly-ass grins and their 'good manners' do not have enough blood in their guts or vim in their spleen to stab and stab and stab again at the rotting carcass of a flabby chicken. Instead, they shilly-shally about, carving oh-so-dainty 'slivers' for their genteel friends. How ugly and cheap it all is! You are all in a sort of prison, the prison of a great lie, a gangrenous lie that springs forth every

Sunday luncheon but which lurks beneath your decrepit creaky floorboards, whining in the dark, throughout every night and every day. And that is the reason why the sex-flow is dying out in the young, and why you and these grotesque weekends of yours usurp my inner energy and then suck it until it whimpers and dies, you pathetic parasites!

May I also say how much I enjoyed the croquet on Saturday afternoon – and how I am only sorry I lost so very decisively to Bertie!

Once again, thank you so much for the most delightful weekend!

Yours ever,

David

D.H. LAWRENCE,
LETTER TO LADY CYNTHIA ASQUITH

The month of October – one of my favourites – is just round the corner, and another chore looms, for October is the month I devote to plumping up the cushions on the sofa in my dressing room. But which should I plump up first – the pink or the pale yellow or the Lincoln green or the navy blue? At the beginning of the month, we will be throwing a ball for some of our greatest friends in order to discuss the matter. Desperately hard work, yes, exhausting, yes, but such are the obligations and duties that come with the ownership of one of our great historic houses.

ANDREW, DUKE OF DEVONSHIRE

September 18th

My first big political test came when Saddam Hussein invaded Kuwait at 3.14 p.m. on August 2nd 1990. As the Defence Spokesman for the Liberal Democrats, I considered that timing was all. So when I rose to speak at our annual conference in Harrogate seven and a half weeks later, Saddam would have known to expect no mercy from this particular quarter.

I roundly condemned his selfish action, telling delegates that, by invading Kuwait, Saddam had proved he was no friend of the Liberal Democrats. I was forthright in my attack, sending out a resounding message to Saddam. 'I would therefore urge him to take the responsible and courteous course and withdraw his troops at his, and their, earliest convenience,' I thundered.

The hall burst out in applause. I received roars of approval. Paddy rushed over to me and pumped my hand. In Volume One of his diaries, he writes, 'Ming made a good speech.' Roy also heaped praise on me. The ovation lasted a full ninety-seven seconds, including interval. The *Harrogate Observer* reported the following morning, 'Some delegates were saying this speech stamped Ming Campbell as potential deputy leadership material.' Prophetic words, indeed!

SIR MENZIES CAMPBELL

Untuck your bed.
Now tuck it up again
And untuck it.
And tuck it up again
Perform this act seven times in a row.
Congratulations.
You have just made your bed for a whole week.

YOKO ONO

September 19th

I'll never forget the time I had the late, great fill his name in later on the show. They don't make 'em like that any more.

I'd admired fill his name in later as a legendary performer ever since I was a lad – though I never dreamt in a million years that one day I'd get to meet my idol!

When the time came to do the interview, fill his name in later walked onto the set with all the customary grace of a legendary performer from the days when the expression 'star quality' really meant something.

Yes, they knew how to make 'em in those days. That's what I thought to myself as I watched him walk towards me with that legendary hand of his outstretched.

I proceeded with my first question, and then on to my second. His replies were fascinating. I asked a third, then a fourth. He answered them all with consummate ease. I listened in awe. They don't make 'em like that any more.

Who'd have thought a young muddy-kneed whippersnapper from Barnsley would end up chatting away to one of the greatest stars this world has ever produced. All in all, my interview with fill his name in later was one of the most memorable it's ever been my privilege to conduct. And I'll say one thing – they don't make 'em like that any more.

MICHAEL PARKINSON

September 20th

You know what really matters? I'll tell you what really matters.

What really matters: that's what really matters.

I said no complacency in 1997. I said no complacency in 2001. And so I think to myself, it seemed to work then – so why not say it again now?

Where we have lost support, we go out and win it back.

Where we have made mistakes, we say so.

So thank goodness we haven't.

People are thinking – do we go back to the Tories? Or forward with New Labour? And I say to them this.

Forwards, not backwards.

Up, not down.

In, not out. Big, not little. Hot, not cold. Start, not stop.

Callard, not Bowser. Torvill, not Dean. Pinky, not Perky.

I believe in you, the British people, as much as ever. And I know that you, the British people, believe in me.

We go so well together. Everyone says so. We always have done. You see, I don't know how to put this. But, well, I think I love you.

So what am I afraid of? I'm afraid that I'm not sure of. A love there is no cure for.

I think I love you. Isn't that what life is made of? Though it worries me to say. That I never felt this way. Before.

TONY BLAIR, LEADER'S SPEECH TO 2004 LABOUR PARTY CONFERENCE

Bosoms we called boobs, a neologism perhaps ill-suited to the well-attested magnetism of those most engagingly pulchritudinous of feminine orbs. This was a tiny aspect of an elaborate and detailed investigation by the males of the species into the feminine mystique in its entirety: a scrupulous weighing of evidence and comparing of notes concerning those delightful birds of the unfeathered variety.

It was at the time of the Six-Day War. One evening I had my wicked way with a lovely lady, who had earlier intimated that she did not perhaps find me entirely repulsive. We procured a decent room, as I remember, at the Cadogan Hotel. Perhaps a little flown with wine, I asked her to don a Martin Amis facemask which I had, with a combination of sticky tape, elastic bands, cardboard and a much-treasured photograph, prepared earlier. The fair damsel was happy to oblige. Thus attired she permitted me to embark on the hugely agreeable pathway to libidinous fulfilment.

CHRISTOPHER HITCHENS

September 21st

It's easy to forget what a truly wonderful drink water is. Whether you are my good friend Madonna or just an ordinary person – and I believe nobody to be ordinary, each one of us is very special – water has much to offer. It may be simple, but it is also democratic and beautifully clear – and it's great for quenching thirst! Try! Whenever I'm thirsty, I drink a glass of water. That's a life-lesson I'm overjoyed to be sharing with you. And if we can teach the unfortunate people of Africa to drink a glass of water whenever they feel thirsty then we will all be doing our bit to help ease their pain.

For me, a glass of cool, refreshing water is the best present anyone can give. I had one yesterday with Cameron Diaz. We enjoyed it together, and, on some deeper level, I think it enjoyed us. But if you want to take your drinking water experience to the next level, you should install the Ultra-Pure Alkaline Drinking System ($900 exclusive of installation) in your home. It filters the water through nine stages to bring you water that balances your pH, readjusts your feng shui, reaffirms your inner self and provides tons of minerals not found in poor people's water. Does that make me feel bad about myself? No. The way I see it is this. The more Ultra-Pure Alkaline Drinking System water I imbibe, then the more Earth I can save and the more I am helping the poor through my example.

Note to self. It's a liberating feeling to step outside our comfort zone, giving more than we think we can afford to help people who don't have it as good as we do.

GWYNETH PALTROW

'So, what kind of filth do you call this muck when it's at home?' I asked the waiter.

I was in a new restaurant in Chelsea and had just been served something utterly revolting on a plate, I forget what but it still had its head on, poor love, and probably its tail too. Not my sort of thing at all, dear.

I told the young waiter that my good friend famous Hollywood movie star Charlie Bronson would never have accepted such disgusting rubbish.

The waiter was about to depart when I noticed his hand peeping out from his sleeve.

'Halt!' I said, and ordered him to stretch his chubby little left hand out before me.

'Yes, I'll be having some of that,' I said. I then dug my fork into his wrist and cut off his thumb.

Yum, yum. With a dab of hollandaise it was really quite tasty. What's more, it came in at fewer calories than a small tub of highest-quality lard. The lad squealed a bit, but I had a word with the manager.

'I can't bear background noise while I eat,' I told him in no uncertain terms, and he had him taken him away.

MICHAEL WINNER

September 22nd

I receive my Prime Minister, a Mr Blair. He informs me of his plans for revitalising the National Health and modernising the railway system.

'This is all very interesting indeed,' I say.

'Thank you,' he says.

'You've obviously put a tremendous amount of thought into it,' I say.

'Yes,' he says.

'Railways are still very popular,' I tell him. 'They are particularly useful if people want to get from A to B and for one reason or another they don't have a driver.'

'You've hit the nail on the head,' he says.

After fifty years as their monarch, I have a wealth of knowledge and experience to offer my Prime Ministers.

'And hospitals form a vitally important part in the health of the nation,' I tell him, adding, 'Though important as hospitals are, they wouldn't be as effective without doctors and nurses – not to mention patients.'

I have had quite a number of Prime Ministers during the course of my reign. One of them was a woman. The others were men.

Mr Blair is busy telling me about nursing shortages in central London when the clock chimes.

I convey to him that our meeting is at an end by making a subtle incline of my head, holding out my hand and saying, 'Have you got far to go?'

I think my Prime Ministers appreciate the sense of continuity that only a Monarch can give them.

As he leaves, I notice that one of Mr Blair's shoelaces is almost undone. I tell Philip about it in the evening. He roars with laughter. He reminds me of the occasion on which the Bishop of Norwich stepped backwards, fell over and broke his ankle whilst taking a service at Sandringham.* By the end, we are both in fits.

HM QUEEN ELIZABETH II

September 23rd, 1889

Entering the market place encased in a suit dark as a cave, and almost as damp, I espied a discarded banana skin a yard or less in front of me. The day before, I had been told a story by a passing traveller of a local man, a waggoner by trade, who had slipped on a banana skin and by so doing had plummeted headlong over a neighbouring escarpment, his fall broken by a party of schoolchildren for whom the day had earlier held much promise.

Not wishing to slip on the banana skin, I took thoughtful action to avert that possibility by stepping sideways. Alas, this action brought consequences of its own, for I thereby stepped onto another banana skin, this one bigger and broader and more slippery than the first. As a consequence my fall, when it came, was all the more catastrophic. Thrust unwittingly into the air and flailing about like a bat, I landed head-first in a great cart marked 'Erasmus Archimedes: Tradesman in Used Banana Skins' and filled to its very brim with banana skins. These banana skins proved so slippery that no sooner had I entered the cart than I was swept straight off it and onto a passing donkey which had been pacing up and down, vexed by the news that its great-uncle had been recently slaughtered, after committing an act of transgression

---

*William Shawcross writes: 'This incident is mentioned in the Sandringham Game Book. The entry reads: "Oct 14th 1989: 7 brace partridge, 42 brace snipe, 1 Bishop of Norwich, 20 brace woodcock."'

against a handsome pony of high-birth. Startled by its unexpected passenger, the donkey bolted, carrying me with it through the town square, across the river, over the valley and into the far hills – in all a dozen miles or more. I arrived home, weary from my travails. Stirred out of her perpetual brooding by my bedraggled return, my wife sought to comfort me.

'The health of the downtrodden man is best served by a banana,' she observed, placing an example of the demon fruit on my plate. To cower like a wretch was my only response, and a deathly silence swallowed the room. Yet this truth will long remain with me: queer are the ways of the banana.

THOMAS HARDY

September 24th

I have always loved writers. And waiters. Writers and waiters, waiters and writers. Of the two, I think I prefer waiters. At least they bring one things.

**HM QUEEN ELIZABETH
THE QUEEN MOTHER**

Our values are our guide. Our guide is our future. Our future is our purpose. Our purpose is our values. Our values are our guide.

So much more to do. So much more to be done. To be done, to be do. Do be do be dum, dum, do be do be do.

**TONY BLAIR, SPEECH TO THE 2001
LABOUR PARTY CONFERENCE**

September 25th

For the past eleven months, I have been conducting a relationship based on mutual sexual satisfaction with Antoinette X.*

I first encountered Antoinette X in a plastic bag at an amusement park in Kilburn. Antoinette is a goldfish, but an extremely intelligent and attractive goldfish with a particular interest in the early plays of Bertolt Brecht. Her body was the most gorgeous slithery orange, and she had a coquettish way with her tail. We both knew in an instant that our destinies were to be intertwined. With two throws of a coconut, she was mine. I settled her in a spacious bowl in a modest out-of-the-way flat in North London. I continue to visit her two or three times a week for evenings of sado-masochistic reverie. I enter the flat as she swims stark naked before me. I say, 'Mmmm, you look good enough to eat!' How I relish the quiver of terror that pulses through her little body!

KENNETH TYNAN

September 26th

Lunch at Harrods with my old mate Mohamed Fayed. Mohamed's a great guy with a terrific sense of humour. Over vintage champagne and a 1911 Château d'Yquem, we agree on how morally repugnant it is that so many top people in the government and the media are prepared to stuff themselves with other people's drink.

Mohamed gives me a top-secret scoop about how Prince Philip and Tony Blair have ordered the SAS to pay off the Yeti. Apparently, the Yeti found out that Princess Anne was behind the Brinks Mat robbery, and there's been this huge cover-up involving Lord Lucan and MI6. We decide to splash with the story on Monday. There have been far too many lies coming from this Blair government, and it's about time someone had the guts to tell the truth.

PIERS MORGAN

---

*Name changed to protect identity.

September 27th

Bumped into a ghastly little woman at a 'reception'. Took her to be one of the waitresses: common as muck, foreign look about her, nasal voice, not a bad bust, decidedly alluring to be frank, tidy-poo hair-do, had her marked down as possibly a cleaning lady, obviously fancied me something rotten, kept giving me the come-on by asking me questions of the 'What exactly is it you do, ooh, that must be interesting' variety.

Was just plotting to offer her tuppence ha'penny an hour to clean out the stables when I suddenly found myself getting the hots for her. Must have been her feet – two, one on each side, quite small, well shod, not bad at all. So I put my arm around her shoulder, volunteered my broadest grin, and whispered into her ear, 'If you really want to know EXACTLY what I do, why don't we bunk up together for a few mins in a little Ministerial cupboard I spotted just out in the corridor. Let me "Minister" to your every urge, know what I'm driving at, fnurr, fnurr?!'

At this point, an oik in pinstripes sidled over to her and said, 'Your Majesty, may I present you to so-and-so?' Crikey, I thought. Smack botties time. Silly really, because one hardly ever fancies Krauts. No sense of humour.

ALAN CLARK

September 28th

En route to Cannes, I catch up on the latest Beeb programming ideas on my iPhone. Our important ClimateChange season – a massive wake-up to the world – kicks off with Ruby Wax and eight other celebrities including David Starkey and Zara Phillips struggling with their skates (hilariously!) in the Antarctic, and continues with an *Imagine* documentary following brilliant artist and all-round state-of-the-art iconoclast Tracey Emin as she creates her latest lighting installation – *I DON WON NO FUKIN SOONARMI* – for her latest exhibition at The Cube. If that doesn't change our attitude to the very real threat posed by climate change then nothing will. Other items scheduled must remain a closely-guarded secret. So let's just say the two words 'genius' and 'my friend Bono' and leave it at that.

ALAN YENTOB

September 29th

As dawn breaks, I find myself listening again and again to *The Greatest Hits of Cliff Richard.*

Cliff: a word at once reassuring yet perilous. A bird – a seagull, a hawk – sits atop the cliff. Is he ready to fly, or will he fall instead with a flap and a screech to his death?

Sir Cliff (or is it *sur* cliff, for he is now, more than ever, surely on that cliff) has always had a way with words. He does not simply have his way with them, since a true comprehender of words is no more their master than he or she is their servant. The triangle of Richard's music, his voices, and his unpropitiatory words: this is still his equilateral thinking.

> Congratulations and celebrations
> When I tell everyone that you're in love with me.
> Congratulations and jubilations
> I want the world to know I'm happy as can be.

Am I alone in detecting an underlying note of sadness, of melancholy, of extreme and nightmarish desolation, in Cliff's signature tune? He states, maintains, avers, that he wants 'the world' to know that he is as 'happy as can be'. But the tone is brutally ironic, as if in morbid acknowledgement, like T.S. Eliot before him, that his is an ambition that is wholly unattainable, for the fast-moving world (whirled?) is too preoccupied with its own thoughts, actions and consequences to concentrate on the state of mind, happy or otherwise, of Sir Cliff Richard.

CHRISTOPHER RICKS

September 30th

Today, I tell Kathleen about Antoinette. Her reaction is dreadfully bourgeois and unforgivably snobbish: how could you do it with a goldfish, don't you realise they only have a limited memory span, this could wreck our marriage, you'll have to change her water regularly, blah, blah, blah. I explain that I plan that Antoinette should accompany us to dinner with Larry next Tuesday.

'How could you do this to me?' she wails, inconsiderately. I point out that she has had affairs with the actor Warren Beatty, the pop singer Jim Morrison, the film director Bernardo Bertolucci and the fictitious time-traveller Adam Adamant over the past year.

'But at least they didn't swim round and round in circles opening and shutting their mouths all the time,' she countered.

How can one ever hope to explain Antoinette's aquiline charm and scaly grace to someone as coarse as Kathleen? No one who has yet to whip a carefree goldfish has ever participated fully in the sexual act.

KENNETH TYNAN

Cabinet all over the shop. We'd got on to Housing, and Clare Fucking Short gave one of her sighs and said to be honest her flat was crying out for a new set of fucking curtains, did anyone have an old pair they didn't want.

So then Peter Mandelson gets up and screams, don't fucking piss with me, I know what you're all doing, you're all out to get me. You're all pretending to talk about curtains when what you're really talking about is me and getting rid of me and swapping me for someone new, well, I've just about had enough of this.

TB says Peter, calm down, and Peter says, bollocks to that, what do you mean, calm down, I'm not fucking angry, don't fucking patronise me! Then Mo Mowlam says, blimey, it's getting a bit hot in here, and she takes off her top and she's not wearing a bra. So Robin Cook gets on his high fucking horse. It ill-behoves us to get mired in trivia, he says. Is it not time we got back to Housing Policy? He asks whether there might not be a strong moral case for a substantial tax rebate for a married man who is prepared to house a single woman, a secretary perhaps, or a personal assistant, in a flat in central London.

John Prescott comes out strong in support, and Mandelson, who's by now wiped away all the tears and given his nose a good fucking blow, says the tax rebate should rightly be extended to all single professional men who have secured loans against mortgages from, say, friends or business partners.

While we are all considering the various ramifications, GB comes through the door, and a bucket of water someone left by mistake on the lintel sploshes down on his head and all over his suit.

GB goes right over the top and totally loses the plot, claiming someone must have put the bucket there deliberately. His judgement is seriously impaired. I tell him in all honesty that a window-cleaner left it there by mistake, and if he wants to check then I have written proof, including a signed confession from the window-cleaner. Out of the corner of my eye, I spot TB trying to keep a straight face. I don't need this shit, mutters GB, before we move on to Transport.

ALASTAIR CAMPBELL

October

October 1st

'You know something, Keith, it really pisses me off, this rock-star-moll image I've been saddled with,' I say when we are lying in bed today.

'Yeah,' he replies sympathetically, and then he says, 'Hang on, it's quarter past. It's Mick's turn.'

Mick's great. Lying in bed with him seems to put things in perspective. 'You know something, Mick,' I say. 'It really pisses me off, this rock-star-moll image I've been saddled with. And the Establishment's always trying to make out we're all on drugs.'

'Don't blag the spliff, babe,' says Mick. A look of agitation comes over his face. 'Hang on,' he says. 'There's something bumpy at the bottom of the bed – go an' see what it is, babe, be a doll.'

So I give Mick the spliff and make my way through the sheets to the bottom of the bed. On the way down, who should I meet but Brian Jones with his familiar hangdog expression. 'What you doing here, Brian?' I say.

'I'm forming an orderly queue, Marianne,' he replies. It's then that I notice a couple of Small Faces, a Trogg and three or four Swinging Blue Jeans behind him.

Something tells me that at the top of the bed Mick is beginning to get restless. 'What's happenin' down there, Marianne?' he says.

'Nothing, Mick,' I reply. Mick can get obsessively jealous, and I don't want anyone to come between us, even the Swinging Blue Jeans. But when I make my way back to the top of the bed, I catch him snogging

Anita and sorting things out with his accountants. But this is the Sixties, and in these heady days, everyone snogs Anita and sorts things out with their accountants, so it's all cool.

MARIANNE FAITHFULL

October 2nd

What is love? Love belongs to itself, deaf to pleading and unmoved by violence. No one can legislate love; it cannot be given orders or cajoled into service. Love is a clear pool. Love is a sunlit sky. Love is a bird in flight. Love means never having to say you're sorry.

My own love for mankind is unfettered and unfounded, a boulder set adrift in a sea of indifference. I love human beings with a love inexorable and incurable, ineluctable and inseparable, like the love of a toenail for its toe, or a sausage – so sage – for its skin. My love is a love for all human beings, for their grain and ebb, for their woof and pelmet, for their sob and trill, for their sock and espadrille, a love unfettered by the value placed on it by the nauseating Thatcherite market economy. My love is a love for all human beings, every single one, unique in their uniqueness. Except for men, of course. And old women, their skins parched and yellow like discarded phonebooks. And futile heterosexual women, prepared every day, every hour, every minute, to act as the cake into which man's knife must plunge. And subservient lesbian women, drifting like zombies as the handmaidens to the words of one so much braver and more passionate and more alive than themselves. Yes – my love is a love for all human beings, save those who, alas, are not myself.

JEANETTE WINTERSON

As the days became weeks, and the months became seasons, and as we fell happily into the habit of partaking of luncheon, that most princely of repasts, *à deux*, there began an inexhaustible conversation about womanhood in all its forms and varieties and permutations, a scrupulous weighing of evidence and comparing of notes. It was the time of Thatcher's disastrous Falklands War. Boobs, bums, or legs? Decisions, decisions. Ours was not the idle sex-chatter of the proletariat, hunched corpulently over their well-thumbed copies of the *Sun*: no, it was not less than a soaring Platonic dialogue between two master-investigators of the female physiognomy.

To all-too-predictable charges of misogyny, the only suitable response is an eyebrow, first arched and then slavishly raised, accompanied by a well-rounded, 'Pshaw!' We simultaneously admired and respected the female of the species, and everything that went on in that scatty little head of hers.

CHRISTOPHER HITCHENS

October 3rd

Michigan: Robin Williams drops round and completely adores the show – it cracked him up. And that guy knows a thing or two about laughter! Of course, backstage Robin was irrepressibly hilarious, giggling uncontrollably at everything I said.

No one is faster than Robin. He's the Einstein of gags – and I don't mean gags of the cloth-tied-round-the-mouth variety! He can take a concept and run with it, turning it upside down and round and round with a range of funny foreign voices and madcap facial expressions! The guy's a fucking genius, and I don't use the word lightly (genius, I mean – not fucking! Which isn't to say I don't like a bloody good shag – far from it!).

So Robin – the man's a god, but bloody nice with it, unlike the real God, who can get tremendously bad-tempered!! – comes backstage and starts one of his brilliant improvs on the word 'backstage'. 'It's not the same as BACKSIDE,' he says, hilariously, in the accent of a crazy

Russian scientist, before switching into his finest Arnold Schwarzenegger voice and adding, 'Because if we slipped BACKSIDE, we might truly be mistaken for ONE OF THOSE' – and he said 'one of those' in his hilarious camp L.A. hairdresser's voice!

Classicarooni!

ERIC IDLE

October 4th

Rembrandt van Rijn died today, in 1669. As an artist, he was fatally flawed. He only ever painted Dutch people. Everyone is agreed that they are not interesting.

V.S. NAIPAUL

October 5th

There's a row taking place between Great Grandma McCourt and me Dad. Oh Jasus, says Dad. Don't you Oh Jasus me, says Great Grandma McCourt. I'll Oh Jasus you when I want and where I want, says Dad. Oh Jasus, says Great Grandma McCourt. Don't you Oh Jasus me, says Dad. I'll Oh Jasus you when I want and where I want, says Great Grandma McCourt. Oh Jasus, says Dad.

But just now and at that very moment the St Vincent de Paul Society is staging its annual march-past, horns a-blowin' and hymns a-blarin' preaching love and peace to all mankind. So hearing the cursin' and sensing a mission, they divert into our kitchen, all five of them, let's call it fifty, no two hundred, so's to break up the arguin' and claim two more penitent souls for the Good Lord.

Oh Jasus, say the pair of them together as the St Vincent de Pauls break into a grand old Irish hymn:

The leprechauns are jigging swell
'Pon this moonlit night
The bells 'pon their caps a-jingle
Their dancing shoes all white
As Cuchulain sits 'pon his throne
Lookin' grand and mighty scary
And 'pon his knee – well, bless my soul –
If it ain't the Virgin Mary!

As the chorus flies hither and thither like an angel in the night, Mam arrives in the room wearing the remains of last year's suet pudding while she waits for her dress to dry after the accident with the sheep dip when it sprung a leak while she was gathering the slugs below it for the Sunday stew, but the leak didn't matter, she said, because the last sheep'd run off with Paddy McGarrigy six months before after Paddy had sweet-talked her into marryin' him with the promise of a pen of her own, only the last we heard of the poor sheep was she'd taken to the bottle and was proppin' up the bar in Mulligan's every Friday night with her pint of stout and a chaser by her side sobbin' her heart out that she'd been blinded by love and Paddy'd only wanted her for her wool, bejaysus wouldn't you know the filthy scoundrel. And Mam says, what in the name o' God is goin' on in here, who're all these people tormentin' my eardrums with their carry-on and Dad says, it's the St Vincents, they're reclaimin' our Souls for the Lord, and Mam says, well I trust they've left their fleas outside and Dad says, fleas, fleas, what are we waitin' for, woman, take all those St Vincent fleas in hand, train 'em to sing and jig and take 'em to Hollywood – we could be sittin' on a goldmine, woman. So Dad rushes outside but he never manages to catch 'em. Alphie whispers he reckons a flea can spot a loser a mile off.

FRANK McCOURT

October 6th

I have sent my detailed analysis of the Falklands conflict to London. It covers two full pages of foolscap, with hardly a single crossing-out. My summing-up concludes that it consisted of a difference of opinion between two major nations, i.e. Britain and Argentina, and that, by and large, Britain emerged victorious. I also include a summing-up of President Galtieri. I say that he is a military man who rose to the presidency, very Argentinean indeed, with a limited sense of humour. London is delighted with my report. And some people still maintain that the job of an Ambassador is all tea and buns, which are actually in very short supply, owing to Embassy cutbacks.

SIR NICHOLAS HENDERSON

October 7th

'What Do You Think?'

A man called Desmond
A bloke called Ron
A boy called Andrew
A guy called John.
They all vanished, for better or worse
And all I had asked them
Was what they thought of my verse.

WENDY COPE

CONGRATULATIONS – AND CELEBRATIONS

The hard 'c' of congratulations clashes against the sibilant soft 'c' of celebrations (a name also given to a luxury selection of chocolates formed, tellingly, of centres both hard and soft – my own preference, incidentally, is for the soft, particularly the Strawberry Crème) like a knife through silk. The effect of emotional uneasiness is both maintained and reinforced by Cliff's devastating employment of words beginning with 'w' – 'when', 'want', 'world' – in the second and fourth lines.

These 'w' words (and the word 'word' is, don't forget, itself a word beginning with 'w') carry echoes of the sadness inherent in words like 'woe', 'weep' and 'wail': in these lines Richard is evidently semaphoring his own turbulent state of mind, by turns desperate for the acclaim of the entire world population for his struggle towards happiness ('I want the world to know ...') yet at the same time poignantly aware that his contentment is only relative ('I'm as happy as can be') to his own, perhaps even greater, capacity for a bitter and brooding unhappiness.

In the third line, 'jubilations', with all its Old Testament echoes of judgement and retribution, rhymes – precisely, uncannily, and with uncanny precision – with the 'congratulations' of the title. And there is undeniable sexual tension, too, in Richard's prolonged rendition of the 'lay' in 'jubiLAYtions' and 'congratuLAYtions' when set against the emphatically standoffish 'shun' of 'jubilaSHUNs' and 'congratulaSHUNs'. Seduction versus rejection: it is the greatest artists who take risks, and what could be riskier than for Cliff to bare his deepest sexual misgivings with such purgatory bravado?

CHRISTOPHER RICKS

October 8th

TO RONALD BIGGS ESQ

Dear Darling Ronnie,

Just a note to congratulate you and your company on a most excellent robbery. How supremely gratifying it must be for you that everyone but everyone is already describing it as the Great Train Robbery. Tell me, dearest Ronnie, did you wear corduroy on the big day? It does look so very, very becoming with a stocking pulled casually over the head, finished off with a lovely warm Aran pullover in cream or lilac.

JOHN GIELGUD

October 9th

The State of Britain, Part Four: In this truly moving piece of dialogue, the main character is a brilliant yet sensitive playwright, who some people say is based on me but is obviously NOT me at all – I'm not Welsh. The playwright character, Daffyd Hare, confronts what he sees as the malaise in post-colonial Britain:

JACK: Cigarette?

DAFFYD: No thanks.

JACK: You don't want a cigarette?

DAFFYD: Not at the moment. No thanks.

JACK: Don't smoke?

DAFFYD: Only when I stop to think about the malaise in post-colonial Britain which stems, directly or indirectly, from our national sense of dislocation, springing, whether consciously or not, from our deeply rooted inability to shed the sense of past glories, a failure which may or may not be rooted in our concurrent inability to face up to the challenges of the future, to develop and expand those institutions that are crumbling around us, unloved and unwanted, fostering an abandoned generation without pride or sense of purpose. (He frowns. Something is on his mind.)

JACK: Yeah, I keep meaning to give up, too. I did once, for a couple of months, but then I went back. Mug's game, really.

DAFFYD: You're right there, Jack.

JACK: It's not as though I even like the taste, much. How about you?

DAFFYD: I'd relish the taste more if it didn't make me remember the days when hope beat in our hearts, when it seemed as if this country was marching forward into a new age, an age of optimism, an age in which society would look after those who were unable, for whatever reason, to –

JACK (looking at his watch): Lordy be, Daffyd – is that the time? I must be going. Cheerio, then. Lovely talking to you.

DAFFYD (frowns): I've always wanted to know the answer. The answer to one question. A question that has haunted me. And the question is. After two and a half hours, is this all it's been about? Is it? Well, is it?

(The lights fade)

DAFFYD: Well – is it?

(The sound of 'Land of Hope and Glory' grows louder. Curtain)

SIR DAVID HARE

A bucket contains water, but water does not contain a bucket.

SHIRLEY MACLAINE

October 10th

New York. They call it the Big Apple – well, it's certainly big, but it doesn't taste very fruity to me, at least not when I last licked the pavement!!

There is a totally hilarious moment when I check into the hotel. 'Don't I recognise you, sir?' the concierge said in a distinctively American accent. Yup, you guessed it, he was a huge *Python* fan – and I was his favourite! He asked if I'd do the silly walk for him, but I said that wasn't actually my one, so then he asked for the Lumberjack song, but I suggested my famous (more like infamous!!! – ed.) Dead Cod sketch. He looked a bit blank (some fan!) but I did it for him anyway, right there in the lobby of the New York Intercontinental, with everyone watching – and by the end I was in absolute stitches!

Paul Simon, Randy Newman, Steve Martin, David Crosby, Bill Murray. All amazing, talented guys – and guys I know very, very well. And they know me very well too, they've all been to my house, bless 'em. I guess it's because I was born with the very precious gift of being able to make people laugh. Seriously – being able to list personal friends of that calibre is very humbling.

Onstage tonight, I gain an almighty roar of laughter just by saying, 'I didn't expect the Spanish Inquisition!' I don't know where it came from – it was totally improvised! – but I must remember to incorporate it into the act, for added giggles. (Did you say Biggles? – ed.) (Why do you think I'd fancy a butch English air-ace, Ed? I'm not gay, you know – and my delicious wife will attest as much after our next Olympic shagathon!)

ERIC IDLE

Do you sometimes get the feeling you just have too much on?

At one end of the room, the kids are crying out for you to teach them how to make that very special detox teriyaki salad with a carrot and ginger dressing. At the other end of the room there's a great new movie script sent you by genius film-maker and all-round fabulous guy Steven Spielberg. And then the phone rings and it's your lovely close loyal friend Madonna Ciccone begging you to step into that favourite old cut-price Balenciaga knee-length dress with your buckle belt and outrageous tartan boots and come with her to the opening of this great new restaurant.

Meanwhile, you are desperately trying to get your butt in great shape while nourishing your inner aspect by learning how to fold napkins in a way that will help the world environment. And how about booking a table for Sunday lunch with your family at this wonderful little corner bistro you've just discovered called The Four Seasons.

And at that moment your personal trainer calls by with this great new recipe for a detox face-cream consisting of oatmeal, butterfly larvae, organic anti-freeze, sunflower seeds, extra virgin olive oil, and liquid Lycra.

How do you cope? The answer is so simple.

Get your nanny to look after the kids, your agent to deal with Spielberg, your kitchen staff to fold the napkins, your environmentalist to mix the face-cream and your lovely PA to book the table at the Ritz.

This frees up all the time you need to step into that classic much-loved dress and go partying with fellow mom and pure genius Madonna Ciccone. You know what? My life is good because I am not passive about it. I invest in what is real. Like real people, to do real things, for the real me.

GWYNETH PALTROW

October 11th

My wife and I were lunching alone with Michael Heseltine and his wife, insert name, in early 1997 at his costly stately mansion in Northamptonshire. We were being served highly-priced food in his Quinlan Terry sun-lounge off hallmarked silver dishes held by his range of liveried well-spoken butlers.

The conversation turned to Jeffrey Archer. 'Let's face it, Michael,' I said, applying the gold Asprey's tongs to the lobster-filled Angus steaks, 'The man's nothing but a name-dropping vulgarian – and Andrew Devonshire agrees with me.'

A junior butler held the looking-glass steady as Michael dragged a Cartier comb through his extravagant locks.

'There are two kinds of shit,' I continued, sagely. 'The complete shit – and the prize shit. And Jeffrey is both.' Over a very decent Petrus (£350 a bottle wholesale), I gave serious thought to the historic view of shits. 'Stalin was a complete shit, Mao a prize shit. John Major's rank of shit we must leave to future historians. But what is beyond doubt is that the man would never listen.'

At this point, Mrs Heseltine interrupted with a question. I glanced at my watch. 'I can give you two minutes maximum,' I said. While she was boring on about whether anyone would fancy a coffee, I seized the opportunity to pass on a healthy bit of advice. 'The world's divided into dogs and grouse,' I said. 'And it's the dogs that bark, and the grouse that fly. If ever you see a grouse that barks, then, God Almighty, the kindest thing one can do is to wrench its head off. White for me, Mrs H – no sugar, and pretty bloody sharpish.'

MAX HASTINGS

Hits on the Katie Price website was down 20 per cent last year, which well pisses me off, so I must get my boobs modernised ASAP. Big, bigger or biggerer? Or maybe I should go for littler, for a change? Basically, after nearly two years with the same old boobs, I'm mad for something well different.

The doctor – phwoar, phwoar and fucking phwoar, talk about a well-fit body but he must be gay because he never even tries it on – shows me the brochure with its full-colour selection of brand new boobs for me to choose from.

'We could do you a pair of the Beckhams for 15 per cent off,' he says, 'and we'd throw in an arse-lift.' But I'm not having no bargain basement, for all his sweet talking. What with the sponsorship, I get all my new boobs for free anyway – and that's before the magazine and DVD rights, so who's fretting?

'No disrespect, doctor,' I say, flicking through the brochure, well bored, 'but I've had all these sizes before. Ain't you got nothing more exciting?'

That's when I have the great idea. It comes like a flash from heaven.

'I'll have a third!' I say. 'Just think! Katie Price with an extra boob! That's 33 per cent extra – the TV companies will go well nuts for it, then we can revise the contract with *OK!*, and the world rights will go for a fortune.'

KATIE PRICE

October 12th

Off to see Roy Jenkins in his office in the Lords before our historic meeting with the Prime Minister at Downing Street tomorrow. We are meeting for fifteen minutes to put the finishing touches to a new beginning for a fresh start.

I tell Roy that, as I see it, it is time to seize this historic opportunity.

'Really? I didn't realise that was the time,' he replies. 'I think we might award ourselves a little glass of champagne, don't you?'

I inform him of my determination to hammer out the fine details before our historic Downing Street meeting.

Roy looks serious and contemplative. 'The bubbles sometimes get up one's nose, don't you find?' he replies.

I come away feeling deeply depressed.*

PADDY ASHDOWN

I tell my manager about my plan for Boob 3. She doesn't think it's such a great idea, she says – she thinks two boobs was more normal.

'Thanks a lot for the vote of confidence,' I reply. I think, I don't need this aggro, I'm not going to be treated like shit, what's she ever done for me, she's history.

'Your fans might prefer the more natural two-boob look, Katie,' she says. 'And anyway, where would you put a third boob?'

Talk about negative. The natural look is all very well if all you want to end up on is *University* fucking *Challenge*. No one disses my ideas and gets away with it. I'm burning with anger.

'I'm Katie Price,' I say. 'I'll put it where I fucking want.' There's a load of body-areas with fuck all going on in them, they're each crying out for a third boob. Top of the head, small of the back, forehead, shoulder, just below the bum, behind the knee, wherever. The guys would go well mad for it – and just think of the publicity, we're talking a quarter of a million minimum from the *Sun* per extra boob.

I decide to consult my husband Pete. He loves my boobs something rotten, and I know he'll be all hands at the prospect of another. 'Sounds great, babe,' he says. 'You put it where you want it. Hey, babe, d'ya wanna hear my latest song?'

'Thanks a lot, Pete!' I scream. 'You just ruined my fucking day! I tell you I'm gonna have an extra boob and you can't even be arsed to tell me where I should fucking put it. And no, I don't want to hear your

---

*Roy Jenkins mentions the same episode in his political journals: 'Eager little fellow from the Liberals dropped by. Didn't catch his name.'

latest fucking song, not now, not ever! And you can put that away while you're about it – I'm so not in the mood!'

KATIE PRICE

October 13th

I'm still fucking fuming, I can tell you. Not for the first time, I'm going to have to go it alone. Recently, I've been going for a more sophisticated market, not just lad mags, so I definitely want my new third boob somewhere tasteful. The doctor tells me he thinks it would look really in keeping if we put it in between the other two. 'The bad news is it'll be a bit of a squeeze,' he says, 'but the good news is that it'll give you two cleavages.'

'That'll potentially double her earnings, doctor,' says my personal business manager, bringing out his pocket calculator. I always have him to hand before any of my major operations. 'And with another bosom in the middle, we can launch a whole new Katie Price Swimwear range, and let's face it, Katie, with all the extra press and TV coverage, they'll never be able to deny you that schoolgirl ambition of yours!'

'You mean I can become Principal Ballerina with the Royal Ballet?'

'With a third boob popping up through your tutu, they so couldn't refuse you.'

KATIE PRICE

October 14th

I am reinventing the umbrella. In the Eighties and Nineties, people used umbrellas just to keep off the rain, hm? But that is so *démodé*. Who are the only people who need to keep off the rain? I tell you who – the people who walk in the streets. And who walks in the streets any more, hm? No one! They have no need to walk, their chauffeur or their pilot, they take them everywhere. So please do not tell me an umbrella is necessary to keep off the rain. If you need an umbrella to keep off the rain, you should destroy yourself immediately, you are quite ghastly.

I have always been mad for the elbow. An elbow is a gorgeous thing. And the elbow patch! The elbow patch is genius! Think of the British country gentleman in his tweed coat with his elbow patch. So chic, so trendy, so sexy! So how do I reinvent the umbrella? I reinvent the umbrella as an elbow patch!

I have a small umbrella – open, of course! please do not be stupid! – attached to my left elbow and another small umbrella attached to my right elbow. So when I sit down at table I am sure no one else can come too close to me or they will be spiked on the chin by my umbrella.

I am now going everywhere with an umbrella open above my head, but only indoors. Outdoors, my umbrella has its own umbrella, so it does not get wet and dowdy. Have you seen that movie – *Mary Poppins*? Mary Poppins will be so huge next year, with her umbrella. And the men, they will put my new range of soot upon their faces, and dance around like the chimney-sweeps, no question.

KARL LAGERFELD

October 15th

Today, I begin writing a commentary to that most profound of all Welsh verses, 'The Sun Has Got His Hat On':

What exactly do we mean when we say that the sun has got his hat on? It is, to my mind, an immensely rich and in many ways hugely meaningful image, from which many useful issues not only have arisen, but will continue to arise. Some of these issues concern hats, and their role in today's multicultural society; others concern the sun, and its continuing importance and validity for all our citizens, regardless of race or creed, in this, the twenty-first century. I trust that a fuller exegesis of this remarkable lyric can and will offer a vast amount to, as it were, 'chew on'. Today, I tackle 'The'.

What exactly do we mean by 'The'? Overwhelmed as we are by the sense of possibility in that extraordinary first line – and I quote, 'The sun has got his hat on' – it is all too easy to overlook that comparatively small but to my mind hugely important word 'the'. Fascinatingly, the author could have chosen to employ the indefinite article (i.e. 'A sun has got his hat on'), but instead he chose the slightly longer and less generalised 'The'.

What, then, do we understand by that 'the'? All of us, during the course of our daily lives, use the word 'the' probably rather more than we think we do. 'I am just popping out to THE shops,' we might say, or 'I wonder who will win THE football match later today.' Yet the shops and the football match are two quite different things: one would not pop into a football match, for instance, in order to purchase a half-pound (or the equivalent metrical measurement) of Brussels sprouts; nor, conversely, would one expect to kick a ball around in a greengrocer's shop without incurring the understandable displeasure of the greengrocer in question. So, in a very real sense, it all comes down to context.

DR ROWAN WILLIAMS

October 16th

'The sun has got his hat on'. So what exactly do we mean by 'sun'?

That which most of us recognise as the 'sun' can be spotted in the sky at some point during all but the most cloudy or 'overcast' of days. By appearing with such dramatic regularity it is, as it were, offering itself up for discussion, and I hope and trust that any such discussion will be both open and wide-ranging, offering a variety of possible conclusions, each one of them applicable to the particular background of the person or persons engaging in that specific debate.

But I think we must, as a society, take every possible care to distinguish the 'sun' from the 'son', with which it has much in common, including a first and a last letter, but from which it nevertheless remains wholly distinct in 'meaning'. If the son has got his hat on, then that may be as a result of some direct parental advice on the suitability or otherwise of appropriate headgear. But if, on the other hand, the sun has got his hat on, that is a matter of altogether more universal concern.

DR ROWAN WILLIAMS

October 17th

'The sun has got his hat on'. Leaving aside for one moment the feasibility or otherwise of placing a hat on the sun, what would be the purpose? The reason most of us wear a hat in hot weather is, I would suggest, to keep the sun off our faces. But if one WERE the sun, then there would, I think, be little point in striving to guard oneself against this particular danger by donning any sort of headgear, for the heat would itself be emanating from one's own face.

Whether or not the sun should wear sun-screen, or any other form of preventative lotion, rather than a hat, is a matter perhaps best left to our colleagues in the wider scientific community.

DR ROWAN WILLIAMS

October 18th

You know what I love? Opening my heart to new experiences. Yesterday, I saw a new color, I didn't recognise it, it was kind of yellowy. I asked a close friend who I totally trust, I said, what would you call that kind of yellowy yellow color? He said he'd call it yellowy yellow, or even just yellow.

And you know what?

That was one sacred moment.

BRAD PITT

October 19th

Cherie. That's not a Christian name I often hear as I walk the bulldog down my tree-lined avenue. Far from it. You hear plenty of good, trusty British names. Bert. Dave. Fred. Jane. Judy. Eileen. Yes, and even Norman. But – forgive me – I can't once recall a Cherie.

'Hurry up, Cherie!', 'Hands out of pockets, Cherie!', 'You'll get a sound spanking, Cherie, when your Dad gets home!', 'Take your coloured friend elsewhere – I'll not have him in this house, Cherie!'

Doesn't sound right, does it?

Could this be because Cherie is not a 100 per cent British name after all? Sounds foreign to me. Cherry, yes. Cherie no.

To my ordinary British ear, the word has a peculiar, almost Eastern, ring to it. Frankly, it wouldn't surprise me to find it had pitched up from India or even Pakistan. I am no expert, but to me the word Cherie suggests all-night biryanis, beggars on street corners, cholera, foul-smelling joss-sticks and skinny old men in National Health specs wearing next-to-nothing telling us how to live our lives before being filmed forty years later by overweight bleeding-heart touchy-feely wishy-washy liberal cry-babies like the self-styled Lord 'Dickie' Attenborough.

Of course, if the trendy new Prime Minister of this once-great country chooses to run around with an Indian wife, that is his own concern.

But it frankly gets my goat that the so-called People's Prime Minister can't come clean about his predilections. A word in your ear, Blair. Isn't it high time you forced your Missus into a sari? Oh, and don't forget to lock up those valuables when she finds her way indoors!

NORMAN TEBBIT

October 20th

Quite sunny but with some light drizzle.

I have asked my ministers to come up with an answer to the Irish Question. What is the question? The question is Irish. That much we have established. But if Irish is the question, what on earth is the answer? Heaven knows. I suspect it may be Irish. If we have an Irish Question, why not an Irish Answer? It would seem appropriate in the circumstances. But it really is high time we sorted out the question and the answer, or the whole thing might begin to grow tiresome.

Luncheon of roast lamb and a selection of vegetables. Stamps, then bed at 10.50.

HM KING GEORGE V

October 21st

'The sun has got his hat on, Hip! Hip! Hip! Hooray! The sun has got his hat on and he's coming out today!'

There is, to my mind, no reason at all why the sun should not, as it were, 'come out'. That is entirely a matter for him. But should he then expect to be promoted to a senior position within the Anglican Communion? This is a question posed, but not, alas, always answered, by this haunting verse, and it is a question with which the Synod may expect to engage for some decades to come.

DR ROWAN WILLIAMS

Yesterday, I got my extra boob. Fantastic. No peeping, fellas – or at least not 'til the deal with Sky TV and *Nuts* magazine is all signed and sealed (pictures including the kids, bless 'em, 50 per cent extra per kid, please note: I'm a very private person, so anything extra's got to be paid for, fair dos).

Royal Ballet here I come! Next week, I'll be squeezing into my new tutu and going up to claim my new job from whoever the bloke is who's in charge. Let's hope he's not one of *them*! I'll tell him I'll be Juliet in *Romeo and Juliet* or I'm not being nothing, thanks very much. Never underestimate Katie Price. I know what sells, and if you've got Jordan with her 33 per cent extra bosom at the Royal Ballet, well, you've got a fucking sell-out on your hands. (And that's not all, guys!)

KATIE PRICE

October 22nd

A reception at B.P. for leaders of the Commonwealth, many of them in colourful national dress. They love bright colours, particularly shiny coloured beads. They shake my hand with a natural sense of rhythm.

I observe that most of them have a far keener sense of history and tradition than many of their British and European counterparts – they bow quite beautifully and treat me with the very greatest respect and devotion. There is no doubt that we in the West must move with the times, but there is always a danger of moving too fast, and losing something very precious in the process. In this day and age, deference should never be a dirty word.

'May I present the President of Somalia, Ma'am,' says my Foreign Secretary.

'And where are you from?' I ask him.

'Somalia, Ma'am,' he replies, with a deep bow.

'That must be very convenient,' I say. 'Though hot.'

It is conversations such as these, conducted between friends in the family of nations, that constantly afford me hope that a better world lies ahead of us.

This evening, my son Andrew turns up. He is divorced. 'I was just passing by so I thought I'd just pop in to say hello,' he says.

'Have you been waiting long?' I say, setting him at his ease. 'Have you done this sort of thing before? Keep you busy, do they?'

HM QUEEN ELIZABETH II

October 23rd

How one yearns for one's lost youth! I felt this ever more intensely today as I photographed Noddy Holder and his young male friends from the 'pop' group Slade. How full of vim they are, how like Greek gods in their platform heels!

Noddy himself is Zeus, so manly and unscrubbed, his skin like a plucked but still sadly undefrosted chicken, his sideburns as lush and unharvested as a verdant grove on a Cephalonian hillside in June.

As I position him for a shot in profile, Noddy's nostrils quiver like a steed's mid-gallop. He is a very sensitive and exceptional person. His figure in his tight satin bell-bottoms, his hands and arms – they are all so very masculine, his rough peasant hands deeply reminiscent of poor, dear Diana Cooper's, yet somehow more elegant (in my view Diana's hands were vastly overrated, and much improved in the studio photographs by my last-minute addition of a pair of Maid Marians).

Sadly, I do not take to the loathsome guitarist 'Dave' Hill, not one bit. He is an uppity youth, with little to recommend him, as spotty and overblown as poor, raddled Elizabeth Taylor, but with nothing of that porcine female's saving vulgarity. And what a dreadful racket he makes! 'Skweeze me, pleeze me!' he yells as I attempt to adjust his lime-green and puce silk waistcoat.

'I have no wish to do either,' I respond, testily.

CECIL BEATON

October 24th

This morning, I spoke to a person or persons about something, and he, she or they made his, her or their opinion about whatever it was I had just said, if anything, perfectly clear. I then either agreed or disagreed with him, her or them, and we decided either to discuss it at a future date, or not to discuss it at all. But this is a private matter which I do not intend to go into.

DAVID BLUNKETT

October 25th

On the wireless this morning, the newscaster – a Blairite, let's make no bones about it – tells me the disc-jockey John Peel has died up a mountain in Peru.

Needless to say, the newscaster – fully paid-up, incidentally – won't reveal whether Peel was pushed by a member of the Secret Services working in conjunction with the fascist regime out there. Well, he couldn't, could he – otherwise they'd do him in too.

What a bleak day for democracy when even a Radio 1 disc-jockey is pushed head-first off a mountaintop, just for playing a few tunes from the Hit Parade. Quite terrifying, really. What an untrustworthy man Blair really is. Of course, it wouldn't have been Blair himself, he's far too crafty. He'd've despatched his Foreign Secretary, little Jack Straw, up that mountain on his bicycle, equipped with a pair of gloves so as to avoid any tell-tale fingerprints. Frankly, I feel quite sickened.

At lunchtime, the book launch goes splendidly. Tony Blair comes up and says how much he enjoyed reading it. What a lovely fellow he really is.

TONY BENN

Pugs are common, and so are labradors, King Charles spaniels, terriers and dalmatians. When I last met Queen Elizabeth the Queen Mother she mischievously whispered to me that she thought corgis were awfully common. She giggled uproariously when I promised not to pass it on. I thought it best not to mention that giggling uproariously was common. When she died, a quarter of a million people marched past her body. It's terribly common to allow a quarter of a million to march past your body. Chairman Mao did the same, which proves my point. After umpteen years, Mao really should have done something about that grubby little blue romper-suit. He might have looked fabulous in tartan, but, being common, he lacked the imagination.

NICHOLAS HASLAM

October 26th

At lunchtime, I was driven in my vintage Rolls – one of several, I might add – to the beautiful luxury home of my very good friends Sir Michael and Lady Shakira Caine. To his great credit, Michael is a tremendous fan of all my films.* He says I always bring them in under budget, than which there is no higher praise. Too many of your arty-farty types bring in their films way over budget, and often forget to include a decent rape scene. Yet they persist in passing themselves off as film directors!

The food on offer at Michael's was far too fatty. By the end of the meal, I'd left most of it on the side of my plate. But I was still feeling extremely peckish. As the woman next to me – a complete nonentity – was holding forth on a subject of no interest, I couldn't take my eyes off her lovely lean arms. 'I'll be having some of that,' I thought to myself. I then sank my teeth deep into her lower arm, and helped myself to a decent mouthful.

Scrumptious! For main course, I summoned the waiter, got him to drop his trousers and tucked into a delicious slice of left buttock topped off with double cream. That still left me with the problem of dessert, so I reached over the table, grabbed the head of the Lord Mayor of London and took a superlative bite of nose.

A splendid repast, and no need for cheese. Evening weight: down a full 2lbs. Looking at myself naked in the mirror this morning, I had a stroke of genius: eat yourself, and you'll lose double the weight, whilst saving money you would have spent on eating riff-raff. So I'm having my surgeon remove a nice couple of slices of my own delicious stomach, for my chef to braise over a low heat with shallots and Beluga caviar. And now everyone be like me just by following my diet! My message? Eat more of yourself and others, my dears! After all, it's only human!

MICHAEL WINNER

**Death Wish 1* (1974), *Death Wish 2* (1976), *Death Wish 3* (1981), *Death Wish 4* (1987), *Death Wish 5* (1989), *Death Wish 6* (1991), *Death Wish 7* (1993), *Death Wish 8* (1994).

In these modern times, people go to quite extraordinary lengths to avoid upsetting dwarves, or 'little folk', as we are no doubt expected to call them. If one passes a dwarf in the street, it seems one is forbidden by an unspoken taboo to pass comment on his lack of inches, however noticeable and indeed objectionable that lack may be. I am no dwarf – far from it: my friends tell me that I am of a perfect height – but if I were, I would resent such pussy-footing. Of course, I suppose it is possible to go too far in the other direction – dwarf deportation on any major scale would be unworkable, though one imagines they might profitably be stacked – but henceforth I will make pointed comment along the lines of 'Oi! Shrimpy!' whenever I see one scuttle past my ankles. Dwarves would be the first to admit that they do not respond well to obsessive mollycoddling. Only by such frank and honest means will the dwarf population regain the dignity that is their due. And the example would be chastening to others who might even now be entertaining the temptation to shrink.

SIR PEREGRINE WORSTHORNE

October 27th

JOHN: Why is it only married couples who divorce one another? Is there something about marriage that encourages divorce, do you think?

ROBIN: In the vast majority of cases, divorce comes about after married couples 'fall out' with one another. But of course, if they had remained single, they would not then be in a position to get a divorce.

JOHN: Or if they had never met one another in the first place?

ROBIN: Certainly.

JOHN: So it follows that two people – let's call them Person 'A' and Person 'B' – should never actually meet if they want to avoid the awful prospect of divorce?

ROBIN: They are certainly increasing their chances for a potential divorce in the years ahead if they first get to meet one another.

JOHN: And what's the best way, then, for Person 'A' to avoid meeting Person 'B'?

ROBIN: Well, if they live in different parts of the world, and are in different socio-economic groups, then that's half the battle won.

JOHN: But surely they might still meet? On holiday, for instance.

ROBIN: Certainly that's a risk.

JOHN: So what's the best place to go on holiday in order to avoid meeting your future wife, and the whole thing ending in a distressing divorce, awful for the children and potentially ruinous to the inner psyche?

ROBIN: We're venturing into very difficult territory, here, John. It's advisable to consult your travel agent on this one, I think.

JOHN: Quite.

JOHN CLEESE AND ROBIN SKINNER

October 28th

The stone in my shoe has been there for six months, for Chrissake, and no one's done a blessed thing about it. Every time I put my shoe on, there it is again. In our 'enlightened' society, women are indoctrinated not to complain when there's a stone in their shoe. Instead, they're forced to choose between a stone in their shoe – or a stone in their shoe. What kind of choice is that?

At the end of the Millennium, there's simply no choice, stonewise. It makes me so angry – and I'm darned if I'm going to take it any more.

GERMAINE GREER

Went to the theatre last night. Very posh do. Classy progs. Plush seats. Curtain up. Yummy lollies in the interval. *Hamlet*, it was. Bit wordy. Not much action. Only decent bird goes and gets herself drowned halfway through. Set in Denmark, of all places. Hero moons around doing bugger all for three or four hours. Not a single tune you can hum. Yawn, yawn. Can't see it catching on.

HUNTER DAVIES

October 29th

The fox-hunting season commences. For chasing Mr Reynard, there is no animal I would rather ride on than the horse. The donkey is too stubborn, the camel too slow, the duck too flighty. I once rode to hounds upon the back of a chihuahua, but we had not leapt the first fence before the wretched beast perished beneath me, thoughtlessly leaving me to wrap it round my neck as a surprisingly effective head-scarf and to leap the fence all by myself.

The English horse is a creature of strength and beauty unsurpassed. This merry morn, I ascended my doughty steed. Seventeen-hand horses were snorting and heaving to every side, their buttocks rippling with muscles like the seething wakes of ocean liners. Dobbin's neck was arched, his head down, with the bit held firmly in his teeth; his feet were dancing on the road, his tail swishing provocatively to and fro, and great surges of life rose through his quarters, invading and inflaming me on their way to his heart and to his head.

Ah! Most equine of steeds! A novice, I climbed into the saddle and from this great height looked out o'er the clear view of yonder English hills. A crack of the whip, a crick of the spur, and Dobbin was up and away, like winged Pegasus flying o'er lofty Mount Olympus! Never had I felt such a sensation, for I was now travelling backwards at a great gallop, the swish-swish-swish of Dobbin's mighty tail beating heavily into my visage. But where was his head? Through the hairs of his tail, I searched for his head. Did not every steed perforce have need of a head? With a start, I realised I had ascended my mount with a degree of incorrectitude. I was facing the rear.

Civilisation continues through adherence to established codes. I did not intend to discommode the hunt by calling my horse to a halt and turning around in my saddle. Instead, I employed Dobbin's tail as reins, turned my riding hat around and urged my noble steed to proceed backwards, thus maintaining my dignity at no cost to my fellow horsemen.

ROGER SCRUTON

Foxes are so common! No one should wear a tail in public! And as for whiskers, they aren't just common: they are very very VERY common!

It's also terribly common to be chased by hounds. Where do you end up? Either getting filthy dirty down some dreadfully cramped little hole – or ripped to shreds! And there is simply NOTHING more common than being ripped to shreds!

One should avoid celebrity foxes at all costs. Basil Brush? The absolute pits! That awful throaty laugh! Common, common, common! Has he never heard of lozenges?

And what of the other famous foxes? Sam Fox is DESPERATELY *passé*, dear. Appearing topless on Page Three of the *Sun* is terribly common. Always has been, always will be. And as for Charles James Fox, it was always very common to oppose William Pitt. He really should have known better.

Edward Fox wasn't at all common until he played that awful little man who tries to assassinate President de Gaulle. Assassination is very common, ATTEMPTED assassination even more so.

And Liam Fox is common too. There's no one more common than a Conservative frontbencher.

NICHOLAS HASLAM

October 30th

A cloudy day, but not unpleasant. Breakfast at 7.30. We motor to Portsmouth, arriving at 12.45.

I learn with regret that the Irish Question remains unanswered. Luncheon at 1.30. Henry of Prussia comes to see me in the evening. Very Prussian. 'And tell me, Henry, how is Prussia?' I say. He kindly informs me Prussia is well. I show him my stamps. He takes the most keen interest. As I reach for the twenty-third volume, he remembers a sudden appointment back in Prussia and takes his leave.

Bed at 11.30.

HM KING GEORGE V

October 31st

Statistically, as few as 2 per cent of men are ever forced by their parents to wear a brassiere, yet as many as 72 per cent of women have been told to wear brassieres by their parents at one time in their lives. Why the imbalance?

'When I strangled my younger brother to death with my first brassiere, I was made to feel guilty by my father, who told me he would undoubtedly lose his temper if I ever thought of doing it again,' writes one correspondent. 'The experience of this brutal chastisement has stayed with me all my life, and I am now in my ninth year of trauma counselling.'

From this, we learn that of the 23 per cent of teenaged women who strangle their younger brothers with brassieres, an astonishing 92 per cent have a sense of guilt forced upon them by one or both parents. What right has society to enforce such strong guilt association? Answer: none whatsoever.

SHERE HITE

All those years of my valiantly (foolishly? quixotically?) standing up for British cinema are not so much disregarded as despised.

I felt this most strongly and – yes – upsettingly when the woman behind the counter in the bakery served a nondescript fellow before me even though he had quite clearly come in after me. How dare she?! How bloody DARE she? If this is the way they treat a man who has spent the best part of his life struggling on a pittance to revive British cinema, well, I sometimes think that Britain thoroughly DESERVES to sink beneath the pus spewed out by one great septic tidal wave.

'Now what can I get you sir?' the wretched woman says with a sly, ingratiating smile. I realise in a flash that she is in no sense an intellectual. I am about to ask her if she realises that I am the director of last year's Cannes prize-winning film – but, oh bloody hell, why should I bother? The working class never seem to care the foggiest who's on their wretched side, who's batting for them against this bloated, destructive age. For all they care, I might as well be one of them!

LINDSAY ANDERSON

November

November 1st

The arrival of the Prince of Wales has delighted everybody here in our Paris Embassy. He is quite brilliant at shaking hands with everyone, and walks with a natural ease by moving one leg in front of the other. The French adore him, of course, and since his arrival British exports have boomed, with two pairs of British driving gloves sold in the Lyons area alone. After his official duties are over, HRH lets his hair down, retiring to our drawing room to delight us with his imitations, which he performs quite brilliantly.

'Have I done my Neddy Seagoon?' he says at 2.00 a.m.

'No, sir – that would be priceless,' I reply, and he does his Neddy Seagoon for the fifteenth time, while we all applaud wholeheartedly. The role of today's diplomat, working at the coal-face of modern life, is not to be underestimated, even in this day and age of 'highspeed technology' – electric toasters and so forth.

SIR NICHOLAS HENDERSON

November 2nd

It doesn't take a genius to guess that the electric toaster was designed by a man. Why? Because it's lousy for putting in the dishwasher. Every time I put my electric toaster in the dishwasher, it fucks up, and I have to go out and buy another one for Chrissake. For 92 per cent of men, the dishwasher is merely a means of irreparably damaging toasters, leaving their wives to toast bread by hand, leading to 33 per cent body burns, and bogus research suggests that a further 17 per cent have attempted at some point in their married lives to stack their wives in a dishwasher before turning the knob to Rinse. It's even been said that women are sexually turned on by the dishwashing cycle. Oh yeah? This kind of made-up statement makes me hopping mad. How DARE anyone give it the time of day – let alone repeat it in print?

GERMAINE GREER

I had that Primrose Shipman, wife of the late Dr Harold, in the office this afternoon. (If you knew what I know, you'd realise he was a first-rate doctor, lovely man, very caring, very considerate, on the shortlist for the Nobel Prize – but the snooty, patronising medical establishment were jealous, weren't they?) Anyway, lovely Primrose is trying to reinvent herself with a new diet book to promote, so she's looking for a whole new rebranding to go with it.

She was letting things get on top of her, so I slid the old box of Kleenex Extra Strong across in her direction and said, 'Have a good weep, love – that's it, all better, let it out. 'Scuse us a minute, love.'

So while Primrose was having a right old sniffle, I'm on to my friend Simon Cowell of *X-Factor* fame.

'I've got a lovely bubbly lady with me here for you to escort to Stringfellows, Simon,' I said. 'Believe me, there'll be a helluva lot of press interest, particularly if we can persuade the lovely Kerry Katona in her thong to join the two of you at a table with bad-boy former MP Ron Davies. And any chance of Ant and Dec?'

Result? 324 column inches on 'Plucky Primrose's Big Night Out with the Stars'. Result? A helluva lot of interest from the high-ups in her hosting her own knitting show on satellite, and that can't be bad.

MAX CLIFFORD

November 3rd

We have bought a new puppy, Spot, who is quite simply not house-trained. I telephone the Master of St Swithin's, Oxford, and ask him if he'll take Spot on in some sort of undergraduate capacity and knock a bit of sense into him. He says he'll see what he can do. I tell him there's a dinner with Queen Elizabeth the Queen Mother in it for him. He brightens up.

WOODROW WYATT

With Christmas fast approaching, we are all asking ourselves, 'What is holiday spirit?'

For me, holiday spirit is a feeling of warmth, of togetherness, of connectedness. We get that by buying things. That is why 'God', 'All-Seeing', 'Inner Eye', 'Om', 'Buddha', 'Big Buddy' – call him or her (or both) what you will – gave us all these beautiful neighbourhood stores, and, more recently, offered us the candid spiritual privilege of personal renewal by shopping online, thus helping save the Earth.

GWYNETH PALTROW

November 4th

Delighted to hear that Bill Clinton has won the American election. He's what one might call 'a little man from nowhere', so it's a jolly good effort all round. It's always been my firm belief that these people always benefit from a pat on the back from the likes of us, so I take the trouble to send him and his wife a brief card.

LADY ANTONIA FRASER

Barack must be hurting dreadfully, just like me. OK, so he's going to be President, but it must be so overwhelming for him and I know he's feeling a little bit lost and bewildered and in need of TLC from yours truly! So I've been trying to call him all day to offer him lots of lovely big huggies and a right royal shoulder to cry on.

SARAH, DUCHESS OF YORK

Like me, Barack Obama is an internationalist. That is why I had high hopes for Senator Obama. Though he priggishly refused to smoke during his speeches, he was, like myself, of mixed race. But that was yesterday. Since then, Obama has behaved appallingly. If I had won the Presidency, I would never have then accepted it. Barack's acceptance was a typically populist act, and one that discounts him from being taken seriously. By doing so, he has played into the hands of all those who voted for him. It was a truly appalling and indeed disgraceful thing for him to have done.

CHRISTOPHER HITCHENS

Barack has been elected President. I'm going to leave it for later. Overwhelming numbers of people were urging me to stand for the Presidency last year, but I'm like, no, it's high time America had its first black President. After that, America might just want its first black woman President – it's a secret, but I am actually black – but let's wait and see, shall we? One thing's for sure, though: if and when I become President, I plan to change the title of 'President' to something a whole lot less formal, and much more humble. Like 'Top Carer'.

HEATHER MILLS McCARTNEY

The Master of St Swithin's College rings to ask if our new puppy Spot might muster a Grade 6 in Latin O-Level. 'I'll ask him and get right back to you,' I say and put down the phone. I immediately telephone the King Pin of the O-Level examiners and invite him to dine with my friend Queen Elizabeth the Queen Mother. I phone back the Master of St Swithin's. 'I think we can get Spot a Grade 5,' I tell him with confidence.

WOODROW WYATT

November 5th

'Another Poem About Men'

I look in the fridge
And find it empty
But nothing rhymes with empty
So I look again
And find a hen
Which gives me the chance
To make this another poem about men.

WENDY COPE

Spot is accepted as an undergraduate of St Swithin's, Oxford. Dropping him off on his first day, I mention to the Master that we've been rather hoping he'll get a chance to row for the college. The Master tells me that as far as he knows they've never had a puppy rowing for the college before. I happen to mention there's a place on the board of the Tote coming up. The Master thinks for a while, and says there's really no reason why Spot shouldn't make a very useful cox, just so long as he can produce the necessary swimming proficiency certificate.

WOODROW WYATT

November 6th

I put a call through to the Chairman of the Board of Swimming Proficiency. 'I was wondering if you've ever had the chance to meet my dear friend Queen Elizabeth the Queen Mother?' I ask.

WOODROW WYATT

You know, sometimes I worry that eliminating negativity is, like, a negative process, I think, like, should I really be eliminating anything, I mean, doesn't negativity have a right to live and exist on this planet without, like, being eliminated?

MADONNA

November 7th

I had a day to spare so in the morning I took the underground train from Westminster to Sloane Square. In the afternoon I wrote a book about it.

As I boarded the train at Westminster, I noticed that everyone apart from me was squat and ugly and dishevelled and grimy. The English have never recovered from their loss of Empire, and their faces and bodies have become raddled with self-pity as a result. Among them I felt like an alien: I sensed their eyes glaring at me with undeserved contempt. No one spoke a word to me as the train rattled along. Instead, they buried their heads in their newspapers, pretending to read as they plotted ways to kill me. I knew from their sullen silence that they would like me to fall beneath the wheels of the train. Only then would they smile. I had lived in England for thirty-five years, but never once had I felt any warmth.

The next stop was St James's Park. Opposite me sat a statuesque Masai woman, her body made sleek and strong by her daily hunt for wildebeest in the foothills of the Serengeti, her voluminous breasts swaying gently in the winter breeze. I asked her whether this was the

Circle Line, and before the train had set off she had placed her hunting spear to one side and was howling eagerly in the ecstasy of sex like an addict injected, and her eyes rolled up in her skull and she stared, still howling, with big white eyes like a blind zombie that sees everything. 'Paul! Paul!' she cried – she must have read my name off my clutch-bag – 'You are not only a great writer – but you are all man!!' Afterwards, limp and sleepy, stupefied by sex, she confirmed that, yes, this was the Circle Line. As the train drew into Westminster, she rose to leave.

I never saw her again.

I now realise that I never actually liked her.

PAUL THEROUX

November 8th

I've always loved words. Long words. Short words. Middle-sized words. Words not exactly short, but still not quite long enough to be called middle-sized. In-betweeny kind of words. No matter. I love them all. As a child, making words slant across the page was like making rain. Hey! I could make rain! The revelation impacted on me like a triple orgasm on a deck-chair. See the flowers bloom under my golden rays! And isn't that a rainbow athwart the pastures? Beneath the arbour of the corn-bush, a young rabbit pleasures an older one with his twirling, tinkling, rabbit tongue. The older rabbit has taught him all she knows of love, and now he is repaying her in full. Fill me! Fill me! Yes, I was the God of all I wrote, and, like God, I was going to change the world.

And so I did. Just a year after I wrote *Fear of Flying*, Richard Milhous Nixon resigned from office. Sixteen years later, with the publication of *Horny as Hell: The Feminist Diary of an Eighteenth-Century Lady*, Nelson Mandela was released from prison. And almost exactly twelve and a half years after I wrote *How to Save Your Own Life*, the Berlin Wall came tumbling down. This week, I have a new book out. Whaddya know, a new Millennium is soon to be announced.

ERICA JONG

John Milton died today, in 1674. *Paradise Lost* is really very feeble and old-fashioned. It was fashionable once, but it sells really very few copies these days. A good writer wishing to pursue his craft should not succumb to blindness.

V.S. NAIPAUL

November 9th

I have been sent yet another book about Jack the Ripper. Why do people go on so about poor Jack? As a child, one was taught that if one had nothing nice to say, best say nothing at all. This is a rule that now seems to be disregarded. Most, if not all, of Jack's severest critics never even knew him personally, as I did. Yet their insufferable ignorance seems only to spur them on to greater heights of sheer malice. How one wishes they would simply 'shut up'!

Jack was hugely amusing, a brilliant talker with a clever wit, as well as exquisite courtesy towards women. Needless to say, these qualities are never mentioned. Instead, his small-minded critics concentrate their efforts entirely on what one might call his 'one little weakness'.

Oh, the ghastly suburban tedium of those blinkered dullards!

DIANA MOSLEY

November 10th

Throughout the known and – deservedly, to my mind – unknown world, the owl silently rejoices in his reputation for wisdom, unaccountable though that reputation may be to his peers. My entire life has been, and will doubtless continue to be, and, later, to have been, overshadowed by the unearnedness of this reputation. Theologians, philosophers and scientists have made me welcome in Copenhagen, but they have eschewed the central question. So let the question be submitted: if the owl is so very wise, why does he only eat uncooked mice, which he is, furthermore, forced to catch for himself, disgorging the remains of their prey, indigestible and undigested, in unattractive pellets or castings? Why have I refused to add my signature to manifestos, appeals, protests with many of whose propositions and urgencies I would otherwise concur but whose deification of the owl strikes me as unworthy and for-uncalled? No owl has ever held down a post in a university of any international reputation, nor has an owl ever been known to have presented first-rate research from primary sources on a subject of even secondary importance. In essence, the etymological accord of 'owl' and 'howl' is factitious; nevertheless, upon passing that smug bird in an aviary, I invariably find myself submitting a silent yet, for all that, hideously anguished howl.

GEORGE STEINER*

Shops have abandoned salesmanship. I visited several this morning, looking for a halfway-decent blowpipe and poison darts with which to despatch an irritating cat that has taken it upon itself to prowl around in our grounds.

The man – if you could call him that – in W.H. Smith looked completely blank. 'We mainly do magazines, books and stationery, sir,' he whined. Excuses to that effect also came from the assistants in Woolworth, Rumbelow's and Hallmark Cards.

Eventually, I took pot luck at Dixon's, where the female assistant told me offhandedly that they just sold electrical goods. 'Right!' I said, slapping £50 on the glass-top counter, which turned out to be far too frail for the job. 'I'll have an electric chair. And make it small enough for a cat.'

The brighter reader can guess what happened next. Yes: Dixon's sell toasters and record-players and electric toothbrushes and heaven-knows-what-else. But they do not sell electric chairs for cats.

I returned home cursing the inadequacies of the British High Street. When you see how many cats there are – sometimes even inside

*From *My Unbitten Rooks* (2002).

people's houses, dammit! – you are left staggered by the retail industry's failure to plug this particular gap in the market.

I would normally despatch it with my 4.10, but my wife tells me it's illegal. I should have known. Soon this despotic Blair government will have killed off everything that's worthwhile about the English countryside. Believe me, it won't stop here. First, they make it illegal to pepper a cat to an early grave. Next, they'll force you to 'apply for a certificate' if you want to despatch your old grandmother to a gentler place, even if she's proving the most profound irritation to herself and others.

MAX HASTINGS

November 11th

To some sort of outdoors 'do' at the Cenotaph. I went along to get regally drunk, but everyone was standing stock still, and saying f— all.

As per usual, it fell to yours truly to liven things up a bit, so I told the one about Diana Dors and the elephant. When I'd finished, I roared with good-natured laughter. But I was reckoning without them all having left their senses of humour at home. What a lot of stuffed shirts.

So I turned round and said, 'Hey, lighten up, you guys!' Someone had to say it, and I was the only one there with a) the courage and b) the sheer bloody sense of occasion.

PIERS MORGAN

November 12th

More rain in the night. Five degrees of frost this morning.

Lord Roberts arrives with news from the Front. Thousands killed. Quite chilly, but with occasional sun. So much more enjoyable fighting in halfway decent weather. Marked my new stamp catalogue during afternoon and early evening. One stamp suffers slight nick. Most regrettable.

Dinner with May. Bed at 11.15.

HM KING GEORGE V

Graffiti spotted on a wall: DOWN WITH FEMALE'S THEIR ORL TART'S. This made me so hopping mad that I got out my trusty felt-tip and corrected it to DOWN WITH FEMALES. THEY'RE ALL TARTS. My campaign for a better-educated Britain continues apace.

KEITH WATERHOUSE

November 13th

Here I am in my own house, bought with my own hard-earned money, thank you very much, so don't tell me I didn't or I'll bloody thump you for being so aggressive, and I'm standing down here at the bottom of the stairs looking up and I'm sorry it may sound stupid but I've always had this feeling when looking upstairs that there's going to be someone on a higher step looking back down at me, that's why I've always preferred to travel in lifts, or 'elevators', as the up-their-own-arses brigade call them, because at least when you're all stood in a lift you know everyone else is on the same level and there's no one above you looking down on you thinking bloody hell he's inferior. Y'know, sometimes I've travelled in a lift with lah-di-dah bigwigs all posh and that and even though I've been dressed up in a suit and tie I've known in my gut they're all busy thinking I'm the bloody lift-operator and thinking to themselves, why don't that inferior lower-class man stop giving himself airs and start pressing the buttons like we employ him to do and that kind of attitude really gets to me, it really does I want to give them a good thumping and tell them look, chum, I've got as much right as you to travel in this lift and if you want to go to a particularised floor then why not just punch the buttons for your own bloody self?

JOHN PRESCOTT

November 14th

So I'm standing naked in front of the mirror searching for anything to tell my lovely lovely readers about when in a flash of inspiration it suddenly comes to me.

I'll remove a limb!

Flushed with excitement from head to toe, I hurtle downstairs in search of my most expensive designer kitchen knife (£65 from Seraitier of Bond Street). Found it!

Then I hurtle back up to the mirror again and prepare to make the Big Decision.

Which limb?

If I cut off a finger or toe it would eventually pay for itself, as that would give me an annual 5 per cent saving on nail varnish. But these days who gives a toss about fingers and toes? I might go to all that effort only to find my lovely lovely readers couldn't give a toss about it and give me no feedback whatsoever, ungrateful bloody so-and-sos.

What about a leg? If it worked for that boot-faced sourpuss Heather Mills, it'll work for me. It would give me columns galore – not only six or seven about how I managed to cut off my own leg with a carving knife, but three or four about how much I love hopping in the country, and at least another half-dozen on how no one in my hard-hearted village has shown any sympathy what-so-bloody-ever for a young woman who's struggling to come to terms with a new disability, thank you very much.

LIZ JONES

The Queen Mother is no beauty, bless her. She is even, dare I say it, a bit common, with a perfectly ghastly habit of interrupting one when one is talking of subjects beyond her.

I held the table – a dull philosopher and his dreary wife; my publisher;* a ghastly, spineless politician (possibly the Prime Minis-

---

*Lord Weidenfeld, whose memoir *Remaindering My Good Friends* also recounts this incident.

ter?) and his equally ghastly wife; a couple of vulgarly famous film stars and a boorish poet – utterly spellbound with all the latest gossip from the Victoria and Albert Museum. The Keeper of Ceramics has fallen out with the Under-Keeper of Miniatures after hearing that one of the Secretaries in Stuffed Animals had mentioned that the Director of Engravings had taken a dislike to an early work by the Assistant Director of Porcelain.

Inevitably, this news rendered the table speechless. It was the Queen Mother who was the first to chip in. Alas, she was desperately muddled.

'And apparently they all absolutely loathe the new Director,' she said. 'They say he's a self-serving, publicity-mad, social-climbing ponce.'

'Correction, Ma'am!' I laughed. 'You must be thinking of someone else! You see, I am the new Director!'

Poor dear, she gets her names very mixed up these days. The food incidentally, was filthy. Needless to say, I received many admiring glances for my broad-brimmed scarlet fedora and purple crushed velvet knickerbockers, not unmixed with a certain amount of envy from the ladies.

SIR ROY STRONG

November 15th

On the other hand, if I cut off my leg I'll never be able to kick anyone ever again, and that breaks my heart. I could cut off my head, I suppose, but then I could never wear my beautiful Philip Treacy hat (total cost £650) again without it falling off and that would be a total but total waste of the massive £650, no kidding, it cost me.

Back to square one (story of my life! talk about to hell and back!).

But then I'm thinking – what about the skin?

I've always had a troubled relationship with my skin. Now it's too wrinkly, now it's too spotty, now it's too saggy. Whatever! All in all, as my osteopath always said (before I had to get rid of him for talking behind my back), I've never been happy in my own skin.

So it has to go!

LIZ JONES

Everyone is going on about Lucky (Lucan) having killed that nanny of his. Honestly! She wasn't even a very good nanny, or so I'm told.

ANNABEL GOLDSMITH

November 16th

Our weekends were spent relaxing at Chequers. It was a 'stockbroker-with-taste' sort of place, very Tudor, very Bucks, but the luxury was heavenly.

We once entertained President Khrushchev and Marshal Bulganin there, both clever and very Russian. I placed President Khrushchev next to Maurice Bowra. Maurice entertained him with hilarious stories of Bobbity Musgrove staying at Pringles with the Dotty Herberts and getting into the most frightful trouble with the Snubby Boothams in the 1920s. We learnt afterwards that Khrushchev didn't know the Musgroves or for that matter the Herberts or even the Snubbies. And he had never been to Pringles!!!

The following week, Anthony told us that the Cold War had taken a turn for the worse. Very tiresome, given all the effort to which we had gone.

CLARISSA EDEN

Ouch! Ouchitty-ouchitty-OUUCH!

It's hard to put into words the pain involved in peeling off all your own skin. But it's worth it in the end. You make an incision on your tummy with a sharp knife, then peel upwards, and keep on peeling, so that eventually you're pulling all your skin over your head just as though it was an expensive skin-tight cashmere sweater by Stella McCartney.

Next, you start pulling the rest of your skin from your tummy downwards, so that eventually it comes off at the feet like a pair of Wolford tights.

Hey presto! You're left looking in the mirror at a Whole New Me! I may be a bit pink and I may be a bit gooey – but at long last I don't have to live in my own skin!

LIZ JONES

November 17th

The Book of Common Prayer. The title says it all.

NICHOLAS HASLAM

November 18th

Sign spotted in the back of a car: 'Honk If You've Had It Today'!! Had WHAT, I wonder???!!!

HRH THE DUKE OF YORK

November 19th

Typi-bloody-cal! I donated all my own skin to the village to make a new flag for the village hall – and they turned their ungrateful noses up at it!

LIZ JONES

November 20th

How I wish I had my own skin back, and how I really really hate myself for peeling it all off.

LIZ JONES

November 21st

From my earliest days, I've always been in love with cinema. It has occupied all my care and attention from as far back as I can remember. My quest for beauty in the cinema is never-ending. Like, when I was filming *Raging Bull*, about this lonely guy, full of anger – a role played, after many months of sitting in a gym being punched by one of my favourite actors, Bob De Niro – I wanted to capture the real beauty of Jake La Motta having his nose punched outta shape.

Again and again, I referred back to Italian masterpieces such as Caravaggio's *Death of the Virgin* and Giorgione's *Tempest*. Again and again, I would rerun scenes from great old movies such as *Bicycle Thieves* and *Citizen Kane* to see if they contained angry loners being punched senseless. Then, for forty days and forty nights, our ninety-strong crew stayed in that boxing ring. We miked up Bob's gloves and his nose and for this sequence I even strapped the camera to his chest, so you can go with the hit. In the movie, the scene lasts just five seconds – you see the glove coming – cut to the nose – then to the glove – then fist hits nose – cut to blood spurting out, like in a Canaletto fountain.

Then Bob has the line: 'Uh.' Simple but beautiful, but Bob had to get to know every damn part of his character before he could get to grips with that line. He said to me, he said, 'Marty, what does a guy actually feel when he has his nose punched? What do you think he's going through?'

'Bob,' I said after a lot of thought, 'Bob, I'd guess he feels kinda – how'd you put it? – beat up.' So we settled that Bob would say: 'Uh' with a kinda hurt, kinda beat-up expression – angry, yeah, lonely, yeah – but also kinda, well, beat-up.

So we filmed for a month, never quite getting the beat-up expression I was after. That: 'Uh' just didn't sound beat-up enough. But today I pulled Bob to one side, set the cameras going and punched him with great force in the nose. 'UH!' he said, 'UH!' – giving us a choice of two perfect UHs for the final cut.

'Jeez, Bob,' I said, 'you're so instinctive.'

MARTIN SCORSESE

November 22nd

Halfway through *Two-Way Family Favourites*, I hear that President Kennedy had been shot in Detroit. Typical! He's just gone and interrupted my favourite record! I was just thinking of going to America, and now he goes and gets himself assassinated. Men! I mean, talk about upstaging. The assassination was quite interesting at the beginning but the initial excitement wore off by tea-time.

JANET STREET-PORTER

The day Kennedy got shot, a hundred years ago or more. A top exec from Paramount rings to say, hey, he's just wild about my classic movie scene in *Basic Instinct* when Sharon Stone uncrosses her legs and for a split-second you *see it all*. Says he wants to offer me $2.2 million to write the same scene – tender yet meaningful – into *Thirst Lady*, a biopic about the sex life of Jackie K.

I'm all done by midday. The Dallas scene is a stand-out. For reasons of dramatic tension, I make the first and second shots blow the head off the driver of the vehicle, giving JFK the chance to grab the wheel and make the hi-action getaway.

JFK (wiping a pint of the driver's blood off his brow, changing to top gear, and driving away at 170 mph): Jeez, Jackie, there's a mean bastard out there. That bullet was meant for me!

JACKIE K: Stay cool, Jack! Let's get the fuck outta here!

Jackie moves to the front passenger seat. In doing so, she crosses and uncrosses her legs. For a second, the audience clocks that she is *wearing no panties.*

As if from nowhere, a historic third shot rings out. It just misses JFK, and instead zaps through the diamond button holding Jackie's tight-waisted $7,000 Chanel jacket together. Jackie is wearing no brassiere, so her tits pop clean out.

A cheer erupts from the crowd. Eighteen floors up in the Dallas Book Depository, Lee Harvey Oswald puts down his rifle, grabs for his binoculars and begins pleasuring himself.

JFK (laughing good-heartedly at the wheel): Woooh! Dallas sure ain't seen a show like this before, honey!

JACKIE K: This excitement's sure as hell made me horny, Jack – let's drive somewhere kinda private and make love!

JFK (swerving car to a halt, ripping off his shirt): I heard there's a grassy knoll somewhere near!

JACKIE K (pulling off her skirt): Too right there is, big boy!

JOE ESZTERHAS

I do not gloat. Far from it. Absolutely not. Nothing could be further from the truth. Nor do I rejoice in the pitiful – and, to her former colleagues, painfully embarrassing – state to which the previous Prime Minister, a Mrs Margaret Thatcher, has been reduced. When I heard the news of her resignation following the resounding humiliation meted out to her in the first ballot, I did not rejoice. This was no time for jubilation. One does not delight in the misfortune of others. One looks to the long-term future of this country and its role in Europe, of course one does.

Instead, I sat by myself contemplating the long-term future of the country and its role in Europe with a decent spread of gulls' eggs and vol-au-vents and some very acceptable Pol Roger champagne. As a small dance band struck up a few 'up-tempo' tunes in the corner of my drawing room I found myself tapping my feet. But let me add this. It pained me to witness scenes of Mrs Margaret Thatcher's obvious distress, visible disappointment and crushing humiliation on the *6 O'Clock News*, the *7 O'Clock News*, the *9 O'Clock News*, the *10 O'Clock News* and on *Newsnight*, and all over again a couple of times on video. Though my neighbours may well have heard great bellows of laughter emerging from my chambers, these were only intermittent and my deepest sympathies remained with her. I would not know, but I imagine it cannot be remotely amusing to realise the country has decided that enough is enough and they have had just about as much as they can stand of your shrill, womanly bossiness. She never concealed her jealousy of me and my rapport with the people, but I am now more than happy to wish her a very long retirement.

SIR EDWARD HEATH

November 23rd

I greet the Duke of Edinburgh, dear old friend and quaffing partner, with a friendly slap on the back. As always, I am delighted to find him in robust form. 'Who the hell are you?' he says, with his usual gruff good humour. 'Have we been introduced? Get to the back of the queue!'

I roar with my trademark laughter. It is his little joke. The last time we bumped into each other, just fifteen years ago, he said exactly the same thing. His pretending not to know who I am has become what one might call a 'standing joke' between us.

Of course he knows exactly who I am. In 1968, I was privileged to be presented to him when he honoured the offices of the *Spectator* with a royal visit. We struck up an immediate rapport. 'What do you do, then? Bugger all, I suppose!' he quipped. I immediately applauded this brilliantly quick remark.

'And stop that infernal clapping!' he added, in that familiar tone, before passing on to the next person with a characteristic stamp of his foot. It was at that point that I realised how very much we had in common. We had that all-too-rare thing, commonly known as 'rapport'.

Today, I approach him as he turns on his heels. I inform him that I have – for my sins! – been granted privileged access to his 'better half'. 'She may well like to be presented to me,' I add, agreeably. 'We have a great deal in common. She, too, is a lover of the Great Outdoors.'

'Some people are the bloody limit!' replies the Duke, in mock indignation. A born comedian!

'Absolutely!' I say with a chuckle, setting him at his ease. 'Couldn't have put it better myself! I must say, M'Lud, you are simply MARVELLOUS for your age!'

GYLES BRANDRETH

'The Owl and the Pussy-Cat'

The Owl and the Pussy-Cat went to sea
In a beautiful pea-green boat.
They took some honey, and plenty of money
Because they were fucking Yanks
Sucking the shit out of the arse of the poor.

HAROLD PINTER

November 24th

There was a time when I could outperform all but the most hardened imbibers, a generous slug or ten of Mr Walker's amber restorative being my tipple of preference. This was between the Tel Aviv massacre and the Soviet invasion of Afghanistan. I now restrict myself to no more than a couple of bottles of halfway-decent wine for elevenses, and then a couple more as an accompaniment to luncheon, with Mr Gordon's gin firmly ensconced in the driving seat for the remainder of the day. As an enthusiastic participant in the delights of Mr Dionysus, I offer no apology for passing down these simple pieces of advice for the young.

Never drink before breakfast unless the day of the week has a 'u' in it. Martini goes surprisingly well with Corn Flakes, while a medium-dry sherry remains the perfect accompaniment to Mr Kellogg's admirable Rice Krispies.

Don't drink to excess before appearing on Mr Logie Baird's magic lantern. Admittedly, I once appeared on Dr Dimbleby's *Question Time* after getting wholly blotto on a flirtatious bottle of tequila, but I was careful to discard the day's meals between impassioned pronouncements on Senor Pinochet's foul regime, and I was assured by even my most perspicacious friends that the dribble of vomit on my shirt front would have been mistaken by viewers for an embroidered paisley tie, so I think I got away with it.

It's much worse to see a woman drunk than a man. I don't know why this is true but it is, it just is, I don't care what you say, it just is and you can take that from me and anyway that's not what I said, take it back.

CHRISTOPHER HITCHENS

November 25th

We drove through the night, deeper and deeper into the pitch darkness. It was really really dark all around us. We didn't need anyone to tell us that this was fuckin' night-time – you could see it from the way it was so dark.

'It's dark, isn't it, dude?' I said to Ewan when we got to where we were getting.

'Dark,' he repeated. 'Very dark.'

'Jeez – but I guess we'll get some daylight in the fuckin' morning,' I said. 'Otherwise we won't see anything. It's that dark. Dark. Dark.

Dark. Y'know, dude, that's the worst thing about night-time: it's so fuckin' dark.'

CHARLEY BOORMAN

November 26th

I'm sick of dealing with fucking wankers, I said to the Queen. You get all of the shit and then they fuck you up the backside.

She was sympathetic, looking down at her toes, then along the line of losers waiting to be presented.

Basically, the woman's bloody angry, and the way she vents her anger is just to stand there in silence, grinning malevolently and holding out her hand like she's challenging each newcomer to a fucking arm-wrestle. Sometimes she can't help herself, and she lets all that pent-up anger out with one great big fuck-you wave.

Her look this morning said who-needs-this-shit, and I know how she was feeling. Like her, I was in total fuck-it mode. I've had it up to fucking here.

I asked her how the Christmas bollocks was going. The Christmas what? she said. The Christmas Fucking Message, I said. She said, oh, fine, she was thinking of saying something along the lines of the need for all human beings to live together in harmony. You don't want to do it like that, I said, you want to tell them that they're all a load of fucking bollocks, because that way you'll look like you know something they don't know, and it'll play well. But I could tell she wasn't listening by the way she began talking to someone else, forcing me to shout.

I felt like crying. Sometimes I don't know why I fucking bother.

ALASTAIR CAMPBELL

November 27th

Victoria Falls. This must be one of the wettest places I've been to in a long, long time – wetter than Droitwich in January, and that's saying something! Victoria Falls was named after Victoria – though it's not known whether she actually fell or not! Every day, year in, year out, literally masses of water goes over the high rocks, creating an amazing waterfall, formed of lots of water. Certainly a sight to remember, and almost Pythonesque in its total unexpectedness. Somewhere, a long way away, people are doing sensible things like watching cricket or gardening – and here am I standing beside the Victoria Falls wearing a daft hat for the cameras! Makes you think!

MICHAEL PALIN

The path up the hill is not steep; it is the hill that is steep.

SHIRLEY MACLAINE

November 28th

Enid Blyton died today, in 1968. True, the Famous Five are preferable to the Secret Seven, but, being English, both groups lack a third dimension. Enid Blyton never travelled down the Congo. She never exposed herself to anything. She never got her hands dirty. Was she a lesbian?

V.S. NAIPAUL

Had Professor Steve Hawking on the show this morning, and we switched off his voice-box for a giggle and did farty noises instead, cracked us up that one did, and took him down a peg or two. Classic! Like the time Gerri Halliwell came on and I told her to get her tits out, or when I did the whole show sat with a bucket on my head, or when I did a poo into a teacup live on air, or when the Kaiser Chiefs came on and I asked each of them to name which one of Girls Aloud they'd most like to shag. Before I came along, British radio used to be full of posh wankers with silver spoons up their arses talking about the balance of fucking payments and stuff, but now it's a lot more like real, a lot more human.

CHRIS MOYLES

November 29th, 1922

Dear Lady Ottoline,

I cannot tell you how thoroughly we both enjoyed staying with you last weekend. Everything was so perfect – the scintillating conversation, the delicious food, the excellent wine, and all miraculously brought together to perfection by the finest hostess in the country!

By the way, I do hope I didn't cause any undue offence at dinner with your guests on Saturday evening when, just as that lovely soup was being served, I tore off my trousers, pulled out my aroused member and began to chase your buxom serving wench around the dining-room table.

I noticed that your first thought was that the tomato soup in the wench's great bowl was being tossed hither and thither over your well-dressed guests. How typical of you and your feeble servility towards the pathetic silliness of propriety that you should care more for the laundering of clothes – those absurd chains that keep man from his true self – than for the sex-flow that keeps man alive and is the only honest expression of animal energy that exists on this miserable globe.

And when I eventually caught up with her, and managed to grapple her to the ground, and was struggling to grasp her bountiful delights within my needy palms – then you implored me to forbear, you rang your bell and insisted in your cheap and degraded voice that there was 'a time and a place for everything'.

Do you realise what a loathsome thing you are? You make me ill. I wanted to light a flame, to warm my body against the heat of a real woman's naked form, to worship the sun-god of the sex-flow – and all you could think of to do was beg me hysterically to desist! You and your sort have a disgusting attitude towards sex, a disgusting desire to stop it and insult it. You are like a worm cut in half, with one half discarded in a bin while the other half wriggles around in a kind of grey hell.

Nevertheless, the main course was absolutely delicious, and I know that everyone also thoroughly enjoyed the pudding. And the rest of the weekend was every bit as heavenly! You were really extremely kind to entertain us all so extravagantly. Once again, thank you so much for a really wonderful weekend.

Yours ever,
David

D.H. LAWRENCE,
LETTER TO LADY OTTOLINE MORRELL

November 30th

There was an *awful* lot of shopping in the Eighties. When we went into shops, we'd often take out our money from our Armani wallet then buy something – *and take it away with us.* Food shopping in particular was very voguey. And *after* you had bought the food and taken it home – *you would sure as hell want to eat the stuff.* The world was divided into those who ate it by themselves and those who ate it in the company of others, brought in to supplement their *lifestyle.* In many ways, food taught us how to reinvent ourselves. But it left us feeling confused. And a *teensy bit guilty*. This was the boil-in-the-bag, very *Next*, pre-Major culture of the post-Bowie era, with perhaps a dab of *Neighbours*, and what it said was this: 'There's an awful lot of *stuff* around, and we've got a *momentum* going, so let's *run with it* and – fingers crossed – soon the stuff with the momentum will *thingy itself*!' So being someone who bought food from shops in the Eighties and then ate it became one of those *terribly defining* things.

PETER YORK

December

December 1st

I am at home when a parcel is delivered. It is a set of blank pages. I recognise it instantly as a new work by Pinter. To my horror, I recognise the silences as our own. They are all there, for the world to see. He has obviously decided to break the silence surrounding the silence. Can I ever forgive him?

JOAN BAKEWELL

I always treat myself to a splendid shopping expedition to the delightful market places of the Auvergne at this time of year. It's the only way to find exactly the right chipolatas for Christmas. Let's face it, chipolatas can be fearfully boring simply served up on a plate. Some years, we bind them together with splendid Christmas ribbons in wonderfully rich reds and greens and hang them over the eighteenth-century mirror above the drawing-room mantelpiece. Other years, we find they make a very effective Christmas tree decoration, every branch hanging with three or four shiny little chipolatas. Magic!

SIR TERENCE CONRAN

Whatever faults I may have as a politician, if any, I can honestly say that throughout the course of my political life, I have been a man of the strongest principle. That's something not even my closest political allies would wish to contradict. Let's not beat about the bush. Time and time again, I came very close to resigning from the Callaghan government. For instance, I bitterly disagreed with Jim and the rest of the Cabinet over incomes policy, defence, Europe, Northern Ireland and crawling cap-in-hand to the IMF. I frequently said: 'Frankly, Jim, I'm not going to take it any more, my principles won't let me. I have no choice but to resign.' But – and this I may say is typical Jim! – whenever I stood up to him, he somehow always managed to avoid being in the room.

TONY BENN

December 2nd

I have been working on my Christmas message.

It is not going well.

'Traditionally, Christmas is the season when many of us, young and old alike, take stock of the year that has passed and ask ourselves why we bother …'

'Christmas is a time when our thoughts inevitably turn to family. We ask ourselves, over and over again, why just one or two of them can't for the life of them occasionally – just occasionally – do something right for a change …'

'In this, my Jubilee year, as I have travelled up and down the length and breadth of the country, I have had occasion to meet a great many of you. Time and time again, I have been struck by the very real way in which you just stare at me as though I were some sort of performing seal …'

No. I can't seem to hit the right note. Perhaps I will have a little lie-down.

A knock on the door. It is my son, Edward.

'Hello Edward,' I say, informally.

'Hello Mummy,' he replies.

We shake hands. What's that expression everyone uses these days? That's it. We are a close-knit family.

'Have you come far?' I ask.

'Not really,' he says. 'We don t live all that far away. Though the traffic was quite busy.'

'There are a lot of cars on the roads these days,' I say. 'You sometimes wonder where they are all going!'

'Yes!' he agrees.

We have a smile.

'You can't help but wonder,' he says, 'where they are all going!'

'Yes!' I agree.

Jester, my senior corgi, puts his head round the door. That means she is in need of one thing! 'Have you had your chocolate drop, Jester? Have you? Have you?!! Has mummy forgotten your choccie drop? Has she?!! Good girl!'

'Well, I'd better be off then,' says Edward. 'Sophie sends her kind regards.'

'Ah,' I say, dipping into my secret cache of chocolate drops. 'One drop, two drops – three drops! Who's a clever girl, then!'

Edward lets himself out.

HM QUEEN ELIZABETH II

December 3rd

TO BERNARD BERENSON

My dear BB,

You ask me to tell you about the cat which sat on the mat: was he a feline of any real distinction, and did his chosen sitting arrangements prove acceptable? There is little, I fear, to say on the matter, or, to put it another way, on the mat, though the mat upon which he felt inclined to place himself was as inherently 'mattish' as one might have supposed.

Little is known for sure about the cat in question. Cats are, in my experience, ill-suited to the rigour of an ancient University; their conversation, being little more than a relentless succession of overblown miaows, invariably fails to excite or to scintillate. It is, I would add, hard to think of a cat of one's acquaintance who exhibits any real intellectual distinction. Is the Cat in the Hat related to the Cat on the Mat? Might they, perhaps, be one and the same? These are the questions historians will be tempted to ask over a bottle of hock for many centuries to come.

You ask for any gossip from Oxford about the wider world, if there is such a thing. I am reliably informed that the USA is going downhill. For all its talk of sky-scrapers and – heaven forfend – 'big bucks', I have it on good authority that it will soon be roughly on a par, socially, economically and intellectually, with the Isle of Wight.

The roses remain in bloom. They disappoint, smell unctuous, and have little to say for themselves.

Yours ever,

Hugh

HUGH TREVOR-ROPER,
LETTER TO BERNARD BERENSON

I have never successfully masturbated to Hugh Trevor-Roper's writing, though I have to certain remembered scenes in J.K. Galbraith, and I find my dust-jacket photograph of William Golding powerfully erotic. Among English authors, I have masturbated successfully to the weekend essays of Roy Hattersley and some of the novels of Margaret Drabble, though Michael Holroyd's three-volume *Life of Shaw* seems to me too long for sustained masturbation.

NICHOLSON BAKER

December 4th

Death is the snare in God's drumset, the pot-noodle in the scabby puddle, the dandruff in the bouffant, the zit in the plug-hole, the mouldy slice of pig in the two-door saloon fridge.

MARTIN AMIS

December 5th

I love to build a snowman. The absolute best way to build a snowman is out of snow, so it is best to pick your time of year with care. Snow in the summer is rare, unless you are somewhere snowy.

These beautiful snow-based figures we call snowmen put us in touch with our creativity, and remind us that though some of our fellow human beings may not be blessed with legs, they are still able to rejoice in their own identities and to live richly satisfying lives, at least until they melt.

In these hectic, recessiony days, few of us can find the time to build our own snowman. My good friend the internationally-acclaimed designer Tom Ford has come up with a fine solution: The Tom Ford Personal Snowman Maker ($3,450 from Macy's, snow extra). This must-have invention will construct an instant snowman on your behalf (eight different designs available, among them a profound Rothko snowman in deep reds and blacks, and a moving and inspirational Third World snowman). It takes just thirty minutes for your snowman to be ready for everyone to admire, saving you precious time for personal growth and/or investment renewal.

Your kids may find the snow unpleasantly cold to the touch. Note to self: remember to make space under your family Xmas tree for The Tom Ford Junior Personal Snowman Maker ($4,600).

So many great gift ideas! We are living in exciting times. We are confronted with the challenge of sustaining our food, our water and our environment. It is up to each one of us, Mother Earth's wayward children, to buy as many gifts as we can for those we love, such as my good friends divine songstress Norah Jones and leading film-maker Sam Mendes. The more we buy, the better off we will be, and the more those less fortunate than us will benefit. All human beings, particularly the poor and downtrodden, love to see others enriching their own lives. Yup. It's a win–win.

GWYNETH PALTROW

December 6th

A corncob pipe. A button nose. Two eyes made of coal. It's the self-styled Frosty the Snowman. I'm sorry, but that's not someone I want my kids to go out to play with. For crying out loud, where are the relevant authorities when you need them?

ALLISON PEARSON

December 7th

Why is a T-shirt called a T-shirt? That's a question David and I often ask ourselves.

The conclusion we've come to is that it's because it's a shirt. Otherwise, it would be called the T-trouser or T-shoe, or whatever.

Picking a T shirt may not be easy but trying it on is even more difficulter.

Basically, a well-made T-shirt generally comes complete with four holes. There's a medium-sized hole for putting your head through, two smaller ones for putting your arms through, and then there's a big one which is basically for your body. If you get it wrong by just a matter of inches and try putting your head through an arm-hole, you could end up in intensive, so whatever you do you must be careful to aim right.

And that's not all. The other nightmare is finding you've put it on back-to-front. If that ever happens to you, my top tip is to get your assistant to take it off for you, then put it on you again, only this time the right way round. Alternatively, you can try taking your arms out through the holes, then turn your T-shirt round 180 degrees, then put them back in again. Sometimes David makes the major mistake of turning it round 360 degrees and then he gets cross when he finds it's still the wrong way round.

Congratulations! You have now bought a fantastic super-sexy new T-shirt! When you get it home, be sure to try it on. That way, you get to enjoy it at least once before it seems old and boring, and you have to go shopping again for something newer.

VICTORIA BECKHAM

December 8th

Reread the poems of W.B. Yeats. Very Irish.

ANTHONY POWELL

There's one thing that keeps me awake at night. What if underage carol singers, in all their wide-eyed innocence, bless 'em, knock on the corrupt door of the disgraced Gary Glitter?

And what if the man himself opens the door, clad in his one-piece silver bodysuit, singing, 'Do you want to be in my gang, my gang, my gang?' and beckons them in?

It doesn't bear thinking about. Let's hope those little mites have the sense to answer him with a defiant 'Definitely not, you sick former superstar pervert!' and run away as fast as their little feet can carry them.

ALLISON PEARSON

'While Shepherds Watched their Flocks by Night'

While shepherds watched
Their flocks by night
All seated on the ground
They were bombed to smithereens.
That wiped the stupid grins off their faces.

HAROLD PINTER

December 9th

Britain is in the grip of Christmas Decorations Fever. We may not have any cash in our pockets, but at least we have our paper-chains and our tinsel. My only worry – and it's a worry I share with millions of mums, the nation over – is that sick, creepy convicted rapist Barry George – formally acquitted for the brutal murder of Jill Dando – will turn up at our door with a mad look on his face. What a way to ruin a family Christmas. It just doesn't bear thinking about.

ALLISON PEARSON

Art is an umbrella that lets in the rain.

KENNETH TYNAN

December 10th

My husband Andrew is easy to feed, thank goodness, and seldom complains about what is put before him. On Shrove Tuesday last year, he polished off one of our new table-mats under the impression it was one of chef's pancake efforts.

Unlike me, Andrew is a terrific pudding person. He also particularly loves what people on television will insist upon calling seafood. This dish successfully combines his two great passions!

JELLYFISH CUSTARD

1 small to medium jellyfish
2 pints water
Custard, preferably from milk fresh from your own herd
Bring the water to the boil. Chef will show you how. Now plop the jellyfish into it.
Boil for ten to fifteen minutes, until it has stopped wriggling.

Dollop your lovely fresh custard all over it.

Serve with either freshly-baked crackers or a crisp garden salad, depending on season.

DEBORAH, DUCHESS OF DEVONSHIRE

December 11th

It makes me see red when I hear of a mother giving her little toddler the class-A drug Ecstasy for Christmas. No, it hasn't happened yet, thank God, but it's the kind of thing that could happen on every street in Britain. And believe me, I'll shed no tears when I see the wicked perpetrators behind bars.

ALLISON PEARSON

For some years, I have planned to embark upon a novel to show the truth of human existence as more light-hearted, easy-going and optimistic than I have previously portrayed it.

It would concern a troubled man, but one of great decency, a forester by trade, known to all as Tobias Smethwick of Tottingdean. In the clearing of a wood, this Tobias, too poor to buy himself a horse and cart, stumbles upon a handsome woman of carefree beauty and gracious manner. Her name, she tells him, is Katharine.

Tobias courts Katharine, who, after some years, agrees to marry him. Together, they have five children, who love them with the same intensity with which they continue to love one another. Throughout the next thirty-odd years, Tobias and Katharine are too impoverished to buy a horse or a cart, but they remain content in each other's affection.

The final scene would see their five children and their twenty-three grandchildren together assembled to rejoice in the fiftieth anniversary of the enduring marriage of Tobias and Katharine. Then from out of the dark fog, a messenger arrives, bearing a telegram. He hands it to Katharine, still carefree, still beautiful, still gracious. She reads it out. 'YOUR FRIENDS AND NEIGHBOURS WISHING TO CELEBRATE A HUSBAND AND WIFE WHO THROUGH THEIR ETERNAL GOODNESS AND CHEER HAVE BROUGHT UNTOLD BLESSINGS TO ALL THE PEOPLE OF THEIR COUNTY HEREBY PRESENT THEM WITH THE HORSE AND CART FOR WHICH THEY HAVE SO LONG WISHED.'

The story ends with the sound of the horse neighing merrily outside, as all those in the room throw their hats in the air and cheer.

This morning, I lift my pen and dip it deep into its inkwell, ready to sally forth on this, my first joyful novel. I decide to show all those who have for so long attacked me for the bleakness of my outlook that my conception of the world has changed for the sunnier, and that I now regard Providence as the true ally of the virtuous, rewarding decency with good fortune, and turning a blind eye to misdemeanour:

CHAPTER 1

Melodious Birds Sing Madrigals

It was early in the Spring when Tobias Smethwick of Tottingdean, a forester by trade, took the path through Copper Wood. Reaching a fork, he decided, he knew not why, to take the left hand trail. This trail took him to a clearing, and in that clearing was a young lady, dressed all in white. Tobias recognised her at once as the most beautiful and virtuous young lady upon whom he had ever set an eye. She looked so intensely living and full of movement as she stood in the silent clearing, bathed in bright March light. High up above, a solitary magpie whistled its morning tune.

The young lady gasped.

'I did not mean to startle you,' said Tobias. 'Quite the reverse. My only wish is that she who glorifies nature with her beauty, should herself be glorified by the very nature that encloses her. I beg you, madam, to vouchsafe me your name.'

The young lady turned to Tobias. She had, she thought, never seen a young man upon whom she so yearned to imprint a sweet kiss. Above them, the magpie continued to sing its melodious madrigal.

'Sir,' said the young lady, playfully shaking her head, 'my name is Katharine Habnorden of Wainfleet. I fear it is hardly proper for us to be here, conversing. Yet something strange within me stirs. It is almost as though fate had intertwined our destinies here, forever, in this sunlit clearing.'

'O, my Katharine!' he exclaimed, and moved to kiss her.

High above, the magpie swooped down upon a twig. The twig cracked and hit a thin branch. The thin branch, hollow from decades of weary incline, fell onto a larger, heavier branch, which, stirred by the sudden jolt, plummeted headlong sixty feet or more, and landed on the youthful skull of Tobias Smethwick, splitting it in twain.

'O,' exclaimed Katharine, as her chance acquaintance collapsed cold at her feet.

The magpie flew to another branch, on another tree, there to sing his same sweet madrigal, indifferent to the tragedy that had unfurled in the Copper Wood below.

'O,' exclaimed Katharine, realising, in that tragic instant, the impossibility of ever again finding happiness.

Damnation! With one slip of my pen, I have created the very magpie that conspired to destroy my finer intentions! Tomorrow, I shall start another novel, and this one will indeed be cheery.

I think I shall call it *Jude the Obscure.*

THOMAS HARDY

December 12th

Today I took three of my colleagues out for a slap-up Xmas meal at the Savoy. Take it from me, that costs.

'Okay,' I said, 'have whatever you want from the menu, and I'll pick up the tab. Generous offer, and I never go back on my word. You got forty minutes from … NOW! – so you better eat your bollocks off, do I make myself clear? I said, do I make myself clear?'

The waitress comes, and they was ordering like there's no tomorrow – starter, main course, the whole bloody bollocks. But from the outset they made some serious mistakes.

Gareth goes first. Orders the prawn cocktail. 'The prawn cocktail!' I says. 'What you want to do that for, Gareth? You must be out your tiny mind!'

'Oh, Sir Alan!' says Gareth, 'I've always liked the pink sauce what they comes with.'

'Don't you "Oh Sir Bloody Alan" me, my son,' I says. 'You bloody what? You bloody what? You always liked the pink – don't give me that! You're sending me a suicide message, my friend. Pink sauce costs nothing. You know what sort of mark-up they're asking on that pink sauce? 800, 900 per cent. And he says he's always liked pink sauce! What kind of bloody fool is that? You order a prawn cocktail, you're going to get dished, my friend.'

'Actually, Sir Alan,' says Gareth, 'I just changed my mind. I'll have the pâté.'

'That's your second mistake, my friend,' I says. 'Place like this, you don't just say, "I'll have the pâté." You say, "Look, mate, what's the best price you can do me for the pâté?" Or else the waitress will never respect you.'

''Ow'd you know the waitress's name was Else, then, Sir Alan?' says Gareth.

'Gareth – you're fired!' I says.

I've held to the same rule all my life. In the dining-out game, keep your eye on the ball, or you'll be kicked to death by your own team.

Rule Number One: Never chop and change, my friend. It sends out all the wrong messages, and you'll get your head sliced off.

So we're all settling in nicely, having a bit of a chat – remember, team leaders, always encourage your team members to have a bit of a chat but IN THEIR OWN TIME – when a waiter comes up with this bloody great basket, asks us if we want some.

'What's the product?' I says.

'Bread, sir,' he says.

'How much, my friend?' I says.

'It's free, sir,' he says.

'I'll take the lot,' I says. 'Then fill your basket up again, bring it back here, and I'll take that load too.'

And that's precisely what he did. Be under no illusion: if you're offered something, and the deal's to your advantage, buy up the stock before they up the price. I didn't get where I am today by settling for a single bread roll when I could have had dozens. When I get behind a project, I give it 200 per cent.

'Henry,' I says to my number three, 'we got here what? Twenty, twenty-five bread rolls? But they're not buttered, are they? Big mistake! Listen here. What I want you to do is butter them, then go round the tables and pitch directly to them, offering them READY-BUTTERED bread on a decent mark-up. These are big businessmen, men of the world, captains of bloody industry, leaders of the business community – they're not the sort of clientele who wants to waste valuable trading time buttering their own bread!'

Rule Number Two: Focus on the bottom line. In the world of restaurants, it's dog eat dog.

So Henry's finished his buttering and he's off round the restaurant with his bread basket, Gareth's out on his arse, and I'm left looking at this piece of fancy white cloth in front of me.

'Whatya call this, then, Denise?' I say to my secretary.

'It's a napkin, Sir Alan,' she says.

'That's as may be. And what would you use this "napkin" for, Denise?'

'Wiping your mouth and hands, Sir Alan.'

'What they charge for 'em, you reckon?'

'Nothing, Sir Alan.'

'Nothing! I got this right? They're handing out good clean linen, asking the punters to cover it with muck, then spending time washing it and ironing it and whatever – AND ALL FOR NO CASH BLOODY RETURN? They must be stark staring bloody mad! Off you go, Denise!'

And with that, Denise is off to negotiate with the management vis-à-vis taking a hundredweight of paper serviettes off our hands, which we pick up wholesale for a tenth of the price. The bottom line is there's no downside to waste matter: there's always cash in getting rid of it.

Rule Number Three: Never underestimate me, my friend, because you'll be making a fatal mistake and I'll sue the bloody pants off you.

My dining companions might have been otherwise employed, but my solo meal's the pig's bloody bollocks. OK, so I don't like cabbage, never have, but in the eating-out game you got to roll with the punches.

Exactly forty minutes on, I tot up the bill on my Amstrad calculator, but the battery must've gone. So I settle the bill through a subsidiary company based in the Caymans, and I'm being transported back to my boardroom in my personalised Bentley, registered in Hong Kong. From my vehicle, I ring through to the office on my Amstrad mobile phone. Then I ring again, and again, but I still can't get a bloody peep out of it. 'What a pile of bloody toot!' I say to my chauffeur, throwing the piece of crap out the window.

Rule Number Four: Never be content with second best.

SIR ALAN SUGAR

December 13th

Drop-dead gorgeous and so totally to die for. That's what went through my mind when I set eyes on hunky top people's Chancellor Gordon Brown last night.

At the time I was going out with TV weathercaster Ian McAskill. What is it with me and weathermen? To give him his due, Ian certainly knew what to do with his hands. But our relationship wasn't going nowhere. For all his talk of sunny spells I never felt he was interested in me for myself. It was time to move on.

I had recently had my bosoms made bigger once more. I needed someone who'd be interested in them for themselves.

It was at a celebrity Yuletide reception at top club Number 11 Downing Street. From the start, I could tell Chancellor Gordon fancied me something rotten. And believe me the feeling was neutral.

He couldn't take his eyes off them, for starters. Talk about fiscal expansion! I could see he wanted me like mad. But after we had been formally introduced I spelt out my rules. I didn't mind a bit of a kiss and a cuddle, for friendship's sake. But we wasn't to go all the way for a month, or four weeks, whichever was the shortest. And nothing kinky, mind.

As I ran through the rules, that mouth of his hung open like a dog's. To his colleagues, he may have been Chancellor of the Whatever. But to me he was so just a great big bloke.

He may have looked gorgeous with a fantastic body, but Gordon turned out to be a right shit through and through. Frankly, he didn't know how to handle a woman. There I was, dressed to kill in my all-in-one skin-tight black catsuit, and within a few seconds he had turned to talk to someone else. I can't remember if he even touched my boobs to be honest.

What is it with me and politicians? Gordon let me down big time. But it would never of worked. Okay, I could of ended up the Chancellor's wife, but what's so great about Downing Street? I'd imagined it would be a top-of-the-range luxury mansion. But it was just a normal house, nothing special. I've seen better up Brentwood.

Anyway Gordon was such a sad pathetic loser, with his tongue hanging out and that. I was better off without him. But I'm a survivor. I knew I had to ignore him and keep my dreams alive. Luckily, exactly thirty seconds later who should elbow up to me but one very tasty guy with glasses.

'Hello,' he says, holding out his hand in the general direction of my famous chest. 'I'm Dr David Starkey.'

What is it with me and top TV historians?

KATIE PRICE

December 14th

Don't get me wrong. I've nothing against turkey at Christmas. But one thing's for sure. When I see that great big turkey sitting there on the serving dish come lunchtime all wrapped up in silver foil, I'll be double-checking it's not naked convicted sex-pervert Gary Glitter before I start dishing it out with all the trimmings.

ALLISON PEARSON

December 15th

I always say that there's nothing quite so voluptuous as a Christmas turkey. When I see it there, all bronzed and sizzling on our dining table, its legs akimbo, its plump breasts so vast, so juicy, so succulent, so beseeching – yes, in that instant I know the meaning of *l'amour*.

We all have our own ways of handling the seductive charms of the moist turkey. Some probe, others delve. Some dive deep, deep, deep, while others prefer to give all their attention to the skin, imbibing that gorgeous scent through whatever orifices come to hand then licking, tearing, gobbling and – oh yes! – swallowing.

Turkey is, to my mind, best consumed within the softly enfolding afterglow of a full moon. Oh, to nibble on the most slender sliver of breast as the silver-blue light shimmers enticingly upon its juicy curves! Then, and only then, can one fully experience the tastebud heaven that is turkey. On a more practical level, I always store at least three or four turkeys ready-cooked in my deep freeze for when the next full moon comes a-calling. There's nothing my friends and family like more when setting eyes on a full moon than to rush to the deep-freeze for all the pre-cooked turkeys they can carry. And if a frozen turkey is at first a bit on the hard side – well, who's complaining, ladies? Not me!

NIGELLA LAWSON

December 16th

Chez Moi. Perfectly ghastly church service *au matin*. Vicar plump, ill-shaven and brutish, ditto choirboys, clad in simply hideous turquoise and shrimp vestments, utterly unwaisted, did less than nothing for their podgy little piggy figures, great fat bottoms swaying this way and that.

We are forced to drone our way through 'Away in a Manger'. What sort of a bedroom is that? Those first-century Jews were so stubbornly lazy and drab when it came to making any effort at home decoration.

And if there was no room at the inn, they should jolly well have got their secretary to book them one in advance. Given the choice, I would frankly rather be Away in a Mansion: infinitely more accommodating, and so much more glamorous. Even Away in a Manager might be preferable, though one would have to do something about those awful lapel badges they insist upon wearing on their cheap, ill-cut, two-piece suitings.

Three Kings, albeit from the East, would be a godsend at that time of year, I suppose, but what on earth were they thinking about when they went on to admit all those rank, soggy, common little shepherds, with ghastly soiled sheets for headgear, and nothing but 'open-toed' sandals – sandals! – for footwear?

Babies are quite bad enough, but no one should countenance sheep, let alone oxen, in the home. One must, of course, remain ever-grateful that one was not invited oneself for that first Christmas – in Bethlehem, of all places! So suburban! Yet with a few elegant swags and drapes, some simple yet sympathetic lighting and a hairdresser with just a touch of style, one could have improved their image no end. No more the dowdy 'Virgin' hiding behind that ugly blue headscarf and shapeless robe: I would have dressed her in the most marvellous cobalt silk ballgown, displaying the merest hint of cleavage, perhaps with extravagant bell sleeves, her hair teased and swept back.

Would she have needed a handbag? In her position, she might, I suppose, have been able to get away without one, but I personally would have gone for something petite but gracious, yet – a diamond here, an emerald there – positively dripping with understated wealth.

As for Joseph – nothing to say for himself, terrible dried-up old brute, bearded and grubby, mottled wind-swept cheeks, fingernails bitten to the core, all the while casting those furtive, chip-on-shoulder, dark looks this way and that, unwanted hanger-on *par excellence* – I would have sent him packing.

CECIL BEATON

'God Rest Ye Merry, Gentlemen'

God rest ye merry, gentlemen
Let nothing you dismay
Except you've just
Had the shit blown out of you so you're
Not so fucking merry now, are you, chums?

HAROLD PINTER

December 17th

Ingredients: One 12lb turkey
900g good sausage meat

Your fresh young turkey will come trussed and bound, naked but for great swathes of string tightly bound around its chest and its legs and its *derrière*. 'I am your obedient slave!' it seems to be saying. 'Do with me what you will!'

But all naughty turkeys must learn their lesson. Ignore its beseechings. This is the time to leave it just as it is, unable to move, while you go off and enjoy yourself. Why not pour yourself a delicious warm bath, full of the most exotic oils and unguents? Return to the kitchen in your own good time and you will find the turkey still there, still trussed up and rigid, its body almost quivering in anticipation of what you are about to do to it.

You've had your fun. Now is the time to act! With a few deft strokes, slide your fingers all over its body, removing every last bit of string or trussing from your turkey and thus shaking it free of all bondage. Immediately, it will seem to expand. Now go deep within and wash the inside of your bird with ice-cold running water. Never mind the drips! How glamorous it now looks, how liberated! The sight of the washed turkey always reminds me of Anita Ekberg dancing in the Trevi Fountain in *La Dolce Vita*. Call me silly, but for some reason I've always had this thing about water glistening on the bare shoulders of a naked turkey.

Drain well, and blot dry with kitchen towels, taking care to pamper those hidden crevices. I've always loved to guide my fingers delicately through all those inviting nooks and crannies, playing my beloved turkey like a grand piano. Sometimes I will invite friends over for a turkey-blotting party. One by one, we all take it in turns to smother the bounteous bird with all the love we can muster.

Pre-heat the oven to 200°C/gas 6

Take your turkey and, using your fingertips, pry. Wiggle some space between the skin and those vast, accommodating breasts. Into this space, squeeze your sausage meat, pushing, pressing, coaxing and surging so that it covers the whole breast, in all its magnificent glory. Some people prefer to use oil all over, just to give it that faint but undeniable *frisson* that always comes when fingers touch skin. Others like to dress it in something fabulous from Vivienne Westwood. *Chacun à son gout*, as they say in *La France*. Now, from on top of the skin, mould it with your outstretched hand so that the breast is voluptuously but smoothly bulging. By now it should be yielding to your every touch, and begging you silently for more.

Secure the flaps of skin over the oozing cavity with a meat skewer so that the sausage meat doesn't escape during the roasting. If, despite all your warnings, it does manage to escape then you will be left with no alternative but to whack it back in with a resounding thump. Another skewer may well be in order, methinks! Ouch! Be sure to let that little turkey minx know who's boss!

Or, if you're feeling a little more frisky (and, frankly, with all this fluffy snow around who jolly well isn't?), then why not bundle the flaps of skin into a La Perla thong (or, for that very special occasion, a diamond-encrusted midnight-blue thong from Agent Provocateur, who have just opened their brand new Eroticadeli food-and-panties store in London's exotic Covent Garden)?

Now squeeze your turkey breast securely into a skin-tight tin and let it roast for about two hours and forty minutes, basting periodically. An excellent idea for a get-together with friends and family is to throw a basting party, where between ten (10) and twenty (20) guests take turns to open the oven door and, clutching tight to your most curvaceous and voluminous ladle, pour those fragrant juices all over the outstretched bird, thus keeping it wonderfully juicy and moist. Baste! Baste! Baste! More! Yes! Yes! YES!

NIGELLA LAWSON

December 18th

How dare the snow target MY house and MY garden?

GERMAINE GREER

December 19th

We are met by Blair dressed in tight jeans and a white open-necked shirt.

It is not every day the Prime Minister greets the leader of the Liberal Democrats, so I attempt to set him at his ease. 'That's a beautiful clean white shirt,' I congratulate him. 'It suits you.'

He thanks me.

'A new Prime Minister,' I tell him thoughtfully, 'must always be in possession of a clean white shirt. You have already won popularity from the public. But dressed in this clean white shirt you will also have won their respect. You have done yourself a power of good. Well done.'

Meanwhile, Roy (Jenkins) is keenly surveying the Prime Minister's Downing Street office.

'A word in your ear, Tony,' he says. 'I always found it best to keep my desk clear of what one might call "excess paperwork". Between ourselves, all the – how should one put it? – *premiere league* Prime Ministers have maintained a tidy desk. I say, that's a very agreeable-looking Pouilly-Fumé you have there!'

At this point, I step in. 'I wanted to take the opportunity to tell you how I see things,' I say.

Sadly, Tony has an urgent appointment, so cannot stay for the whole of my overview.

I come away feeling deeply depressed.

PADDY ASHDOWN

December 20th

Ever since I wrote yesterday's blog about how to stop wars, zero new wars have begun. My readers have obviously passed on the news to their friends, and the word has got round. I guess this means I must be doing something right!

MALCOLM GLADWELL

December 21st, 1924

Dear Lady Diana,

I'm not sure I have ever enjoyed a ball quite so much in all my life. What a glorious hostess you are, with your natural effervescence and your sheer *joie de vivre*. Everything about your party – the dance-band, so frenzied in its repressed sexuality; my fellow guests, fed on the sodom-apples of avarice yet straining to be free, to experience their animal selves under the sun and the stars; the champagne, spurting and flowing like the semen of a savage – was quite simply tip-top.

Thank you, also, for showing me again that a woman's sex is in itself dynamic and alive, that it is a power in itself, beyond her reason, and of itself it emits its peculiar spell, drawing men into the delight of desire. So why when I asked you to come outside and to tear off your clothes and to surrender your naked body to the impress of the moon's volcanic manservant (me) did you say so coldly that you would prefer to dance the next rumba with your dreary little castrated cottonwool husband?

Oh why is England so dead and wretched? Why are its people so immune to all feelings, all urges? You made haste to return to the ball, even though I promised you there and then that I would happily tear off your garments and take you in my hands and thrust my John Thomas into your rose petal again and again and again. And all you could say was that now was neither the time nor the place! What kind of false and mealy-mouthed reply is that, woman? Never was an age so spineless! Never was a country so enfeebled! You and all your kind are an insult to humanity, you are like dying beetles, wriggling with your pampered legs in one last pathetic dance of death.

Might I also compliment you on your wonderful guests? I had many very pleasant chats throughout the evening, and feel that my wife and I came away from the ball with a number of quite marvellous new friends!

With very best wishes to both you and your charming husband,

Yours ever, David

D.H. LAWRENCE,
LETTER TO LADY DIANA COOPER

December 22nd

Never EVER cook a chipolata. Too much effort! At this time of year, there's a tremendous amount of drivel talked about frying or grilling your chipolatas. But there's absolutely NO NEED. Save yourself time by following my advice. When I was married to Terence, we'd always serve chipolatas raw in a salad with chicory and endives. To cheer them up a bit, you can always sculpt them into lovely flower shapes – minced pork lends itself wonderfully to azaleas and primroses. Chipolata daffodils as a salad centrepiece can lend a wonderfully hopeful note of spring cheer to a cold December.

SHIRLEY CONRAN

December 23rd

Now, where was I? How was it for you? At this stage, I always enjoy a favourite cigarette. And relax. By now, the skin of your divine turkey should be a delicious all-over brown. If you want some idea of how the well-basted turkey should look, just think Halle Berry emerging in her skimpy bikini from the storm-tossed sea in *Die Another Day*. For a skimpy-bikini effect just like Halle's, why not wrap a wafer-thin sheet of buttered foil over the upper curves of this most generously proportioned and altogether desirable of farmyard animals?

When you think it's ready, press and – yes! – pierce your turkey with your long blade, preferably around that luscious area where the leg meets the rest of the body. Take it slowly, very slowly. Just lie back and wait, letting those precious juices trickle out. Lick! Lick! Lick! Mmmm!

After it's all over, why not pull a cracker or two – or better still, get a close friend or two to pull yours for you? Mmmmm!

Fabulous! Don't stop!

NIGELLA LAWSON

December 24th

Darling Diana Cooper has given me a gold wristwatch. Bless her. Tilted at a certain angle, I can see my face in it. I will not breathe a word against Diana. This is just one of the reasons I keep a diary, to write words rather than breathe them. Diana was always the most sparkling conversationalist and divine beauty. I am so very full of sympathy for her now that she has turned into a wrinkled old sow and a Grade 1 bore, incapable of giving even her closest friends anything more original than gold wristwatches for Christmas. How my heart goes out to her!

An Yves Saint Laurent floppy bow-tie from my dear old friend Wallis Windsor. I dote on her. She was never what one might describe as a 'beauty', but she had a certain something, namely the then Prince of Wales. She was witty, in a caustic, boot-faced, daggers-drawn sort of way, but her looks now make her rather more suited to the Ghost Train at Chessington Zoo, I fear, than to a Royal Palace.

Tring! At the unearthly hour of 8.30 p.m., the doorbell goes. 'Good King Wenceslas looked out, on the feast of Stephen!' sing a motley group of embittered carol singers, their cheeks pinched and scarlet in the freezing cold.

'I care not a fig whether Mr Wenceslas looked out or not!' I exclaim, slamming the door firmly on their grotesque faces. 'He may have styled himself Royal, but he came from what is now Czechoslovakia, and is of no consequence whatsoever! Be off with you!'

Oh, the sheer crude ghastliness of Christmas! As a great admirer of Lord Jesus, I know he would be absolutely horrified at what he has set in motion.

CECIL BEATON

When President George W. Bush spoke of the notion of an 'axis of evil', what exactly did he mean? What did he mean: exactly? By 'axis' did he mean two or more chopping tools usually made of iron with a steel edge and wooden handle? No: because then he would have said 'axes'. So did he mean an unspecified number of motor vehicles licensed to ply for hire and usually fitted with a meter? No, again: because then he would have said 'taxis'.

It all goes, ineluctably, countervailingly, to form a sentence that must end, finally, with a question mark: in other words, a question. Let us take a look at Tony Blair. Tony: Blair. It is by now generally recognised that he is the British Prime Minister, a fact rendered accurate by checking in reference books. Blair feels that British interests are best served by continuing to ride on the back of the American elephant, even as it trumpets its emancipation from the influence of Europe. But in doing so, he perhaps forgets one of the primary features of an elephant: the elephant has a trunk. And with that trunk, it can suck up as much water (H_2O) as it needs, and then it can blow it all out in one great hose-splurge, splose-hurge, power-showering all those who stand in its way.

Should elephants continue to be kept imprisoned, however humanely, in zoos? Or should we as human beings (HBs) feel morally obliged to devise some form of alternative accommodation better suited to their needs as wild animals? And will the American elephant, as ridden by Blair, be willing to accept the need to be on display to paying customers – or will it turn its trunk on them, perhaps with countervailingly devastating results?

MARTIN AMIS

December 25th

I got Kelly a puppy for Crimbles. Kelly loves, loves, loves puppies, she really really does. Don t ask me what fucking sort it was, but I tell you that puppy was fucking expensive, bless it, what with the diamonds we got put into its collar and tongue, the liposuction, the tummy-tuck, the arse-lift and the tail-job.

So Kelly's all over her beautiful new puppy, patting it and that, and she says she's going to call it Cuddles. 'So why you wanna fuckin' call it Cuddaws?' I say.

'Cos it looks like it wants a great big fuckin' cuddaw. So what you gonna fuckin' do 'bout it?' says Kelly. Bless!

So Cuddles it fucking is. At least for an hour, but then it only goes and fucking shits and pisses all over the new settee.

'What the fuckin' fuck's that?' says Kelly, pointing at the poo.

'That's fuckin' poo, that's what that is,' I tell her.

'Urgh! I don't want this fuckin' dog no more! Get me a new one!' she says.

'So what we gonna fucking do with the old one, after all what we spent on it?' I say.

But at that point the problem's solved because Ozzy comes in and sits on it.

'Look what you just fucking gone and done!' I say to Ozzy.

Ozzy stands up and looks back down at the dead puppy.

'Funny,' he says. 'I can't remember eatin' that.'

SHARON OSBOURNE*

Civilised conversation has always been desperately, desperately important to me, never more so than on Christmas Day. One simply can't afford to leave it to chance. So once the designer bell has sounded for luncheon and everyone has foregathered around our festive Conran-designed table, shaped from a unique and to my mind tremendously beautiful combination of elm and ground elder, I insist that the conversation begins forthwith. It's probably a tremendous failing of mine, but I'm not one of those people who can stomach aimless chit-chat about this-and-that. So it's all eminently civilised, with a beautiful hand-printed Conran-designed conversation-sheet for each member of the family and allotted guest, detailing the topic of conversation, and suggested opinions, for each of our six courses.

I always have a decent book of famous quotations to hand, one for each diner. It's the only way to keep it interesting. And we always conclude each conversation with a deliciously light-hearted yet comprehensive summing-up from myself. It's a splendidly enjoyable procedure, and makes the whole business of Christmas-talking so much more relaxing for everyone involved. My secretary then types out the minutes on Boxing Day and we circulate them for everybody to enjoy by New Year's Eve.

SIR TERENCE CONRAN

I spend Christmas – an outdated festival at the best of times, without a genuinely radical bone in its decrepit body – watching old *Fawlty Towers* videos. They help me grapple with the problems faced by the

---

* *The Sad Short Life and Sudden Death of Cuddles* by Sharon Osbourne (with Andrew Motion) became the runaway 2008 bestseller in the Waterstone's Misery Memoir Top 10.

dispossessed middle-aged who wish to make a living within the catering sector in the post-colonial era. That people can laugh at the emotional traumas and economic dilemmas of Basil and Sybil Fawlty, devoid of any historical perspective on the genuine problems faced by the service industries in twentieth-century Britain, tells us a lot about the depth of ignorance residing in this country today.

POLLY TOYNBEE

December 26th

Boxing Day at Windsor Castle is always very much a time for 'taking it easy' and 'having a bit of a chuckle'. At eleven o'clock sharp, Prince Philip comes into the State Drawing Room with one of his famous Whoopee cushions. He then blows it up, forces each of us in turn to sit on it, and roars with laughter. Tremendous fun! Then the Prince of Wales reads a few verses from Kahlil Gibran, explaining what they mean to him personally. Finally Prince Edward enters in his stilettos dressed as a buxom serving-wench, his face painted with rouge and mascara, and recites a comic monologue in a very humorous cockney accent. The moment Prince Philip gets up, walks out and slams the door, that's our signal for offs – a most memorable ending to another happy Christmas.

VISCOUNT LINLEY

So we leave them there in the stable, all alone now that the Kings have scarpered and the shepherds have (finally!) cleared off. What does the future hold for the Infant Jesus? Well, he certainly wasn't backward in coming forward! But for all his fame (largely posthumous, I might add), he earned a fraction of what I earn – AND he never made the cover of the *TV Times*.

DAVID STARKEY

We gave Cuddles a beautiful send-off. We spent a shitload of money hiring José Carreras and that fat one, Jessye Norman, that's it, and the orchestra and chorus from the Royal Opera House for the afternoon and flying them over for Cuddles's funeral, mind you we got most of it back from MTV, who was filming it live.

As that little gold coffin was put into the ground I don't mind telling you I was in a terrible state, sobbing, sobbing, sobbing. I was in my funeral dress which the lovely Vivienne Westwood, a personal friend, had designed specially for the occasion.

I wrote a poem, 'For Cuddles', which I read out at the graveside, choking through the fucking tears:

I loved you little Cuddles
Your lovely fur and tail and head
Til Ozzy came along
And squashed you fucking dead.

It choked us all up, I read it so beautiful. But that's the kind of person I am, I wear my heart on my sleeve, and that's why the public warm to me, because they know I'm the kind of person who'll give a little puppy a good send-off, even if it's driven me to hell and back by shitting over my new settee.

SHARON OSBOURNE

December 27th

Today I have completed my new biography, *The Secret Life of Nelson Mandela*.

It's not his full name, of course. His middle name is Rolihlahla, but it's not something he boasts about.

In fact, he keeps it deathly quiet. 'Nelson hates you to call him Rolihlahla,' says a former colleague. Others maintain he spent all those years hiding away on Robben Island just because he hated being teased about it.

'Let's face it, he could have come out fifteen, twenty years earlier,' whispers a former internee, too anonymous to be named, 'but he always lived in fear of that old taunt.'

Even now, for all his 'dignity' and 'old age', if you creep up behind him and shout 'Rolihlahla' into his ear, he'll leap from fright. 'It's as though Nelson is scared of who he really is,' says a former teenager.

For the purposes of my biography of Nelson Mandela, I conducted 2,804 interviews over five years, a fair number of them with those who had either encountered someone who had encountered the man personally or had almost encountered someone who had.

And yes, I uncovered many cold, hard facts that Mr Mandela would prefer to keep under wraps. For instance, where precisely was he between 1963 and 1990?

'He certainly wasn't at home,' says one former neighbour. 'Oftentimes I would look through the window, but he wouldn't be there.'

The extraordinary truth that I am now able to reveal is that Nelson Rolihlahla Mandela was unavailable for one reason, and one reason only. He was not at home because he was in prison.

'That explains so much,' says a former complete stranger, astonished by the dramatic discovery I unearthed after interviewing 3,914 people across a period of seven years. 'I always wondered why he was keeping such a low profile in the neighbourhood – and now I know.'

Even now, Nelson Mandela doesn't like to talk too much about his 'forgotten' years as a disgraced jailbird. It seems it's a secret he would rather keep hidden.

'We had Nelson and his wife round for dinner a month or two ago,' says one former world statesman, 'and at no point during that meal did he mention his spell in prison.'

Since childhood, he has needed to present himself as open, warm, and cozy, and conceal the part of himself that is a hard-bitten, avaricious, biscuit-consuming ex-convict.

'That's why he wears those colorful shirts,' says a former colleague. 'These past twenty years, I've never once seen him in prison uniform. It's as though he wanted to sweep his past under the carpet.'

Mandela's weight has long been a cause for grave concern among friends and colleagues.

'Some years, he'll add on pounds – other years, he'll lose pounds. There's nothing you can say to stop him,' says one former employee. 'It's like, one day you offer him a cookie, and he takes it. The next day, you offer him a cookie and he says no thanks. He's so unpredictable. The guy's in emotional turmoil. He's literally out of control, cookie-wise.'

Many see Nelson's relationship to cookies as inherently unstable. Sometimes, he'll consume an entire cookie in three or four bites, like a deadly man-eating shark hellbent on spreading terror among underage swimmers. Other times, he'll just nibble at it and maybe even leave it, as if he's in denial. And he'll never offer his cookies to anyone he regards as 'unworthy'.

'I've observed Mandela meeting pop stars and potentates, presidents and princes,' says one seasoned observer, 'but I've never once seen him take a pack of cookies from his pocket and offer them around.'

Denied cookies as a child, is he now attempting to assert control over those who might otherwise deprive him of them? He may have risen to be the best-loved man in the whole world, but when a plate of cookies is placed in front of him Nelson Mandela is still that terrified little boy. Many of the 4,217 people I have interviewed for my book over the past twelve years have expressed deep concern that he is in cookie-denial, and has yet to confront his cookie-based traumas.

A high-ranking cookie expert from a leading mid-west university who has studied his case over a number of years says: 'I have found it impossible to lay my hands on any records of the number of cookies Nelson Mandela has eaten between 1990 and the present day.'

He concludes, alarmingly, that the cookie records must have been destroyed by a person or persons unknown. This is confirmed by repeated attempts to extract a precise amount from Mandela or his confectioners. They have all been rebuffed.

'There's a wall of silence around Mandela and his cookies,' says one former expert. 'It's as though the guy's hiding something.' If so, it is a secret that, many believe, has governed his life.

There is no foundation for the rumor that Nelson Mandela was born to a comfortable white middle-class family in Johannesburg and only decided to change his skin color because he thought it would make him politically more acceptable.

But there is no doubt that many of the 5,793 people I interviewed over seventeen years for my biography of the man had vivid memories of him growing up white.

'Sure, Nelson was a major figure in the struggle against apartheid,' says one former complete stranger. 'But who's to say on which side?'

One former associate recalls: 'I asked him recently if he was ever white, and he said no. And you know what? He sounded almost aggressive, like he was in denial.'

Nelson Mandela has convinced himself that he is – and has always been – a black man in South Africa. And, former colleagues say, he is determined that others believe it too, no matter what it costs.

'In public, he goes out of his way to come across all black and dignified,' says one former onlooker. 'But if ever you try mentioning that in private he dresses up as Elvis and hollers "All Shook Up" on the karaoke, he'll have his office deny it till they're blue in the face. And that's the kind of guy he is. He'll do anything in his power to stay on that pedestal. Nelson just has to be in control.'

And this is what I've found during the course of interviewing over 6,978 people over the past twenty years. In a funny way, it's almost as though he was terrified of the truth.

KITTY KELLEY

December 28th

Pass away and go to heaven, much overrated but not without its modicum of fanciful charm. The golden gates, written up in such hushed tones by the guidebooks, prove a tremendous disappointment: garish, garish, garish. How one longs for a little English restraint! Instead, one suffers the iniquities of the worst excesses of Italian bravado. They are largely Romans up here; homos, too, I shouldn't wonder.

Am met at the gates by St Peter. Like many a bearded man, he is full of himself, with an excessively beery air about him. One would have thought that by now the greeter at any halfway-decent club would have been persuaded by the powers-that-be to take a razor to his chin.

St Peter welcomes me warmly, but there is far too much touching and – one shudders to think of it! – Christian names all round. He is scruffiness personified – not only the hairs sprouting from every orifice but the lack of any collar or tie. It all reminds me of a cocktail party given by Mrs Foley in Eaton Square in early 1947 to view the Stoke Edith needlework hangings in her drawing room: quite well done and perfectly civilised, but unkempt, disordered and somehow louche.

After the formalities – name, profession, date of death, and so on – one is introduced to this angel and that, none of them forthcoming. They speak in hushed tones of Satan. I seize my cue. 'Not one of the Yorkshire Satans?' I say, but I draw a blank. It is only too obvious that they have no idea. I remind them that in the chilly autumn of 1933 I spent a delightfully wicked weekend with Sir Cecil and Lady Cynthia Satan at Damnation Hall, just outside Scarborough. Once again, they contrive to look nonplussed. I suspect them of stuffiness, though I refrain from mentioning the feathery protuberances that spring so unashamedly from their backs: wings indeed! The sure sign of a homo; quite possibly a wop homo at that.

The Archangel Gabriel makes an entrance. He smiles in the sweetest, kindliest way. I fall head over heels in love with him. He sparkles.

JAMES LEES-MILNE

December 29th

Current favourite flowers: magnolia, japonica, fuchsia, Queen Mum.

SIR ROY STRONG

So chilly it might almost be winter.

Motored to Charing Cross Hospital to meet soldiers back from the Front. Many of them without arms and legs, so extremely lucky to be in the Army at all.

Stamps.

Boiled chicken for dinner with Mama. Bed at 11.15.

HM KING GEORGE V

December 30th

Off to the clouds, to an intimate *soirée* to meet my fellow new boys. The very sight of them fills me with gloom. Left-wingers abound, ghastly people voicing noisy, modish opinions – all faith this, hope that and charity the other. To my horror, I am introduced to a squat little woman, no taller than an umbrella, her skin coarsely lined and burnt to a crisp, all in all a slightly chinky look, her unimpressive and ill-laundered robes dishevelled and riddled with dust. 'And who let you in?' I felt like hissing, just as Gabriel informed me that she was known as Mother Teresa (of Calcutta, of all places!). If this is democracy, God help us. 'Do you happen to know Debo?' I ask, in a vain attempt to break the ice. 'Oh, but you should! She's an absolute treasure! Chatsworth is heaven. Or heaven *sans* riff-raff, if you follow me.' M. Teresa looks back at me with a look of gormless incomprehension.

Oh, why on earth does one bother?

JAMES LEES-MILNE

December 31st

It has been an odd sort of year.

In June, there was an intruder on the Palace roof, making a terrible racket with an electric guitar.

I asked who it was.

It turned out to be an old lady called May.

Needless to say, once one had got in, there was no stopping them.

By the end of the day the garden was absolutely jam-packed and no one could do anything about it. One simply had to grin and bear it.

Though I didn't bother to grin.

I saw a lot of the Prime Minister during the past year. We have regular meetings. He greatly values my tremendous wealth of wisdom and experience.

It is my duty as Monarch to advise and inform. 'My son Edward pointed out that there was an awful lot of traffic on the roads this morning,' I tell him.

'That will be the cars,' he says.

'And lorries,' I say. Lorries are for putting things in.

'Yes. Cars and lorries,' he agrees. Once again, he has been able to draw on my vast wealth of experience.

'People getting from A to B,' he adds.

'That doesn't sound very far,' I point out.

'They might be better off walking,' I say, giving it some thought. 'Perhaps the third lane of the motorway could be reserved for pedestrians, with cars and lorries in the first.'

The Prime Minister says that is one idea he has never thought of. He will look into it.

I am pleased my idea seems to have caught on.

'... which would leave the second lane free for horses and carriages and so forth,' I add.

I ask after his wife: 'How is your wife?'

They do appreciate it when one shows a bit of personal interest. He says his wife is well.

'Well, goodbye,' I say, getting out of my chair, shaking his hand and leaving the room.

This is his signal to depart.

HM QUEEN ELIZABETH II

At last, I find myself with an *entrée* to God the Father. His house may indeed have many mansions, but to my eye every one of them is fearfully *déclassé*. I fear it would have been rather more accurate for the scribe in question to have declared that His villa had many chalets. The furniture, too, is not up to much. Nevertheless, I take pains to persevere through the ghastly piped music of the assembled harpists, and attempt to set God at His ease. After much struggle, I make a little headway. 'It's awfully noble of you to allow so many of what one might call the Great Unwashed into your Kingdom,' I venture, 'but have you ever considered the benefits of the long red rope? We found them a tremendous boon at the National Trust for cordoning off the more, shall we say, private areas of a home from those who have little or no idea of how to behave within their confines. I would be only too pleased to oversee any cordoning-off programme you may care to initiate.'

Just as I am getting into my stride, an archangel bangs a gong and announces that dinner is served. At last, I arrive at the front. 'Big Mac, Filet-o-Fish or Chicken McNuggets?' asks the presiding angel. I fear there may have been some awful mistake. I am in the wrong place.

JAMES LEES-MILNE

I reread *The Oxford English Dictionary*. It has no narrative drive, no characterisation at all, and is far too wordy. What on earth were they thinking of?

V.S. NAIPAUL

Over dinner with prominent members of the new administration, I quietly take out my diary to jot down what everyone is saying. The room falls silent while my fellow guests take out their diaries, too. I glance down at my neighbour's diary. 'Over dinner with prominent members of the new administration,' it begins, 'I quietly take out my diary to jot down what everyone is saying.'

What a feast we will all provide for historians of the future!

LORD RUNCIMAN

ACKNOWLEDGEMENTS

For the past twenty-one years I have been writing a fortnightly celebrity diary for *Private Eye*. This has been the fulfilment of all, or almost all, my ambitions. I am very grateful to my friend and editor, Ian Hislop, and to everyone else who works there, especially Hilary Lowinger. Thanks, too, to my agent Caroline Dawnay.

I have written a number of new pieces for this anthology, particularly in the area of days gone by (Hardy, Woolf, Lawrence), but I have also resurrected, and in many cases reworked, parodies that originally saw the light of day in *Vanity Fair*, the *Daily Telegraph*, the *Daily Mail* and the *Guardian*. My daughter Tallulah helped me excavate them.

Without my wife Frances I would have gone potty, or pottier. Every morning she works downstairs, writing books about tragic Russians, while I work upstairs, trotting out jokes. It seems to me that for the past twenty-odd years we have maintained the tragic/comic balance at an even keel.

This book is for my mother, and in memory of my father.

C.B.

INDEX